Within school walls

Within school walls

THE ROLE OF DISCIPLINE, SEXUALITY AND THE CURRICULUM

AnnMarie Wolpe

R

ROUTLEDGE
London and New York

First published in 1988 by
Routledge
11 New Fetter Lane, London EC4P 4EE

29 West 35th Street, New York NY 10001

© AnnMarie Wolpe 1988

Printed in Great Britain by Richard Clay Ltd, Bungay, Suffolk

British Library Cataloguing in Publication Data

Within school walls: the role of
discipline, sexuality and the
curriculum
1. Great Britain. Schools. Students.
Sex roles.
270.19'345'0941

ISBN 0415 008 360

Contents

Acknowledgments   vii
Introduction   1

PART ONE: *Discipline and Control*   17

CHAPTER ONE *Within these walls*   19
CHAPTER TWO *Classroom behaviour*   36
CHAPTER THREE *Girls and boys at school*   57

PART TWO: *Sexuality*   *95*

Introduction   97

CHAPTER FOUR *Sexuality and moral order*   102
CHAPTER FIVE *Sexuality in the school*   122
CHAPTER SIX *Sex and everyday life*   144

PART THREE: *The Curriculum*   177

CHAPTER SEVEN *Knowledge and control*   179
CHAPTER EIGHT *The curriculum at Berkeley*   201
CHAPTER NINE *The curriculum and work*   227

EPILOGUE   246

Notes   272
Bibliography   279
Index   289

Acknowledgments

This book is the outcome of collaborative work between the staff and pupils of Berkeley School, without whose help and cooperation nothing would have been achieved.

The welter of material was patiently and efficiently transcribed by Daphne Clench and Shirley Webb who, over the years, were enthusiastic, helpful and very encouraging. They were directly responsible for my resumption of the project at a period when both time and energy were at a low ebb.

The Nuffield Foundation awarded me a grant enabling me to carry out the last set of interviews and to begin the final assessment.

I am grateful to Harold Wolpe, Elizabeth Wilson, Pippa Brewster and Mike Cole for critical comments on the book and to a number of people who have commented on sections of the work, in particular Tanya and Talal Asad.

Finally, there is my family who have patiently nurtured me through the long period that this book has taken to reach completion.

Introduction

This book is the culmination of work spread over more than a decade. The empirical material is derived from data obtained at a comprehensive school over two periods: initial work involved two years' 'participant observation' in the school, followed by interviews of the original cohort two years later, and then with some of them as young adults after they had left school four years on. It is, therefore, a longitudinal study. The theoretical perspective governing the analysis of the data represents my own development and those which have occurred both in the sociology of education and in feminist literature. I have had the benefit of these developments in the course of formulating and organizing the data in the form in which it is presented.

The Introduction is divided into four sections. The first presents the background to the study; the second is a brief outline of the methods employed in the investigation; the third summarizes different theories relevant to such a study (indicating both their utilities and their limitations), and the fourth is a brief statement on the order of the book.

Background to study

Arising from an earlier study on the recruitment and career patterns of women in professional engineering, I became concerned with the processes through which female gender roles and gender identity are constructed, defined and reinforced within a secondary school setting. The effect of these differences is apparent in the examination results of boys and girls. It seemed quite clear at the time that girls' school performance was lower than boys' if certain

1

examination results – particularly those relating to academic subjects – were compared.

In accordance with academic convention I developed a working hypothesis which was as follows:

That the specific gender identities with which pupils enter the secondary school tend to be clarified and reinforced by the following factors: a school organizational structure which differentiated between pupils on the basis of gender; the transmission to pupils by teachers through the curriculum specifically and generally via the cognitive and value systems which are confirmatory of differential gender identities particularly in so far as these are related to pupils' future occupational roles which are themselves conceived of in gender terms; the peer-group relationships and culture.

Like so many academic hypotheses it is difficult to read and comprehend. What I was arguing and planning to do was as follows. The hypothesis began from the presupposition that pupils enter schools with already formed gender identities and all that that implies, but that the school system reinforces these identities through a number of different processes. In order to understand these the most productive method would be studying everyday life at the school. The processes needed to be identified and these included a number of formal structural constraints including school uniform, school assembly, the way in which registers are kept, playground facilities, staff hierarchies and so on, all of which automatically contribute to the differentiation between boys and girls and hence to the reinforcement of gender stereotypes. Given this basic structure it was thought at the time that the curriculum and the way in which it is taught would be an important, if not crucial, aspect of the process of differentiation. It was anticipated that obvious differentiation on a gender basis would occur in some subject specialities such as home economics. Other distinctions would have to be identified in what is now known as the hidden curriculum of values and ideas which teachers themselves hold about gender differences and which are transmitted largely undetected in the classroom. A direct relationship was taken as given between the school experience and pupils' future roles in both the workforce and the family. In conventional terms, women's role (irrespective of whether they work or not) is defined in terms of family duties, and men's in terms of the workforce. Finally I acknowledged the fact that pupils were part of a peer group culture which also contributed to the reinforcing of gender roles.

After preliminary groundwork I was lucky enough to conduct the study in a new comprehensive school, which I shall call Berkeley, whose first intake, of 180 pupils, was in 1972. I was able to monitor the developments very closely; I was attached to one particular class and followed it through the school day, accompanying members on school outings, interviewing staff, parents and pupils alike. I was thoroughly immersed in the school and its activities.

The school is in Greater London and has all the problems associated with metropolitan areas. It is located in a predominantly working-class area with a large, mixed group including all ethnic minorities.

In its first year of operation the school occupied the top floor of an old building which also housed pupils who had some form of disability. This created some difficulties to begin with, but territorial boundaries were easily recognized and observed. By the second year the school had taken over the whole of the premises. These measures were purely temporary and plans for the building of a new architect designed school according to the planners' priorities were going ahead. In its third year the school occupied its new purpose-built premises.

In 1974 I got a full-time teaching post and was unable to complete the study. However, I did return to the school in the hot summer of 1976 to interview the same pupils who were then completing their fourth year of school. I had not had any contact with the school during this interim period. I had, fortunately, managed to interview most of the pupils when I received a letter from the headmaster barring me from continuing with the interviews. This came quite unexpectedly and the reasons given were perhaps more complex than those expressed in the letter. The letter reads as follows:

Dear AnnMarie,

Having given my approval to the continuation of your research in school I regret having to write this letter. However, I have become increasingly concerned at the reaction of members of staff who have been approached about interviews either for themselves or children in their care at a time of increasing pressure as we approach the end of term.

I regret, therefore, that I have to withdraw the facility I offered you and I would only be prepared to reconsider a continuation of your research after some close and detailed study of proposals you may have for next term. No doubt you will let me have these detailed notes so that I can see what time factor is involved for both pupils and staff alike. I should add that some of our antipathy towards the resumption of your research has been the erratic nature of this work hitherto which I understand is through no fault of your own but is none-the-less very unsettling in its effects upon the school. With the increasing pressures of work at this stage of the term I feel unable to devote any more of my time to consideration of this issue and I reluctantly must therefore cancel my interview with you on Thursday 8th July.

I look forward to hearing from you.

I replied expressing my regret at his decision and saying that spreading out interviews was methodologically unsound. I did not attempt to return to the school as I did not have the time to do so. Apart from anything else, I had conducted almost all the interviews with the pupils that I required.

Following an award of a Nuffield Fellowship I was able to resume work on the project once again in 1980. At this stage I wanted to interview the same cohort who were now young adults in order to establish what they were doing, how they had effected the transition from school to work, study or home, and what their reflections were on their school careers.

I again tried to establish contact with the school, partly out of courtesy and partly to obtain detailed school records. By this time there was a new headteacher to whom I wrote. He did not respond by letter and following a phone call I made he told me he was seeing the previous headteacher and would discuss this with him. Within a few days I was told that he would not see me at all. He refused to have anything to do with me and gave me no reason at all for his refusal.

It is difficult to establish why I had given offence but this may lie in some of the written material I published in 1976 which included some of the comments made by the headteacher in regard to the issue of sexuality amongst his pupils.

Method

Prior to selecting and beginning work in a secondary school I conducted a number of interviews with educationalists in a range of fields and then found a comprehensive, co-educational secondary school in which I could conduct a 'participant observation' study. The phrase is somewhat of a misnomer: I did not anticipate participating in terms of actual teaching, although it was agreed that I would do so should the occasion arise (which never did occur). However, observation was to be the order of the day and this would be conducted in depth, over at least a two-year period.

Observation techniques overcome the limitations of an interview schedule, which are many (Hindess, 1973), and the advantages of this research technique were spelled out in the now-famous Willis study (1977). I do not want to repeat the same discussion here. Suffice it to say that, at the time the initial work was conducted, there was little available data on classroom interaction as it related to gender differences. What work had been done had largely focused on boys. Nor was there a great deal of information on how the curriculum differentiated between boys and girls, both in terms of the content of the subject matter and the way in which teachers taught. I anticipated at the time that the observations would be rich in providing evidence of a differentiation process in the classroom.

However, there are difficulties of combining subjective observations with a structural analysis, and I found this a major task. This book is an attempt to build a bridge between these two. The shift from the macro level of structure to the micro level of interpersonal relationships is not an easy one to maintain, nor is the interrelationship between these two levels simple to establish.

In terms of research conditions I was extremely fortunate. The head gave me *carte blanche*. As far as the top echelons of the school hierarchy were concerned, I was able to discuss many aspects of the school and its development with the head, I was allowed to sit in on the planning sessions he held with his deputy headmaster, I attended all staff meetings, and was given information by the Chairperson of the Board of Governors. The staff were asked to co-operate with me and they seemed to accept my presence there without any noticeable difficulty and I could move freely about the school. The presence of a resident research worker added to the prestige of the whole development.

I recorded all meetings and interviews on tape and in addition kept daily notes of observations which were also transcribed. By the end of two years I had a huge volume of material. This was augmented by the subsequent interviews.

The nature of my research project was known to the headmaster but not to the staff. I believed that if they knew that I was primarily interested in gender differentiation it would have had an effect on the way in which they answered questions or presented material to me. As far as they were concerned I was monitoring the development of the school and even when one or two of the teachers would turn to me and say 'What are you doing?' they never stopped long enough to listen to my answer.

It was an exciting time in the school because the newly appointed teachers were extremely enthusiastic about the school and its prospects. In that first year many of the younger teachers devoted a great deal of time outside their normal duties to consolidating their work in regard to team teaching – Humanities and English were to be interdisciplinary – in setting up activities out of school hours, and in conducting home visits. They worked long hours beyond the call of duty and their enthusiasm was contagious – the pupils and many of their parents played an active part in the school and its development.

During the second year certain changes began to occur which were largely tied up with the head's concern that some of his members of staff conflicted too publicly with him and constituted a threat to his authority. A number of these teachers left the school at the end of the second year for a variety of reasons, one being the head's ability to block their promotion and keep them in subordinate positions. Originally the school had been designated as a community school. This constituted one of the areas of concern for the head and so in the second year that designation was dropped.

Aims and theoretical influences

This book sets out to examine the processes in school which contribute to the firm fixing of female gender identities at the micro level of the classroom. Although the analysis focuses on classroom interaction, account will be taken of structural conditions, specifically class and ideologies.

In the course of conducting the analysis at the micro level, several theoretical positions are critically appraised, particularly some of the current feminist accounts of girls' overall level of under-achievement. There is no one single feminist theory on education. There are a number of different strands which will be discussed in the relevant sections throughout the book. However, just as there has been a tendency, as Stebbins (1987) points out, of a sectarianism in the sociology of the classroom between neo-Marxists, symbolic interactionists and functionalists, many feminist accounts have failed to exploit some of the important insights made by other analyses, including those concerned with the structures of class and ideology. This book is concerned to re-insert multi-dimensional factors into feminist accounts of girls' education.

The important contributions on how class and ideological structures intersect in the education system were derived largely from the work of French Marxist writers, Althusser (1971) and Poulantzas (1975). Their major concern was primarily with the reproduction of capitalist relations of production, and Althusser's essay on ideology and ideological state apparatuses was to have a great impact. Within this overall framework analyses were made by Bourdieu and Passeron (1977) who spoke of 'cultural capital' which is transmitted by and stored in the schools. 'Cultural capital' acted as a 'filtering device in the reproduction of a hierarchical society'.

These structural analyses added a dimension to the new sociology of education which had dominated sociology during the late 1960s. This latter work drew on the sociology of knowledge as well as contributions made by ethnomethodologists. What was argued was that 'Knowledge ("transmitted" in education) is neither absolute, nor arbitrary, but is "available sets of meaning", which in any context do not merely "emerge", but are collectively "given".' (M. Young, 1971, p. 3). To comprehend fully the interaction process 'the curricula, pedagogic and assessment categories held by school personnel' were regarded by Young and others as crucial to understanding the schooling process, and studies on classroom interaction became all-important (Hargreaves, 1967, Hargreaves et al., 1975, Ball, 1981).

But through the influence of Marxist analyses sociologists of education turned their attention fully to the reproduction of social relations of production with the schools being seen as a vital part of this process. Bowles and Gintis (1976), for example, conceived of education as the means of the reproduction of the class structure and as the mechanism for equipping new recruits to the workforce with the appropriate values and ideas (ideologies) about their role in the labour force. They introduced the concept of the 'correspondence' principle which was that 'the organization of education – in particular the correspondence between school structure and job structure' (p. 13) occurred at the level of social relations. They said:

> The structure of social relations in education not only inures the student to the discipline of the workplace, but develops the types of personal demeanor, modes of self-presentation, self-image, and social–class identifications which are the crucial ingredients of job adequacy. Specifically, the social relations of education . . . replicate the hierarchical division of labor. (p. 131)

This was achieved through the working of the hidden curriculum and ideological structures.

Although Bowles and Gintis recognized inequalities in terms of gender and race and 'adult male supremacy in the household', gender differences did not comprise an important aspect of their study. Their main concern was to demonstrate the role of economics and they said that: 'the roots of unequal incomes and inequality of opportunity alike lie not in human nature, not in technology, not in the educational system itself, but in the dynamics of economic life' (p. 89). This economic reductionist analysis presents the educational system as functional for the capitalist economy.[1]

But there was a growing dissatisfaction with the radical analysis expressed in reproduction theories based on the economy, and its failure to deal with the individual actor.

Willis (1977) changed all this. Concentrating on youth and shop floor culture he described how working-class lads rejected formal education. His analysis drew on the theoretical developments from the Centre for Contemporary Cultural Studies (CCCS), Birmingham University. The studies emanating from the Centre concentrated on forms of cultural reproduction and Willis was able to demonstrate how working-class 'lads' colluded in their own continued subordination in the workplace as a direct outcome of their adherence to their youth sub-culture. They rejected education; they were not concerned with escaping from the working-class ghetto. Willis emphasized the role of cultural formations which generated the resistance of working-class lads to the dominant culture while still at school. He argued, unlike Bowles and Gintis, that working-class youth reproduced their own inequality. Where the 'correspondence' principle had failed to provide an adequate explanation for the phenomenon of working-class rejection of educational opportunities, in spite of the expansion of educational facilities, the notion of cultural reproduction seemed to present an answer.

Willis' important contribution heralded the concern with the 'importance of human agency and the notion of resistance'. As Gordon (1984) says: 'Willis' analysis explicitly sets out to challenge the mechanistic notions of [social] reproductions which have dominated the structuralist position' (p. 1). The concept of resistance has proved a popular analytical tool emphasizing the role of cultural reproduction. Willis' influence has been extensive, even though critically received by some (the most recent being an accusation of romanticism by Walker (1986)).

Aronowitz and Giroux (1986) have considered some of the problems associated with the concept of resistance and argued, correctly, that resistance theorists face two tasks:

> First, they must structure their own assumptions to develop a
> more dialectical model of schooling and society; and secondly,
> they must reconstruct the major theories of reproduction in
> order to abstract from them their most radical and eman-
> cipatory insights. (p. 73)

These authors have highlighted the tendency of resistance theorists to submerge or overlook the insights gained through reproduction theories.

But all this work has been almost exclusively male oriented. The Centre's main focus of interest was the spectacular male youth sub-cultural groups.[2] Analyses were not made of girls' groups as McRobbie and Garber pointed out (1975). As for resistance theories, there has been only limited analyses made of gender differences (Anyon, 1983).

Just as girls were invisible from youth sub-cultural studies so were they from all the studies on education. In the late 1960s, we began to address this serious omission through, *inter alia*, a critique of theories of education, which, whatever their approach, tended to treat the school population as homogeneous in terms of gender, ignoring the specificity of girls' position. It was clear that these approaches could not account for the differences in educational experiences of boys and girls and so several of us turned to examine classroom interaction. It was assumed that such an account could only be made through an analysis at the micro level, that is at the level of individuals, and this, in turn, led to a focus on classroom interaction.

Amongst many feminist writers there was a general dissatisfaction with Marxist analyses which were seen to ignore totally the specificity of women's condition. Some writers have dismissed all Marxist analyses on the grounds that the determinant role accorded to the economy results in its inability to account for women's subordination. Thus:

> All varieties of Marxism, whatever their internal differences, see the oppression of women as ultimately following from our relationship to the economic system: they see our oppression as following from our connection (or lack of it) with production. Thus, our subordination to men is not theorized in terms of the benefits which accrue to them, but in terms of the benefits of capitalism. (Mahony, 1985, p. 66)

These benefits reflect the patriarchal nature of our society, according to Mahony. She, as with many other feminist writers, draws on the notion of patriarchy. But patriarchal relations, according to her analysis, must override all other forms of relationships. For example, although MacDonald (1981) acknowledges patriarchy her work is dismissed by Mahony because she 'sees patriarchal relations as being maintained in the interests of the sexual division of labour which benefits capitalism' (p. 69). The major factor, according to Mahony, is the universal power that men are said to exert over all women, particularly over women's sexuality within heterosexual relations.

Patriarchy and patriarchal relations have been variously described as Segal (1987) has pointed out, but common to all the accounts is the control over women's sexuality:

> 'Patriarchy' has been defined in a variety of ways within different feminist frameworks and discourses: as a social system of male domination, as the power of the father in the family, as the universal principle and symbol of male domination, or as men's power to exchange women in order to form kinship groups. But central to all these definitions of

> patriarchy was men's power over women's sexuality and fer-
> tility. (p. 49)

Some have represented the ultimate manifestation of male power as their control over women's sexuality. Whatever the case may be, all accounts establish male power as a universal principle thereby failing to differentiate between the various forms of power. There are no social formations involving gender differences which are not attributed to patriarchy. According to this formulation, the source of male power must be derived from an essential quality: by virtue of men being men, this power can only be biologically deter-mined. Thus the notion of power in the context of male domination over women is a form of biological essentialism and as such can never be altered. Furthermore given that its source resides in maleness, its existence is not subjected to questioning. Its existence is invariable.

Some male writers have also begun to use the terms patriarchy and patriarchal relations when talking about gender differences. Willis, for example, who was not concerned with working-class girls, dealt with gender matters through an assertion of prevailing patriarchal relations. Introducing and using the concept of patriarchy appeared to make it unnecessary to explore gender differences more fully. It is as though the act of acknowledging unequal power relations between men and women is sufficient.

So the general form of patriarchy is used to explain differen-tiated forms of male power which occur in relation to various social conditions. Such an account is quite inadequate. The differ-entiated forms of male power can only be accounted for by anal-yses which take into consideration the specific conditions which give rise to these situations.

Take, as an example, differentiations which exist in relation to class. Men from the middle class may well have power over women in both the middle and the working class but the nature of this power would differ according to the relationship of the men to the particular group of women. It may be determined through the labour market, or it may be determined in the home. Whichever form the differentiation takes, it is the form of power that needs to be defined and then discussed in relation to the specific conditions which give rise to the form of domination. Male power may then be identified as taking different forms reflecting specific social formations and periods. This formulation rejects the notion that all women are victims of an indiscriminate form of male power. Indeed, women are not always powerless. Middle-class women may well exert power over black, working-class men. In spite of the feminization of poverty, the rise in the number of families headed by women may be seen as an indicator of women assuming power within families.

The question which now needs to be addressed is how the concept of patriarchy has been applied in the analyses of girls' education. There have been complex theoretical accounts by Deem (1978) and MacDonald (1981) which have combined the notion of patriarchy with accounts of economic and family structures. But over the past few years there has been a growing literature which confines itself to an analysis which presupposes an overall male dominance through patriarchy. This work has been concerned to identify where this occurs and what effect it has. Three main areas have been identified: classroom behaviour, sexual oppression within the school, and the curriculum.

The studies of classroom behaviour have been concerned to demonstrate that boys behave in a dominant way detrimental to girls' academic progress and development of self-esteem. The unintended consequence of this work has been to establish a stereotypical profile of boys' behaviour and one of how girls are said to respond. As for sexual oppression, the feminist literature has focused on how girls have experienced boys' behaviour as sexually oppressive, with the girls portrayed as victims of boys' aggression. This focus has led to a narrow view of sexuality within the school. Finally, in regard to the curriculum there have been two distinct areas of interest. The first is within the context of how the curriculum is male dominated as seen in 'male knowledge', 'male language', 'male forms of assessment' and so on. The second has identified specific areas within the curriculum which are necessary prerequisites for access into certain occupations, particularly in science and technology. These areas of the curriculum are heavily male dominated and the work has been concerned not only to identify these but also to seek means of ensuring that more girls study such subjects.

A methodological offshoot of the feminist work has been the extensive use of experiential accounts by girls.[3] In an attempt to counter what has been seen as the inhuman face of Marxist analysis which has ignored the experience of the individual subject, this mode of analysis has gained a great degree of credibility. These subjective accounts of girls' and women's experiences are similar in analytical terms to the phenomenological and other subjective studies referred to above. All such accounts focus on the meanings given to the experiences by the significant actors. But this convergence is not acknowledged by the feminist writers who argue that their methodology is unique and has been developed out of women's experiences (Stanley and Wise, 1983). Furthermore, because the accounts are given by girls these are seen to reflect reality on the basis that it is only girls and women who can fully understand the nature of their oppression.[4]

These studies have resulted in the development of strategies and campaigns to combat the differential practices in schooling which are seen to disadvantage girls. Some have been directed towards raising the level of consciousness of both teachers and pupils about classroom interaction which denigrate girls and affect their work. The curriculum has also been critically examined with regard to its content and the method of teaching in order to break down the existing – albeit invisible – barriers which occur in particular subject areas which are almost totally male dominated. Finally there is a campaign for a return to single-sex schools.

There has been a positive outcome of this work. At the most general level it has contributed significantly to making girls and women visible in the education scenario to the extent that it is now common place, as mentioned previously, for many people to recognize the need to take account of gender differences. At a more specific level it has contributed to the formulation of a number of LEA programmes including some by such huge authorities as ILEA to combat sexism in schools, including the appointment of officers specifically charged with these tasks. At the level of classroom interaction it has had an electrifying effect on many teachers who have been made aware of the way in which the hidden curriculum operates and the part they as teachers play in perpetuating inequalities in the classroom. Such a level of consciousness can only be welcomed.

While the outcome of all these strategies is extremely important in alerting teachers and pupils to the danger of discriminatory practices, they cannot in themselves alter the final forms of division of labour either in the home or in the workplace. The way in which the demand for female labour is generated, and the way female labour is treated, is not simply the outcome of patriarchal practices. It changes according to different social circumstances and over different historical periods as Davidoff and Hall (1987) have so authoritatively demonstrated in their extensive historical study of middle-class men and women in rural and urban English society.

While accepting the importance of gender positioning, the specificity of girls' education cannot be understood outside of the set of social formations in which they exist. These include structures external and internal to the school.

To begin with external factors, the girls' class position reflecting their family background needs to be established. Associated with their class position is the nature of the school they attend. Headteachers may experience relative autonomy in relation to the day to day running of their schools and this is likely to increase with the proposed control they may have over resources, but they are bound by a range of external constraints which in turn determine certain characteristics of the school.

Apart from these external forces there are the structures within the school which create the environment in which learning occurs. These are the disciplinary measures which physically constrain pupils within the confines of the school building. The control over pupils is extended through the teaching of the moral code which sets the parameters of acceptable forms of behaviour, including that relating to sexuality. Finally there is the structure of knowledge and the control which that exerts over pupils.

These three systems of control exist and operate for all pupils, irrespective of gender or any other differences. In order, therefore, to understand what happens to individual groups within the education system, these structural constraints need to be taken into account. The problem then becomes one of combining the structural analysis with an account of the interaction processes of the individual subject. These individual actions and reactions are, in turn, not viewed as unique to the subject but as strongly influenced by external forces of diverse natures. Hence the understanding of girls' education can be successfully undertaken when all these factors are taken into account, and not through comparison with boys' attainment and as an effect of boys' behaviour at school.

It is hoped that this book challenges the onesidedness of so many studies that have appeared and offers a broadly based framework in which the daily working of a secondary school may be viewed. In the face of the continued inroads made into educational provisions in this country it is necessary to conserve and improve the existing facilities. To do so the restrictions imposed by both class and gender differentiation need to be countered. If this book can contribute in any way, however small, to this I will consider the difficulties encompassed in developing the theoretical framework to have been vindicated.

The order of presentation

The book is divided into three main sections. The first is Discipline and Control, the second is Sexuality and the third is the Curriculum. The views of both teachers and pupils are given throughout and discussed in terms of the particular sections.

The analysis begins with what appears to be the very heart of school organization: discipline. Through disciplinary procedures, the distinctive character of the secondary education as a form of rigid social control is established and this affects girls and boys alike. It is necessary to establish what these controls are before one can distinguish how gender differentiation occurs. Gender differentiation will be discussed not only through the administration of discipline but also in relation to classroom interaction and behaviour.

Sexuality is inexorably interwoven with gender identity and, consequently, is likely to play an important part in adolescents' lives. Aspects of sexuality permeate many different facets of school life although they may not be recognized or acknowledged as such. Officially sexuality is subsumed under the heading of moral order and taught in parts of the curriculum. In addition the manifestation of sexuality within the everyday life of the classroom will be identified and discussed.

The curriculum not only represents dominant values and ideologies in our society, but also what constitutes legitimate knowledge. It is in regard to the curriculum, both overt and hidden, that differentiation occurs both as it affects class and gender relations. What is available, to whom and how it is taught, are obvious elements in the process of differentiation within sectors of our school population and has direct repercussions on pupils' future life chances.

PART ONE

========

DISCIPLINE AND CONTROL

CHAPTER ONE

Within these walls

Introduction

The literature on girls in schools focuses increasingly on their reported experiences, particularly in relation to boys. The assumption is that the descriptive accounts of their experiences will provide the key to redressing the imbalances in the educational opportunities for girls.

Thus, for example, girls' descriptions of their experience of sexual harassment by boys in the classroom are used to explain unequal educational achievement between the genders (Arnot, 1984, Mahony, 1985, Spender, 1980, Weiner, 1985). Such work claims that boys' behaviour is the major cause of the apparent failure of girls to achieve in school.

Undoubtedly, the relationship between boys and girls in the classroom is one condition which gives rise to the pattern of girls' educational attainment. But does this exhaust all other relevant factors? The answer is in the negative. Such accounts are one dimensional and ignore factors such as class and ethnic differences, the organizational framework of the school, discipline and other forms of control, the curriculum, youth culture, family influences and so on. All these factors which interact with each other within the schooling system must be taken into account. And this book will attempt to set out some of these complex, interrelated areas.

Any analysis, it will be argued, must take as its starting point disciplinary control because this is at the very nub of school organization and creates the conditions in which the pedagogic purposes of the school may be realized. This then provides the base point from which the analysis of gender differences may occur because disciplinary measures structure the basis under which all other processes within the school operate. Disciplinary measures permeate all parts of school life and *all* participants – female, male, teachers, pupils alike – are subjected to some form of control.

Discipline and its implementation has been examined using subjective analyses (Hargreaves et al., 1975, Stebbins, 1987, Denscombe, 1984). But it is an area which has largely been ignored by many sociologists concerned with structural analyses. This lacuna is all the more surprising given the concern in popular culture for these issues and the expression of a moral panic in the media and amongst some factions in government over what is seen as the absence or decline in discipline. Football hooliganism or the reported increase in crimes of violence is assumed, in these circles, to be related to issues of law and order, which in turn are seen as being affected by the nature of education and child rearing (Wolpe, 1983, Denscombe, 1984). The cause of this alleged change in the moral fibre of the country is defined as the legacy of the permissive 1960s coupled with an overall failure of the education system with its egalitarian philosophy. Teachers and parents, especially working mothers, are blamed for the state of affairs. Obviously, within this context, discourses on discipline are of immediate concern to women: if in ideological terms its failure is attributed to child-rearing practices it follows that there are recognizable implications for women.

Discipline does not recognize gender or other differences. Because of the tendency of many discourses on discipline to take the population concerned as comprising a homogeneous one, it is not surprising that issues related to the general imposition of discipline are not part of the feminist agenda and are consistently ignored by most feminist writers.

It will be argued that it is not possible to begin understanding issues relating to gender differences in school without beginning with an analysis of discipline.

Discipline is recognized as a necessary part of the teacher's everyday life and, indeed, plays a very important role in classroom interaction. Its form and content is often not fully understood and the discourses on teachers' practice focuses very much on their own inherent abilities and qualities.

This chapter will consider the whole issue of discipline. It will focus on the way in which the headteacher conceptualized discipline and control and the measures he proposed to follow to ensure a smooth-running school with minimal disciplinary problems. His views exemplify one of the main discourses in popular culture on this question. Teachers' views will also be represented, demarcating the major difference between the traditionalist and the non-traditionalist which reside in ideological conceptions of what discipline is about.

In order to locate this empirical material within a theoretical context, the chapter will begin with a brief discussion on the way in which popular culture constructs discipline as part of moral order. An alternate form of analysis will be suggested drawing heavily on Foucault (1982). This will provide the basis for understanding those processes involved in disciplinary order. It is only when this has been established that it becomes possible to identify and understand the process of gender differentiation in schools.

Although disciplinary control may be a necessary condition for the containment of individuals within an institutional context, this functionality is not reflected in popular culture. Rather the discourse is usually in terms of moral order. What constitutes moral order is variously described, but there are several common features. Moral order is seen as the outcome of proper supervision and training in the home, correct disciplining in school and the teaching of what constitutes the moral code. It is necessary for each successive generation to be taught the correct moral values of society. It results in the development amongst individuals of a rational process which directs behaviour.

There is an assumption amongst conservatives that egalitarian philosophy and the permissiveness of the 1960s has had an adverse effect on the moral codes of the society. The upbringing of children at home is criticized, and discipline in the schools is seen to be lax. In the 1970s it was presented by the media as a failure of the teachers to maintain discipline. Nor have the terms of the debate altered significantly this past decade, with the problem being attributed to the failure of law and order and the absence of effective discipline in homes and schools. Schools are, therefore, charged with ensuring that pupils are not only taught to behave properly but also learn the fundamental principles of the moral code.

What constitutes the moral code is the subject of debate and analysis, with two major elements continuously referred to. The

21

first relates to all aspects of behaviour and the parameters of what constitutes acceptable social behaviour, and the second relates directly to aspects of sexuality. This latter aspect together with some discussion on the way in which social philosophers conceptualize moral order will be discussed in Chapter 4. For the present the focus will be on general patterns of behaviour and how this links to discipline. The rigid rules governing behaviour and etiquette in the eighteenth and nineteenth centuries no longer prevail. Instead there is a vague and unspecified notion of good behaviour which obviously is class related. For example, rowdiness and aggressive forms of behaviour amongst members of the aristocracy is termed 'high spirits' while very similar behaviour amongst football fans is termed 'hooliganism' (Pearson, 1983). There appears to be some consensus which takes various indicators as exemplars of 'good' behaviour in school, like mode of dress and the observation of certain rituals, such as lining up outside a classroom. These are never questioned but, rather, taken-for-granted indicators. There is a further assumption that correct behaviour is related to academic attainment. If pupils behave properly they are likely to achieve well at school. Finally, correct and proper behaviour is seen to be non-gender specific.

An alternative conceptual framework and one which will provide the basis for the analysis below, is that developed by Foucault in his book, *Discipline and Punish* (1982).[1] His work is complex and raises several controversies including what constitutes power relations. But this is not the place to discuss it. Suffice it to say that he sees discipline as part of the institutional formations and disciplinary procedures as having emerged from a need for various organizations to have 'docile' and compliant people. His account provides the basis for a systematic discussion on both the discourses and the practices of disciplinary control in schools.

According to Foucault, a common feature of institutions is the constant surveillance of all subjects whereby an ever present but subtle coercion over them is maintained. As the term implies, surveillance is a straightforward means of keeping the pupils constantly in sight and under supervision. To achieve this the nature and design of the school premises is important. Dawson (1981) discovered this when he first took over as head of Eltham Forest School. He immediately engaged in some changes to his own office with the installation of a window which gave him instant view of pupils and, with a judicious use of a pair of binoculars, he could extend his range of surveillance.

The timetable which effectively controls the whereabouts of the pupils at any one point in time is a further form of surveillance. The pastoral system is yet another (Sarap, 1982). This system is founded on an ideology of 'caring' for the pupil. This is a recognition that some pupils could experience personal problems which could have a deleterious effect on their education and through the pastoral system these problems could be identified and, where possible, resolved. The pastoral system may employ the expertise of various external agencies such as child educational psychologists, welfare bodies and so on to achieve its aim. In principle the provision is closely linked to the 'child-centred' ideology which has dominated so much of educational thinking over the past fifty years. In practice, however, the pastoral system has become a major vehicle for dealing with the many social problems encountered in large metropolitan schools, and an integral part of the control system. Whilst pastoral care no doubt does provide the basis for dealing effectively with individual problems a pupil may have, the unintended consequence of such a system is to augment disciplinary control over pupils through detailed knowledge of them obtained by surveillance which includes home visits and the personal file system. The range of surveillance is extensive.

All schools employ 'simple instruments of discipline'. These instruments are derived from the needs of the institution rather than the needs of the individual pupil. This is a different shift in emphasis from that of Entwistle (1970a) who analysed discipline in terms of the need of the individual child because of the 'need for regulatory restraints upon human behaviour'.

These 'instruments of discipline' are varied and include a range of strategies and actions such as classroom registers, school assemblies, different forms of punishment including corporal punishment, the adoption of school uniform and so on. An additional instrument, and a very important one, is what Foucault calls 'normalizing judgements' which involve ranking and grading pupils. This 'marks the gaps, hierarchizes qualities, skills and aptitude, but . . . also punishes and rewards' (Foucault, 1982, p. 181). In schools these judgments are effected by streaming, setting, allocation of marks, and, ultimately, the examination system. These judgments assess the pupils and reduce them to what Foucault terms a coherent 'normative order'.

The examination system, an example of a complex and sophisticated form of 'normalizing judgements', is a highly effective tool for controlling pupils. Its effectivity as a means of predicting both study and work capabilities have long been suspect. In an article Desmond Nuttall criticized 'the continued reliance on exams'. He said: 'The experiences of the Open University and comparable institutions throughout the world confirms that exams are poor selection devices within education' (*TES* 18 November 1983). Those who plan to write examinations are in structured situations which reduce the likelihood of their resistance to the school culture if they are to succeed in the examinations. Thus examinations have become a significant part of discipline in schools and there is a positive correlation between ease of classroom control and a high number of pupils taking higher level public examinations. In those schools where end of year and public examinations are not the order of the day classroom control constitutes a major problem. Such schools characteristically have a larger enrolment of working-class pupils than others in which expectations about pupil attainment are high and indeed are achieved. In the former – and inner city schools exemplify this – the emphasis will be on strategies other than the examination system, if classroom control is to be maintained.

With the transition to GCSE (General Certificate of Secondary Education) system and its innovative form of assessment, there is possible room for change. However, it is far too early in the development of this alternate system to know whether the move towards continuous assessment and the development of practical skills will affect this normative process. The GCSE is intended to cater for all abilities and it is assumed that the lowest level pupils will sit examinations for the first time. If this does occur then the system will be a highly effective one of control, and could contribute to increasing the level of attainment of those at the bottom of the pile.[2]

Discipline in Berkeley

Because Berkeley did not aim at developing a high academic profile (for a detailed discussion of this see Chapter 7 on the Curriculum) it could not rely on tests and end of year examinations to maintain control over its pupils. On these grounds it could have been predicted that surveillance, punishment, monitoring truancy and other disciplinary strategies would be emphasized in the struggle to maintain control over the pupils. This was the case.

Berkeley, with an initial intake of just 180 pupils, would hardly experience the range of problems for which inner city schools are notorious. However, Mr Trim, the headteacher, was acutely aware of potential dangers. His previous appointment as pastoral head in a nearby secondary school had alerted him to the important role of headship. As he had worked in the area (an educational priority one with its full complement of social problems), he was conversant with specific local difficulties. He consequently placed discipline high on his list of priorities and was going to make known to staff and pupils alike exactly what his expectations were.

Through his power to define, initiate and enforce some of the specific instruments of discipline Mr Trim's role as headteacher was extremely important. His views were directly linked to the strategies he planned to adopt. At no time did he raise questions such as what are the conditions which necessitate these measures; are the differences between boys and girls significant for the application of discipline; how does the gender of the teachers affect their classroom control; why do pupils resist and how may their resistance be understood; does resistance occur amongst girls as well as amongst boys?

Mr Trim never overlooked an opportunity to express his views on discipline. During assemblies and in everyday situations both teachers and pupils were constantly reminded of these issues. His views on pupils were encapsulated in his message at the first school assembly when he said: 'Nobody can leave until 1979. Now you are almost like prisoners'. Not the most propitious of similes: were the teachers the warders and the pupils the prisoners? Unwittingly he was echoing the similarity between prisons, schools, factories and asylums to which Foucault drew attention.

Mr Trim realized the need to control his staff as well as the pupils. He had already experienced a challenge to his leadership in the first year by some of the young members of staff over the issue of corporal punishment. His initial bonhomie towards all staff members after the halcyon days of cooperative working, had given way to a clear alignment with the older, more traditional teachers whose views on discipline and punishment corresponded with his own. He had distanced himself from those teachers whom he clearly regarded as leftwingers and trouble makers. (This is discussed in some detail in Chapter 7.)

To present his views unequivocally to the large number of teachers appointed in the second year of the school's history, he held a day school. By now his ideas had been sharpened following his first year's headship and these were set out in a working paper titled 'School Atmosphere and Tone, Discipline and Related Matters'.

His position on discipline is clearly identifiable and reflects the discourse in popular culture which links overt outward forms of behaviour to discipline and control. He was concerned with all his pupils, and did not differentiate on the basis of gender.

To ensure his pupils behaved well he said that it was necessary to develop the correct 'tone'. This is another example of Mr Trim's conventional views which correspond with those expressed by Mr Dawson (1981) who quoted the then Senior Chief Inspector of Schools as saying at a headteachers' conference in 1977 that 'that which dictates action in a school is not so much what is actually going on but what people think is going on' and that constitutes the 'tone' of a school. Mr Trim said that he had referred to this on numerous occasions and emphasized that it was a 'subject of considerable concern. Members of staff may disagree violently on what constitutes tone'.

Mr Trim was unable to define exactly what he meant by 'tone'. He related it to behaviour and dress saying 'there is a clear correlation between standards of dress and behaviour and I believe school tone will be assisted certainly in the early years by insistence on school uniform'. Indeed the adoption of school uniform had been widely debated before the school opened. Arguments that it could discriminate against parents who could not afford to pay for the uniform were overcome on the basis that the LEA would assist such people.

He assured the new teachers that parents were '99 per cent behind this policy. There were gains for parents: it was economic for some and for those in financial difficulties there would be aid'. He admitted to lack of consensus amongst the staff on this question, acknowledging earlier protests by the original staff against school uniform on the grounds that it could prove discriminatory.

He located his discussion within the context of the contested area of 'progressive' education displaying his own contradictory position. He did not want to appear 'old-fashioned' but at the same time he did not want to be labelled as 'progressive'. He equated 'self-discipline' with 'progressivism', both of which he regarded in a pejorative way: 'We need to recognise that "progressive" is not synonymous with "new" and that we may well wish to use well-known and tried methods in our attempts to assist the growth of the school.' To avoid being labelled 'old-fashioned' he added: ' . . .

we must always be prepared to radically change our ideas if they are not seen to serve our general aims.' He contrasted 'self-discipline' with 'externally imposed discipline' saying that the 'text books said that the former was preferable':

This is undoubtedly true but we need to look at the other side of the coin. We need to expect and insist on high standards of work and behaviour from our pupils and bear in mind equally incontrovertible evidence that teacher expectation plays a large part in pupils' attainment.

This was the occasion in which he linked pupils' attainment with their behaviour. But he did not pursue the question of levels of attainment, reflecting his overall concern with behaviour.

He did not absolve staff from responsibility in maintaining their own self-discipline but emphasized the need to focus on pupils' behaviour:

Whilst I hope we shall encourage a sense of self discipline and corporate responsibility I hope staff will give meticulous attention to the general behaviour of pupils in their care. We should not accept a slip-shod attitude from anybody, equally we should see that we adopt a consistency of approach which wins the respect of our pupils.

Like Entwistle (1970) who took as axiomatic the 'need for regulatory restraints upon human behaviour', he did question the 'need' to control pupils. He then linked behaviour to the moral order:

Values, which today are considered old-fashioned by some – courtesy, perseverance, loyalty, self-esteem – all, with outer virtues, will occupy an important position in my thinking. These expectations of pupils will be tempered by a depth understanding of individual circumstances which, I hope will ensure our methods remain enlightened, yet consistent in operation.

He wished to avoid the stigma of being labelled 'old-fashioned' through his assertion that his position was one of concern for the individual which was not the case in the 'old-fashioned' views. In this way he was able to claim to be advanced in his thinking. After all, the school motto was 'we care'.

Mr Trim's comments on discipline mirrors that of popular culture (as distinct from high culture and reflecting the culture of everyday life), in so far as he relates it to behaviour and further introduces a class dimension which is often implicit in popular culture. He anticipated that the predominant working-class social background of the school's pupils would constitute a disciplinary problem because of deficits in their home background. It was his duty to ensure that he and his teachers rectified these lacunae and deficits. His position on class differences became more obvious when he discussed the nature and content of the school's curriculum (see Chapter 7).

To maintain overall control in combating truancy he set out certain guidelines and initiated various procedures which all teachers were to follow. And he was to maintain corporal punishment as a major deterrent.

Rates of truancy[3] are particularly high in metropolitan areas and it was estimated that in 1982, ILEA had 20,000 pupils (both girls and boys) absent each day.[4] Mr Trim believed that truancy was an indicator of loss of control over pupils and consequently placed means of dealing with truancy high on the agenda. At a staff meeting he drew attention to a 'survey of inner London [which] showed a very large proportion of kids in large schools played truant, had days off. A survey of our schools will show the same, as I know to my own bitter experience'. To combat this he said that every child was to bring a note if absent and failure to do so would result in the child being sent home. He warned the staff against the possibility of forgeries and said that the tactics to combat this problem would involve closer cooperation with parents. He insisted that pupils would have to bring notes from their parents if they missed a day's schooling and failure to do so would result in the child being sent home. He warned the staff against the possibility of forgeries. All this was to be monitored by the pastoral staff who would act as watchdogs over absenteeism. To be effective the full collaboration of the parents was required. This in turn could be achieved through the 'home links' established by the pastoral staff's home visits.

This instruction was acceptable to the staff, unlike that on corporal punishment on which Mr Trim set store as an ultimate deterrent for difficult cases. Any teacher who rejected corporal punishment was labelled by him as inexperienced or a threat to his authority.

At staff meetings early on in the life of the school the question of banning corporal punishment was hotly debated. Mr Trim successfully overruled what was then the majority's opposition to the retention of this in what one of the teachers described as 'intellectual gymnastics':

Mr Trim said he didn't really like the cane, didn't like using it. But he argued that as long as one member of the staff wanted him to maintain the cane he felt that he had a duty to that member of staff to do so, and he didn't seem impressed by the argument that while nine members of this staff wanted to abolish it he felt that he had a duty to those as well and that didn't sway him. He said that parents expected it.

The acrimony surrounding the retention of corporal punishment continued unabated and feelings ran high when Mr Trim hit a boy whom he had found in a classroom when everyone was supposed to be outside in the playgrounds. Some of the staff's outrage was based on the 'perfectly innocuous' character of the boy concerned. Others pointed out that this happened three days after a staff meeting had resolved that:

> Before any sort of corporal punishment was administered the teacher in charge of the lesson and the child's personal tutor would both be consulted and even if only one of them was in favour then it would not be used.

Some of the staff were incensed that these procedures had been overlooked. The head justified his action by claiming that his smacking the boy did not constitute corporal punishment as such. In spite of his protestations the incident completed the polarization of the staff which had been taking place. It provided the reference point for identifying those who had by now come to be seen as 'leftists'.

Although corporal punishment as such was not used in the first two years – apart from this one incident – its retention was significant. It was unlikely to be invoked, given the age group of the pupils. The absence of older, and hence more difficult pupils, made it unlikely that the pupils in the first few years would resist to the same extent as older pupils. They were likely to appear to be compliant given their youth.

It is important to point out that all the comments on corporal punishment took as given a homogeneity of the pupils and ignored the question of whether corporal punishment could be imposed on girls. There was no possibility that a male teacher in a position of authority would administer the cane to a girl, nor was it likely that a woman in authority would wield the cane on a girl. This is the first indication of a difference which is directly related to gender.

Discussion therefore on corporal punishment must be seen to be only applicable to boys, even though this has not always been the case.[5]

Mr Trim's views on corporal punishment were explicitly stated at the Day School mentioned above where he acknowledged that there was some opposition to its maintenance:

> External sanctions will be the concern of individual teachers although the use of corporal punishment (and I hope it won't be necessary) will be restricted to the head and his deputy only. To date it has not been necessary to invoke this sanction; I hope that it will remain inappropriate. A firm but under-standing approach to pupils can create the secure framework within which personality development can take place.

The retention of corporal punishment was a clear indication of the head's notion of what constituted one of the most important tools in maintaining control.[6] It was a statement of intent and a form of demarcating those teachers who could be identified as constituting a potential threat to traditional authority. He linked this opposition to his complaint that members of staff wanted to participate with parents in decision-making procedures thereby threatening his own authority. He had successfully silenced or eliminated those teachers who had threatened his authority through various means such as blocking their promotion which resulted in their seeking jobs elsewhere. He had also monitored new appointments very carefully, in many cases appointing teachers who were recommended by members of staff who supported his view. By the end of the second year he had redefined the aim of the school expunging the title of community school and emphasizing the role of home links, and family and community links.

Overall Mr Trim had succeeded in creating an atmosphere of 'calm and order'. Miss Cray who left Berkeley after six years had this to say:

> I think that I was conscious that there was an air of calm and order around the place. That was a lot to do with the fact that people like Donald and Bertie [the head and his deputy] were around. I saw that continuing right through until the time I left Berkeley and it was the sort of scene that kids knew. O.K. I am not saying that the discipline was fantastic because of

everything else. But, by and large, there seemed to be reasonable discipline in corridors and around the place generally as well as in individual classrooms.

Mr Trim's strategy appeared to have been successful. Both boys and girls had responded to the ground rules he had established and the school ran with minimal disturbances which affect so many large metropolitan schools.

It is now appropriate to consider the way in which some of the teachers talked about discipline and control and the techniques they employed. Obviously it constitutes a very important part of teachers' lives. Entwistle (1970a) drew a useful distinction between a disciplined and an ordered classroom, pointing out that it is not axiomatic that a teacher well prepared for the lesson has control over the class. The teacher must impose some constraint on individual pupils although he says this does not exclude the possibility of a bond of personal affection developing between the teacher and pupil. When this occurs it is a bonus for the teacher. Although he does not spell it out, he suggests that the teacher has to have specific qualities in order to achieve order in the classroom. In other words it is the *quality and the personal attributes* of the teacher which are important, according to Entwistle.

This view is common amongst most teachers although they may identify two distinctive types of control: traditional and authoritarian and/or liberal. There were representatives of both categories at Berkeley.

The traditionalist favours formal control over individual pupils supporting the ultimate sanction of corporal punishment. School is seen as a potential battleground. The main aim of the traditionalist is to establish and maintain power and control over all pupils and does so using a range of tactics or disciplinary instruments which include all forms of punishment, as well as ridiculing and marginalizing the pupil. The ability to maintain discipline is thought to be dependent on an individual's personal attributes and these develop with experience. Mr David, responsible for handicrafts and design and technology, was such a teacher. He said:

I suppose you would say I was a disciplinarian. I think it pays dividends in the end. I think the kids appreciate it. . . . They like to know where they stand with you, and they probably think you are a miserable old devil at the very beginning. But often they appreciate you later on, especially if it produces good results for them, you know.[7]

He emphasized the need for strictness in the workshop:

I mean it's a constant worry all the time that some child is going to have a serious accident. We get a lot of trivial accidents, cuts and things like that, but . . . er . . . it's a constant worry that somebody is really going to get badly injured one day. Luckily I've never been in that position yet and I hope that I'm not. But you can't afford to be slack at all you know. I mean I have seen handicraft teachers where there has been a riot in the workshop. I have had to go down and sort things out – hammers flying around and things like that, *only because it was a weak teacher there*. I think you learn these things from experience as you go along (my emphasis).

The weakness did not refer to a physical condition but to failure to control; Mr David was small of stature and did not appear to be physically strong.

He set up ground rules for conduct in his classroom and any transgressions were immediately dealt with decisively. For example failure on the part of anyone to line up quietly one behind the other in the corridor outside his workshop before the lesson commenced was not tolerated. When the class did not observe this he immediately picked out at random some of the boys and girls responsible, and made them stand behind his desk, ignoring them completely, whilst he set the rest of the class their work.

When he did turn to them he gave them a lecture on their faults, and then set them the task of writing why they should line up outside the room. On completion they were allowed to rejoin the others. This proved an effective lesson. A watch was always maintained and as Mr David approached the room a warning call was made. 'Look out, he's coming', followed by complete silence. Their apparent good behaviour always won his approval. Mr David's strategy was double-edged, as he subsequently told me:

It also meant that there weren't so many bottlenecks, you know. There were five of them writing while the rest were doing their work. But that's one of the troubles in workshops,

you know. There are always bottlenecks where children have
to wait around for their turn on something or other, and that
can lead to indiscipline. So you try and avoid these and that
was one way. But nothing serious. I knew we would only be
on it for about fifteen or twenty minutes [referring to the pun-
ishment]. They soon caught up.

Mr David provided a recipe for dealing with problems encountered
in teaching a large number of pupils with limited equipment.
Avoiding a bottleneck could be done through setting some pupils
useless tasks. But this also indicates the slowness of lessons, generated by classes that are too large, which may well be one indicator
of why so many pupils seem to be bored in class.

Mr David was in charge of potentially dangerous equipment and
he had to establish his authority from the outset. His strategy applied
equally to girls and boys, although when it came to classroom interaction he did differentiate on the basis of his differential expectations, as will be discussed in Chapter 8.

The tactic of marginalization Mr David used was a common
ploy. Mr Jason, the science teacher, described how he effectively
debarred pupils from doing scientific experiments as a means of
control. He said they always enjoyed doing this and he could make
them feel 'horrible' in the course of preventing them from participating.

The liberal approach to discipline could employ tactics similar
to those of the traditionalist but the ideology differed. The common
link with all liberal teachers is the concern with individual pupils
and their psychological needs. Qualities of mutual trust and cooperation between staff and pupils are likely to be emphasized and
contrasted with control through fear which is attributed to
traditional teachers. For example, Miss Cray, the remedial teacher,
said: 'I relate to kids. I didn't expect to be shouting at kids, but
expected to try and establish a situation where kids were wanting
to work rather than they were terrified not to.' A liberal position
could also be concerned with the home background and considers
difficult children as victims of some form of deprivation or tension
in their homes, ranging from financial hardship to too high an
expectation for attainment on the part of their parents.

Liberal positions on discipline unanimously rejected the use in
principle of corporal punishment although teachers were not beyond
resorting to such a threat when under duress. Mrs White, for

example, had consistent problems with one boy. In exasperation in the staffroom one day she complained how 'he's grinning all over his face like a great big giggling girl and I told him if he didn't wipe that smile off his face I would send him to Mr Burns [the deputy headteacher] who would do it'.

Although she was passionate about the abolition of corporal punishment, the possibility of forgetting one's principles in the course of dealing with some of the tensions in the classroom is illustrated by this incident. Furthermore, it is a clear cut example of the expression of the employment of stereotypical views which will be discussed in the following chapter.

Conclusion

Discipline and its various instruments operate within a school and do so irrespective of the composition of the school. Single sex schools, co-educational schools, state and private schools all employ a range of disciplinary strategies. In this regard the gender of the pupils is quite unimportant. Both boys and girls are treated as an undifferentiated group.

The head's construction of school discipline was in terms of aspects of moral codes of behaviour which he distinguished from a more 'radical' view which he assumed neglected or negated these moral codes. For him moral order upheld the traditional, but worthy conventions of everyday behaviour.

This can lead to two distinct positions in regard to the identification of areas of concern. The first is in children's behaviour and the second is in the role of the teachers in regard to classroom control. Mr Trim was predominantly concerned with the first aspect. The second, classroom control, was outside his area of concern because it was seen as relating to the assumed inherent qualities and capabilities of individual teachers. As such it was not regarded as the head's responsibility. He had to take for granted the ability of his staff to control the classrooms and failure to do so was attributed to the faults of the individual teacher. These views were shared by teachers as well, although they were divided in their views on the methods they should adopt in the classroom.

The head employed a range of methods of surveillance and upheld the conventional instruments of discipline. With the majority of pupils unlikely to do GCE academic examinations the importance of these was heightened. The head recognized this to be the case although his accounting for this need was based on the social composition of the pupils and not on the structure of disciplinary methods.

It was only when corporal punishment was discussed that it became one of the dividing points in relation to gender differences. If corporal punishment in the form of caning could not be used on girls, then there might be some other strategies which the head or teachers consciously or unconsciously applied, assuming that girls require to be controlled in the same way that boys do.

This immediately raised the problem of whether there is a marked difference and what the perception of this difference is between the behaviour of boys and girls and, if so, how control of girls is managed. This leads to a need to focus on the behaviour of both groups.

This has repercussions because of the stereotypical notions about what constitutes feminine and masculine behaviour. The latter is associated with aggression etc., and this is what is seen as needing control within the schools. The concentration on boys' behaviour is reinforced by other related aspects. Absenteeism is so often associated with acts of deviancy and because boys are seen as deviants, the focus of attention is again on boys. The stereotypical view of girls as quiet, obedient, and passive in the classroom and the expectations that both boys and girls have about each other all have repercussions on the way in which teachers behave towards girls. By definition, boys are the problem. The unintended consequence of this is that girls' potential for classroom disruption, violence and other forms of resistance and aggressive behaviour and the actuality of this potential is overlooked or ignored. These are issues which will be explored in the following chapter which will focus on classroon interaction.

CHAPTER TWO

Classroom behaviour

Introduction

In the previous chapter the disciplinary control of all pupils was shown to be a precondition for learning. The range of these controls is established by the headteacher but obviously the major arena for interaction is in the classroom in face to face contact between pupils and teachers. It is in this context that gender differences surface. This chapter will examine the way in which gender differences intersect at the point of pupil/teacher interaction.

Through the presentation of empirical data based on interviews and observations, the conventional wisdom of girls as passive subjects dominated by boys and not given sufficient attention by teachers will be challenged.

It will be shown, drawing on the notion of what constitutes stereotypical behaviour, that teachers' views do confirm these generalized notions. However, their views are not always consistent nor do they reflect the reality of the situation although they do structure the way in which they respond to different groups. There will be a brief discussion of some of the dominant views in feminist literature on classroom interaction in terms of teachers' behaviour and the way boys and girls are thought to behave, with the boys dominating and oppressing the girls. Contrary to this, the classroom observations will show that just as some boys reject school ethics by doing no or minimal class work, so do some girls. Furthermore, other girls may play dominant parts in classroom interaction reflecting their level of commitment to school and a tendency to do well. Finally, some girls may dominate some boys in the classroom situation. All this aims to point out that classroom interaction is much more complex than the stereotypical views would lead one to expect. Furthermore, that these interactions are ever changing and reflect not only the various stages of development but also the context in which these events occur. Thus conventional wisdom is questioned.

There was a reference in the last chapter to Mrs White's irritation and anger with a boy and her threat to send him to the deputy head because he was 'giggling like a great big girl'. His behaviour was disrupting the class and she was clearly not able to control him. She tried humiliating him by publicly referring to him as a 'big giggling girl' and, at the same time, threatened him with corporal punishment. What in effect she was doing was invoking stereotypical notions about girls' behaviour which appeared unpleasant. She implied that giggling was typically female (and irritating at that) and that boys did not behave in this way. She was classifying and generalizing what constituted female stereotypical behaviour.

Over the past few years there has been a trend towards creating a stereotypical view of boys which is being employed as an 'explanatory' framework to account for the form of all girls' education and expectations and life chances. This stereotypical view has identified certain characteristics in boys: noisiness, demand for teachers' attention, need of discipline, pejorative and often violent treatment of girls. It has evaluated these characteristics in terms of all powerful control of boys over girls. These generalizations have also become more widely accepted by those teachers and academic writers who are concerned with issues of gender differences and sexist practices. Ironically this replicates the very problem that in the past we were at great pains to draw attention to, and that is the use of stereotyping which enabled girls' performance at school to be overlooked because of the expectations of what constituted girls' appropriate behaviour. What is now happening is that the set of stereotypical notions about boys has led to expectations about boys' behaviour as a whole. It ignores the widespread differentiation that does exist between boys as well as those which operate within the educational system. Similarly, the stereotypical notion of girls as quiet, devoted to their school work, passive and as victims of boys' oppressive behaviour is not questioned. Working within the framework of stereotyping is sterile whether applied to boys or girls. The use of stereotypes constitutes boys and girls as homogeneous groups, thereby ignoring class and other differences. Such typifications mask the complexity in social relations in schools and also tend to ignore the impact that social forces external to the school make.

Differences in the behaviour of men and women, girls and boys has been the subject matter for social psychologists (Weitz, 1977, Chetwynd and Hartnett, 1979, Maccoby and Jacklin, 1974) whose concern has been with the description of and manifestation of these differences in behaviour. Such work has taken the differences as given and focused more on the plotting of these differences rather than giving an account of how they occur. Much of the work results in the formulation of stereotypical views about gender-specific forms of behaviour.

What constitutes stereotypical behaviour has been largely the subject matter, as well, for social psychologists who take this as a given, and, consequently, non-problematic aspect of people's psychology derived from socialization and which accounts for different behaviour patterns in groups.

Perkins (1979) pointed out that stereotypes are, by definition, typifications or simplifications of common elements which refer to apparent, straightforward identifiable characteristics and predictions of how people will behave. Stereotyping results in the formation of generalizations, and may become part of our culture expressed as beliefs about certain groups. So stereotypical views may be held by groups and are judgmental in nature. The use of stereotyping embraces evaluative statements and these often refer to the performance of rights and duties. In other words stereotyping creates specific roles of identifiable groups in society. Stereotypical views may be held by groups. Stereotypes:

> tend to be thoroughly integrated into a number of practices. They are structurally supported . . . by laws, traditions, institutions . . . stable and definitively central in socialization . . . widely and consistently believed in . . . highly effective in providing people with explanations and definitions of themselves and of others (Perkins, p. 147).

In addition Perkins says that stereotypes are both 'inaccurate or false' in that they 'present interpretations of groups which conceal the real cause of the groups' attributes and confirm the legitimacy of the groups' oppressed position' (p. 155). The views held about specific groups are not questioned; they are deemed to possess certain characteristics and subsequent behaviour towards such groups is regarded as legitimate and justified.

Stereotypical images may become popularized, according to Perkins. The notion of popularization is 'an opaque one' as Riley (1983) pointed out in her discussion on the use of psychoanalytical concepts on child-rearing practices in this country. A clear example of this process may be illustrated by the work of Bowlby, who, as is well known, established a causal relationship between maternal deprivation and delinquency. Bowlby set out to prove, as Riley puts it, 'that separation of the young child from its mother or mother substitute was inherently traumatic. Bowlby's own evidence did not fully warrant the conclusions he drew'. Nevertheless, as a result of the process of popularization effected by various aspects of the media and the dissemination of his work which coincided with a wide literature dealing with problem families this relationship, she argued, became 'a piece of common-sense socio-psychology which lacked any memory of its own origins'.

She says that:

> his work is part of a wider grouping of ideas. For British psychology tends to behave as if it had no history, and could constitute its discoveries on previously unturned ground; a characteristic encouraged by the absence of full accounts of British psychoanalytic ideas and institutions (p. 108).

As with Bowlby's work in the course of popularization the notion 'is employed as if it offered an informative account of a process' but, as Riley bluntly points out, 'it actually explains nothing' (p. 83). In discussing Bowlby's work more fully she says that what occurred was 'the flattening of specificities into generalizations'. Similarly with the generalizations about classroom behaviour.

As will be shown, the processes of generalization and popularization occur within the classroom. The following discussion will illustrate these particularly in the classroom. When examining the work on gender differences in schools the popularized stereotypical views about boys and girls have repercussions particularly in terms of the control over girls.

Teachers and gender differences

In her much quoted article reporting her research in four primary schools (one working-class in a north industrial urban slum, one middle-class suburban 'rural', one council estate school, and a small rural primary school), Clarricoates (1980) produced a check list of teachers' perception of differences between boys and girls. These adjectives form part of the stereotypical view held about girls and boys. They were:

Girls
obedient, tidy, neat, conscientious, orderly, fussy, catty, bitchy, gossiping.

Boys
livelier, adventurous, aggressive, boisterous, self-confident, independent, energetic, couldn't-care-less, loyal.

Clarricoates had this to say about the teachers: 'By providing such ready, stereotyped lists, the teachers betray their own habit of classifying children according to their sex' (p. 39).[1] Did the teachers at Berkeley hold similar stereotypical views? Miss Cray, for example, had no doubts that boys were more 'troublesome'. Mr Sands, a young teacher in Humanities and one of the pastoral team, who dressed well in a thoroughly contemporary manner, gave a more detailed description:

> When it comes to working in the classroom I think that in general . . . boys have a reputation, justly or unjustly, for being noisemakers . . . that girls are the more studious ones, perhaps not so clever: but they want to sit down quietly in the classroom and work. Boys have been given this aura of being noisemakers.
> . . . the boys' voices are higher [he was referring to them before their voices had broken] and perhaps it might be true to say that there are more individual troublemakers amongst the boys and this gives them a reputation. So the girls gang together and say right we will go and sit here and you . . . hear more in the second year now . . . girls saying 'look we only get work done when you come into the classroom because you know how to deal with the boys'. I don't get it from the boys about the girls, but I get it from the girls about the boys. In several classes the girls ask 'kindly come into our room because the boys are noisy and we want to work' and they make their own divide here.

This statement echoes many of the points continuously referred to in feminist writing which canvasses for a return to single sex schools because there is an assumption that girls are more studious than boys, and the latter are the troublemakers who prevent girls from studying and realizing their potentials. Such positions reflect stereotypical views about both girls and boys.

The assumed passivity of girls, which is a variation on Mr Sands' views of their lesser intellectual abilities, was referred to by Miss Leyland who was one of the more experienced teachers and who had previously taught in a boys' only school. She was one of the senior staff, and was in charge of the pastoral group. She also emphasized the troublesome nature of boys and held the view that boys are fundamentally and inherently different from girls. She had this to say about the pupils when they were twelve year olds:

> Boys are very energetic, and they do need keeping down that much more than the girls. I don't know if it is because the boys are like that, but the girls seem to - what would you say? happy, no passive. It might be that the boys are more immature but the girls seem to be terribly passive. As for the work, the boys just don't seem to get down to work or the majority of them you have got to push. But the girls always. You look at your mark book. You have got a solid block which refers to girls and the boys are the ones that you keep in detention because they haven't done their homework.

Mrs Ivory's comments were somewhat different. This was her first teaching job and she did not appear to be daunted by class-room control. She was the research cohort's form tutor. She was somewhat ambivalent about the girls in her group. She thought that some were lazy, identifying them in very pejorative terms. The non-achievers were dismissed out of hand, irrespective of gender. She said that there was 'more enthusiasm on the boys' side' and thought that 'so many of the girls are namby-pamby, trying not to do anything that they don't have to do'. She complained that the two girls she disliked the most were 'coddled too much at home' because of their 'gigantic size'. She was the only teacher to acknowledge her views on ethnic differences. She claimed that the black boys tended to 'talk a lot and the girls were very talkative'. Overall it seemed as though Mrs Ivory preferred teaching the boys to the girls.

Mr David, the craft teacher and the oldest member of staff, anticipated that boys would, in general, be more difficult than the girls,
that this was 'natural'. He referred to boys by their surname and
girls by their given names. However, he said he relaxed this for-
mality in his own tutor group where if he used the surname 'they
realise that I am fed up with them. . . You can only raise your
voice.'

Some of the male members of staff were conscious of gender differences when it came to control over girls. Mr Sands was nervous
that girls could cry if reprimanded and felt this to be somewhat of a
handicap. But it was Mr David who was the most explicit. He said
'you can't do anything about it' referring here to the difficulties he
experienced in controlling the girls. This was the first co-education
school at which he had taught and he seemed to be finding
difficulties in adjusting his method of control over the girls. He felt
that he could only express his disapproval of girls and said that he
would have to be really hard pushed to 'use a slipper on their back-
sides' although in the end he said that such disciplinary action
would have to be in the hands of a senior mistress whom he felt
should be appointed. He tended to be paternalistic towards the
girls. Furthermore he was adept at verbal abuse when he deemed it
necessary and I saw him reduce a child to a quivering state of fear.

To summarize their main comments:

Girls:
studious, sit quietly and work, make their own divide, passive,
lazy, namby-pamby, black girls very talkative.
Boys:
troublesome, noisemakers, energetic, need keeping down, have to
push to work, need detention, more enthusiastic, black boys talk,
boys 'naturally' more difficult.

These descriptions project positive and negative views about
both girls and boys: energy and more enthusiasm attributed to
boys; studiousness, working and sitting quietly were linked to the
girls. Although both groups came in for some deprecatory remarks
on balance can it be said that more positive comments are made
about the boys than the girls? Apart from Mrs Ivory who appeared
to prefer the boys to the girls, there was an ambivalence. It seems
that there is a greater ambivalence about each group's behaviour
than the stereotypical descriptions would lead one to believe.

As for control there seems to be a consensus about boys being more difficult to control than girls. This belief reflects stereotypical views and not necessarily reality. For example, Davies (1984) who was concerned with deviance found some contradictory evidence. She said there were contradictions in her primary sources. Although the actual figures revealed more boys receiving detentions, and being more likely to be caned:

> Yet in contrast to all this, the majority of both pupils and teachers, male and female, saw girls as being 'more trouble'. Girls received more suspensions. Pupils were twice as likely to see girls, rather than boys breaking rules; only one teacher, a female PE teacher, saw boys as 'probably worse in behaviour' (p. 7).

However, the stereotypical beliefs must have repercussions in the classroom. Apart from identifying which these are, this raises, in addition, a number of questions. How marked are these differences in the everyday life of the classroom? Do the observations of classroom life bear this out? Are girls so easy to control? How does this link up with girls' level of attainment? Do the teachers' attitudes affect their teaching and the way in which pupils learn? In other words how are academic advantages related to teachers' attitudes towards boys or girls?

These are obviously important questions but are difficult to answer. Some feminist literature (Spender, 1980, Stanworth, 1983, Mahony, 1985, Arnot, 1984) has highlighted teachers' classroom behaviour and differential treatment of girls and boys. The importance of this work has been to raise the consciousness of teachers about their practice and to provide some guidelines for combating sexism in school (Weiner, 1985, Cornbleet and Libovitch, 1983). The literature tends to combine teachers' behaviour with a discussion of boys' and girls' responses, resulting in generalizations about all three groups. For the present I shall focus on teachers' behaviour and its alleged outcome.

There is the taken-for-granted assumption that there are overall benefits accruing to all boys through the behaviour of the teachers. Sometimes it is suggested that teachers' behaviour is the outcome of the monopoly of teachers' attention (Mahony, 1985). Sometimes it is assumed that teachers themselves favour boys in contrast with the girls (Arnot, 1984). Sometimes it is seen as an interactional situation (Delamont, 1980). Whatever way it is discussed the focus is on the psychological impact that such behaviour may have on individual girls and boys. When it is applied to girls the impact is seen in negative terms decreasing girls' self-esteem (Stanworth, 1983). This type of analysis is important particularly as it has informed policy interventions in regard to the removal of sexist practices and it will be examined in some detail.

As is well known and in the much quoted study by Stanworth (1983), she found that 'trivial tokens of personal attention from teachers are the very signs that pupils looked for in deciding whether or not they are regarded with favour by their teachers' (p. 50). As boys receive a disproportionate amount of attention from teachers, she concludes that girls' self-esteem is lowered. So one of the elements of boys' overall advantage stems from teachers' behaviour. Two assumptions are made here. One is that all girls experience teachers' behaviour in these negative terms, the second is that boys must experience it in positive ways, in an increase in their self-esteem. I shall consider this when reporting on the empirical data below.

Arnot (1984) enlarges on this point. Referring to Delamont (1980), Spender (1982) and Clarricoates (1980) she says that their work has: 'shown us how teachers tend to concentrate their time and energy upon boys in their classrooms, extending more approval *and* more disapproval to boys than to girls' (p. 38). Irrespective of the positive or negative aspect, it is taken as deleterious for girls' progress. But what is the advantage to boys? Do they gain, for example, in self-esteem and confidence through both approval and disapproval: being told to be quiet, or being 'put down'? It is quite possible that the attention received from teachers may enhance their social standing amongst their peers, but it is not clear why it should improve their self-esteem. Why is it regarded as advantageous that teachers spend more time talking to the boys particularly if that time is taken up with admonitions?

In the 1950s this type of action by teachers was not seen in such functional terms as MacDonald (1981) pointed out when she reviewed some of the American social psychology literature which focused on teacher reaction to boys. According to MacDonald well known studies reported on teachers' 'discrimination against boys'. One researcher argued that the 'instructional and managerial interactions with boys were devious strategies for social control'. The discussion then focused on control rather than on the outcome in terms of observers' beliefs about boys' perceptions. By the 1970s the definition of this type of reaction had been recast in terms of boys gaining 'independence, autonomy and activity' through teachers' constant admonitions and has been done in terms of contrasting boys with girls. Boys since then have been seen as benefiting in the long run although similar behaviour twenty years earlier was construed differently. This is a clear cut example of the interpretation of the data being determined by the theoretical perspective that is adopted initially.[2]

There are scattered examples throughout this book of different facets of teachers' behaviour and pupils' responses. This is presented in the context of concrete aspects of school life, such as in terms of discipline, sexuality or the curriculum. What seems clear is that teachers' behaviour is variable and is directly related to particular aspects of the school life. It is not consistent. They may admonish the boys and ignore the girls but this may be in the context of control in the classroom; they may commend girls for some aspects of their work and suggest to the boys that they should emulate the girls; as individuals they may prefer to teach the one group rather than the other. But overall there is a great deal going on in a classroom at any one time and a complex set of contradictory messages which are simultaneously being generated. Because of this I have found it almost impossible to extract discrete examples of teacher behaviour which only favours the boys to the detriment of the girls. Rather I have chosen to discuss the various examples under other headings.

However, because the consequences of teachers' behaviour is linked not only to expressed reactions on the part of girls, but also is intimately connected with the behaviour of boys which is sometimes described as generating the response by teachers, I now want to present observations in the classroom relating to gender-specific behaviour.

Classroom observations

According to several writers, girls' experience of boys in the classroom reflects boys' overall domination of girls. This, they argue, is discernible in many facets of classroom life. Mahony (1985), for example, reports on girls' reactions. She concludes that boys expend an 'enormous amount of time and energy . . . in the social control of girls'; girls are generally 'put down' by boys; boys are dependent on others; a 'great deal of what is said by boys to girls inside and outside the classroom constitutes verbal abuse'; and girls 'service' boys. She argues that all girls suffer from some form of harassment in school and that 'all girls are equally vulnerable to similar treatment'. She concludes:

> In my view it is indisputable that boys benefit from their behaviour towards girls: we have seen how and why they are serviced by girls, how their access to educational resources is maintained and how they are active in structuring relationships of dominance and subordination. In this sense we begin to see that there is a political dimension to coeducation: that of men's power over women. (p. 53)

In her final analysis there is an overall domination of girls by the boys because of patriarchy. This situation gives rise to the monopoly by the boys of what Mahony terms 'linguistic space'. She presents empirical material which she says provides the background for the teachers' perceptions. She says that: 'Over and over again, examples can be found of boys dominating the teacher's field of vision and girls occupying marginal positions' (p. 37). Here is another example of teachers' reactions being seen as determined by boys' actions.

What was the girls' behaviour like in class? How do these generalizations stand up to examination? The following provides vignettes of some of the classroom activities and in reporting on this the data covers the range of levels of attainment, from the extremes at both ends from high level work to those who appeared to do almost no schoolwork whatsoever, and those in the middle range who can go unnoticed largely because they cause no trouble but also their work is unremarkable. The observations refer to the pupils in their first two years of secondary schooling between the ages of eleven and twelve+ years.

While my observations corroborated the sheer physicality of some of the boys, the notes certainly did not portray the girls as passive, sitting down quietly getting on with their school work, oppressed by boys, dominated by them in all spheres of activity. Quite the contrary. Although not physically active they engaged in a number of counter-school activities which took forms different to those of the boys; such as excessive use of body language, verbal wrangles and wandering about the classroom.

Cheryl and Mavis whom Mrs Ivory had defined as being coddled at home were experts at avoiding doing any work and even now, years later, I can recall them well and still wonder at their success. They were certainly not passive: they just did not work in class at all, and, in a very different way to boys, they were disruptive:

Maths lesson: Cheryl and Mavis did absolutely nothing – carried on a conversation. Cheryl pinches Mavis or tickles her back or carries on. She incessantly sucks her hair. She wanders around a great deal during the lesson.

Science lesson: Cheryl developed the sulks and Mavis spent a great deal of time putting her arm around her or asking her what was wrong. This was followed by a lot of whispering and then involving three other girls in their talk.

Cheryl systematically tormenting Mavis – going over to sit with another girl and then calling Mavis and when she responded shrugging her shoulders and ignoring Mavis. The third girl aware of the tensions and went over to comfort Mavis.

It is not known whether the boys did find this type of behaviour disturbing, although both girls were unpopular, in general, with both boys and girls according to friendship tests that were conducted. Continuous talking and whispering with each other was not uncommon:

English lesson: Reading out loud from a book. Shirely, Cheryl and Mavis wrote on their hands and whispered to each other. Mavis' eyes would wander and gaze out in space.

Cheryl tickles Mavis, punches her in the breast, gets in a huff, shrugs her shoulders, tosses her head and waits to be placated by Mavis.

While these two girls dominate this discussion, this does not mean they were the only ones to indulge in this form of behaviour. Work avoidance was not uncommon. Others, like Mary for example, developed techniques of pretending they were doing class work but either did nothing or drew or coloured-in books. What I could not understand was that if I was aware of this, then surely the teacher must have noticed such behaviour but said or did nothing. Throughout, my notes reflect my surprise at the success of both girls and boys in avoiding work. Provided the girls did not disturb others in a loud manner their behaviour was tolerated by Mrs Ivory.

Mavis and Cheryl represented those girls at the lowest rung in terms of academic achievement. Of course there were others who were simply quiet and self-effacing, like Doreen who did not enter into the notes until after I had interviewed her. She was quiet and successfully avoided the attention of teachers as well as of myself. At the age of twenty she confessed that she was illiterate and was trying to teach herself to read from her daughter's story book! Or take Shirley, a non-achiever, who said she did not feel that she had gained much from school. She did not blame the boys for this but laid the blame more on herself. At the age of twenty she said that 'I never used the knowledge learned at school. *I never learnt*' (my emphasis). She thought that people are better able to learn when they are older. 'Probably if you started school when you are sixteen up until you are twenty you could probably absorb a lot more than all those from the age of five until sixteen.' She regularly played truant the older she got.

The group who fell mid-way in terms of ability and who sometimes worked and sometimes not, like Mary, could be very loud and disruptive at times. There did not seem a particular pattern to this because if they enjoyed a subject they would work at it – as Mary did in woodwork – which she would not do in subjects she did not enjoy such as French.

Then there were those at the top end who did work and did settle down and do all the things that girls were supposed to do like Katherine and Carol. These two were at the forefront in all activities as will be discussed below. Furthermore they were assertive and dominant in the classroom situation, far from the passive image that the stereotyping would lead one to expect.

There was the occasion when Robin, a boy of Afro-Caribbean origin, had asked that they be allowed to form a group and write and act a play. This suggestion was eagerly seized upon and the whole class was set the task of writing plays. They were told they could work in groups, in pairs or individually. Robin formed a group with three girls, including Katherine and Carol. Within a relatively short space of time the proceedings were dominated by Katherine who was the director. It was she who read from a book, defined the individual tasks, and by the end of the session they performed a play.

These two girls seldom took a back seat. Eight boys and two girls were to run the classroom's magazine. The four editors were Katherine, Carol, Stephen and Graham, all four comprising the top achievers in the class. At one of the meetings of the group, the editors sat at the head of the table and the others at the other end with their feet up on the table. The meeting was raucous with a great deal of shouting. Unfortunately I did not time any discussions but from the comments in the notes, the boys did most of the shouting, although I noted that both Graham and Carol applied threats to the others and were quite abusive at times. The girls certainly participated fully in the scheme and organized a group of articles.

There was no question at this stage about separation between boys and girls in regard to the classwork. According to Katherine this was general.

> We usually land up working with boys in science where we do experiments. . . We sort of do all different things with different people. There's much more movement in the class than I thought there would be. . . . I'm not talking of physical movement but people working together and more boys and girls working together. . . The thing is that say two boys don't really understand what they are doing then me and Carol and some other girls might well work in a group – all working together to bring them up to the stage that we are – you know or something like that, which helps the class as well because it comes automatically.

Domination of the classroom by some of the girls occurred in the woodwork class. Mixed woodwork classes were held for the first two years (for further details see Chapter 8). Mr David consistently differentiated between the two groups, quite clearly favouring the boys. But this did not deter the girls who answered questions eagerly and appeared to enjoy the lessons fully. Again, those who did well in academic subjects also did well in this class and participated fully. Mary, though not one of the 'high fliers', enjoyed this subject judging by her actions in the classroom.

There seemed to be a chronic shortage, particularly with the more elaborate equipment, and there was often a queue to work with some of this. Mary was particularly adept at not having to queue. Apart from the fact that she was the tallest person in the classroom and was head and shoulders above the boys, if she wanted a particular tool she simply wrested it away from the nearest boy who usually gave it up without a murmur. Time and time again she would get her own way by such tactics: if she wanted something either for herself or a girlfriend, she took it. In spite of being in a minority group – she was black – she held her own in the class. This was also apparent on social occasions such as the disco run at the school.

These examples do contradict the view of the girls as passive, hard working, quiet and 'namby-pamby'. The section below on their failure to accept the school culture provides further evidence of their active, even aggressive, forms of behaviour which contradict the stereotypical image.

What is also apparent is that age factors are relevant to this type of analysis. Initially Katherine and Carol worked consistently in all their subjects. As Katherine reported (see Chapter 6) her emerging sexuality and involvement in socializing took precedence over schoolwork. She clearly lost interest when she was older and behaved in class like many of the other non-achievers. This suggests other factors intervening, such as her sexuality, an issue that will be explored in that chapter. Her withdrawal from school work could hardly be attributed to the boys' domination of the classroom or their aggression.

Playground activities

Having established that girls are far from passive victims of boys' aggression in the classroom, it may be helpful to consider what happened in the playground. Boys appear to monopolize the playground largely because of football, a phenomenon which Mahony (1985) considered drawing on data derived from student teachers' investigations. They found that:

- girls tend to spend their lunch hour in small groups . . . where they are inconspicuous
- boys can be seen to walk directly into or across large open areas, while girls walk around the footpaths. . .
- boys occupy large areas of physical space while girls sit around the edges . . . boys' activities commonly involve large groups and are of a faster and more violent nature
- girls . . . often spectator[s] watching boys' activities
- girls' active games use less space
- boys appropriate space (pp. 26–7)

While there is no doubt that these descriptions reflect the scenes in the playground, if they are placed in context the interpretations may be somewhat altered. The playground activities should be read in terms of the cultural formation both of the school and of the peer group, and take into account factors such as age. For example, Lesley Holly (1985) discussed playtime in relation to the ten-year-old girls she studied. She said:

> Of course when I looked in the playground it was not the case that the girls were passively huddled in groups. They were also racing around but the boys had a large football game organized and monopolized the main section of the playground. This had the effect of restricting the girls to the edges (p. 55).

The question of age obviously has some effect. The younger the girls, the more likely they are to run around and this was apparent at Berkeley. In the first few years of the school's history prior to its move to its new purpose built premises, it had two playgrounds, an inner courtyard reserved for girls only and the other classified as a mixed playground.

However, there was an experiment for a few weeks during which time the inner courtyard was allocated for 'quiet activities' for both boys and girls alike. But this resulted in 'complete chaos', according to the head with children rushing from one playground to the other. It was the boys who were at fault. He said the boys chased the girls around while the girls wanted to play ball or hold hands. He said he had to reverse the decision and the inner courtyard reverted to girls only use, with the banning of balls. It was not long before this decision was reversed and the girls were allowed to play with balls.

The male PE teacher thought that the girls who used the inner courtyard were less mature because he said that 'the girls of that age do play more girlish games such as catch and that'. His comment is interesting; it establishes a causal link between physical maturity and physical activity; those who were still childlike played with balls, those who were mature discarded childish games.

The PE teacher's views were not shared by Mr Sands who expressed straightforward stereotypical views. He regarded the allocation of a girls' playground as congruent with the 'quiet life' that girls pursued voluntarily. He argued as follows:

We have put across that this is the accepted role of the girls in school [being quiet] and the boys are the ones that have all the fun. The girls don't object to it *because it is a socially accepted role*. It happens out in the playground. They stand around and talk; they don't automatically play netball, for instance, in the playtime. The boys automatically play football and chase round and have a fight. The girls will stand around and talk. It's the girls that we have allotted a special quiet playground. I think that we encourage them in the idea that they are the quiet types, and they lead that sort of life. If they resent it, it doesn't show (my emphasis).

Mr Sands' stereotypical views excluded such factors as age, maturity and so on, as the PE teacher had. But no one had put playground activities into a cultural context. Football is part and parcel of male working-class culture, and enters into boys' lives from a very young age. It has a wide media coverage, and the best players become elevated into national heroes. Boys could identify with their local football teams, many of whom had working-class backgrounds, and had reached the dizzy heights of success at a relatively early age. Failure to play football signified failure to be a boy.

There is no equivalent physical activity for girls. None of the games they played were part of their everyday culture as with football for boys. Netball and hockey can hardly be spoken of in a similar vein. Girls who played netball or hockey hardly merited the same attention that the footballers received. Television channels do not compete with each other to show netball matches! Indeed I cannot recall ever having seen netball played on television. It is not surprising that it does not enter into girls' lists of priorities. Consequently the monopolization of the playground by boys, particularly as the girls got older, may not constitute a problem for them.

Girls and boys outside formal school situation

Under different circumstances the stereotypical notions of girls' behaviour did not stand up under scrutiny. Contrary to expectations, some girls displayed a willingness and eagerness to participate actively in physical forms of behaviour particularly when they were in an environment which was new and in which the boundaries for accepted forms of gender appropriate behaviour had not yet been established.

This was illustrated by the events at a weekend camp site in the country, only an hour's drive away from the school. Here mixed groups were taken for up to four days.

On one particular occasion there were twenty pupils – fifteen boys and five girls – all in their first year. The group was fully settled when I arrived in the late afternoon with Mr Sands. We were due to spend the night there.

All the children appeared very pleased to see him, but more so the girls who behaved in a coquettish fashion. After the evening meal and whether through Mr Sands' influence or not, what had started out as a water fight between two boys developed into a full blown war. The children split into two warring factions with boys and girls together. All but one of the girls, Doreen, participated. She was washing up the dishes from the evening meal with the help of some of the parents who had come out on a visit.

Later that night Mr Sands took a group of children to explore the nearby woods. It was very dark and he told them he was looking for ghosts. There was an air of suppressed excitement, tension, anticipation and daring. Only one of the girls, Doreen, joined in.

The following morning soon after breakfast a football game started up and again several girls were involved. At the end of the game Tricia displayed her bruised shins proudly, evidence she thought of her prowess at the game.

How did Mr Sands account for these events in the light of his expectations about girls' behaviour which corresponded so closely with stereotypical views? He expressed his surprise at this and said he was amazed how: 'most of the girls were involved and I found that the girls that I didn't think would be involved in that sort of thing, in fact in school would definitely not be, were there.' He recalled, in particular, the night walk in the wood:

> Although Doreen spent most of the time washing up, when it came to going down into the forest she was the only girl who would do so, and that amazed me about that girl who is so very quiet in school and shudders away from anything what we think is too exciting or boisterous. I mean here she was joining in.

What neither he nor I knew at the time, was Doreen's own private views. Although she appeared quiet and retiring (to the extent that nobody noticed that she could not read in class), she subsequently told me in an interview how she was bored with feminine talk and activities. (There is a fuller discussion of this in Chapter 3.)

Mr Sands did not question his own view but rather sought explanations elsewhere. He attributed this change in Doreen to two main factors: 'freedom' generated by the environment and the absence of precedents which enabled the girls to relax and engage in activities which not only generated fun and enjoyment, but was also in direct contrast to their usual behaviour. He was groping towards a clear recognition of the way in which school is able to control and impose a set of constraints on the pupils. This represented a development of 'sense'. He said:

> This sensible attitude is dormant and is kept suppressed in school. It's only when you put them into a situation outside school, they are able to stand back. They have got nobody laying down barriers for them. They make use of their own reasons, and they weren't in the classroom situation where they – I hate to say the oppression of the school, we aren't oppressive here – but there are rules, there are barriers, and here there weren't and I just think that the natural maturity that they have was able to show itself.

His statement is confused. On the one hand the girls behaved in a 'reasonable' fashion which school prevented them from doing, but on the other hand girls behave in ways different from boys in that they tend to be quiet. Now at school Mr Sands did not question this, but confronted with these differences outside of the normal school environment he was clearly baffled. It is by no means obvious that the behaviour described above could be classified as mature, but Mr Sands did so to avoid having to recognize his construction of girls' behaviour in a stereotypical fashion. I would find myself hard pressed to describe this type of behaviour as mature. Exuberant, fun, lively but not mature. He said that he got the distinct impression that they were saying and doing things that they would not otherwise have done – their conversation was more intelligent, and their sense of responsibility was heightened. As an example of this he discussed the water fight: 'They stopped when they had had enough and they cleared the mess up themselves without being asked.' And when he referred to his discovery of some of the boys sharpening pieces of wood to make 'hatchets', he said they stopped immediately after he had discussed the matter with them. Their responses were sensible. Both in regard to this and getting them to settle down to sleep he said he found them responsible and sensible; they were becoming self-disciplined.

However, by the time he came to the end of this particular discussion, Mr Sands seems to have forgotten his earlier remarks and ended by talking about the girls' 'giggling form of behaviour' and emphasizing the boys' responsible form of behaviour. He could not move beyond his stereotyped beliefs.

Conclusion

From the interviews and observations some tentative conclusions may be drawn. The teachers did hold stereotypical views but, as will be shown in a number of discussions throughout the book, teachers' behaviour was far from consistent and varied considerably. Their beliefs encompassed not only aspects of behaviour but also related to girls' ability.

Irrespective of their beliefs, the fact is that some girls consistently avoided school work. Although I referred to the two most outstanding schoolwork avoiders, the ability not to work was much more widespread. But the nature of girls' school work avoidance in the classroom appears to be less physical and obvious than the boys. They seem to move around less than the boys, and their disruptions are less noisy than the boys. The unintended consequence of this is that this combined with teachers beliefs, enables the teachers to overlook the girls' behaviour. It may appear, therefore, that teachers spend more time on the boys than on the girls but this could involve more reprimanding the boys for their disruptive behaviour than remarking on the girls' avoidance of work.

The disruptive practices varied enormously. On the whole these were done by all ranges of ability, but largely within the middle range. Clearly these were all pupils who would not attempt public examinations, at least A levels, and hence not in the academic stream. Certainly in the class the number of high fliers was small and those who did well tended to be those who did not engage in counter school practices.

The girls were far from passive: the ones whose school work was exemplary participated fully in school work up to the age of fourteen or fifteen. Nor can it be said that those who were not working consistently at their school work had suffered as a result of more attention being given to the boys. They manipulated and controlled their environment up to a point and their behaviour in school seemed to be established at the beginning of their move into secondary school. It is difficult to imagine that had Mrs Ivory spent a great deal of time with either Cheryl or Mavis their performance in their school work would have improved.

Associated with this is the obvious conclusion that girls are active in the classroom and not passive victims of boys' aggressive behaviour. There is nothing to indicate that they were not engaging actively in the classroom activities whether it involved working at their lessons, or avoiding work.

Irrespective of how well girls do at the beginning of their secondary school life, their erupting sexuality and involvement in their peer culture is likely to have an adverse effect on their school attainment, all of which is discussed fully in Chapter 7.

Finally, and this is at the heart of the argument underlying this book, girls in schools in which academic standards are lower than those at select schools which aim to have high academic standards, are, similarly to the boys, unlikely to attempt examinations which would qualify them to try the pathway out of the low level jobs they were likely to get. The reason for this is far more complex than a simplified account of their stereotypical behaviour would suggest. Girls are not expected to excel at school and nor are the conditions available to override these negative expectations. These are characteristic expectations both from their families and many of their teachers.

The girls' failure to work in class and the outcome for them in terms of lower achievement conforms with expectations about their future lives. If the expectations are that work is not an important factor in their future lives, unlike their matrimonial responsibilities, then it is of lesser importance for girls to achieve in academic terms. The teacher is likely to hold this view. To this extent then the failure in class to confront the girls' low level of commitment to school work is the outcome of the stereotypical views held about girls. The teachers' views are integrated into a number of practices and supported by the schools' internal framework, as well as by the labour market in which the girls from a school such as Berkeley could not anticipate working except at the lowest levels of the occupational structure. All this is reinforced by the realistic views about the girls' future in the work place. Teachers at Berkeley knew that the job opportunities for such girls was limited and because of the probability of these girls marrying early and occupying low level jobs the urgency for them to do well at school was less than with the boys whom it was still assumed were the future breadwinners.

CHAPTER THREE

Girls and boys at school

Introduction

The monitoring of disciplinary procedures in the school which set the parameters for acceptable forms of behaviour occurs within the classroom/laboratory situation under the supervision of a teacher. Although discipline applies to all pupils irrespective of differences between them, teachers hold stereotypical views of the pupils which define their expectations and treatment of them even though events in the classroom demonstrate the falsity of these beliefs. This applies in particular to gender differences. An unintended consequence of this is that it provides an environment in which girls may opt out of schoolwork without undue reactions on the part of the teachers. This introduces a different perspective on the processes involved in girls' education. It contradicts the emphasis in some feminist literature which portrays girls as victims of the behaviour of both boys and teachers whose treatment is discussed in terms of being determined by the boys. If girls are not victims, then, presumably, they are active participants in the classroom. They may or may not have this perception of themselves.

In this chapter the girls' and boys' views of themselves as groups will be considered in relation to various questions. These include the following: how conscious each group is of itself; do they have a clear identity which reflects some of these stereotypical views that have been referred to in the previous chapter; how do the girls account for the deviations from what is considered appropriate behaviour; how do the boys conceptualize their behaviour in relation to themselves and to the girls; do their views reflect the oppressive nature of their behaviour that is said to characterize their behaviour in schools; how do both groups understand their resistance to some of the instruments of discipline and what are their views about the teachers? Unsolicited information provided useful insights. These related directly to girls' aggression and forms of counter school behaviour.

Before presenting the empirical data, some of the feminist work concerned with girls' and boys' behaviour in the classroom will be summarized. There will also be a brief discussion of the concept of resistance which will have a direct bearing on some of the empirical material and the conclusions reached.

Some theoretical considerations

As the previous chapter discusses, much of the writing on classroom interaction sets up interconnections between teachers' behaviour and pupils' reactions. It is not always clear from the discussion what causes the specific situations described. In many instances the effect of the situation is assumed to be the cause of the situation: the effect of teachers' behaviour (ignoring girls) on girls (loss of self-esteem) and presumably having the opposite effect on boys (increasing their self-esteem and power) is seen to be caused by boys' behaviour (domination of the teacher, monopoly of 'linguistic space' and so on). So the effect of teachers' behaviour on the personality of girls (their loss of self-esteem) is explained in terms of boys' actions. And boys' actions, in the final analysis, are accounted for in terms of patriarchy. Boys dominate the classroom, including the teacher, because of patriarchy and male power. Although this account is an over-simplification of the arguments, it does constitute the nub of a number of feminist-inspired arguments.

Boys are cast as the villains of the piece, the ones who are largely responsible for the failure of girls to 'achieve' and to leave schools trained and able to compete on an equal footing with boys in the labour market.

This presentation of boys' behaviour, which is derived from observations and from girls' reports on their reactions to boys, has not been corroborated by boys' views. However, what has emerged in the literature is a profile of boys which reflects the notion that 'it is the boys who are a problem for girls in schools' (Arnot, 1984). She says:

> In research such as that conducted by Walkerdine [1981], Stanworth [1983] and Fuller [1980], we get glimpses of the extent of boys' disruption of the classroom; their noisiness,

their sexual harassment of girls and female teachers, their demands for attention and their need of disciplining and their attitudes to the girls in their class as the silent or the 'faceless' bunch. (p. 38)

There are obvious problems in drawing a general conclusion from disparate studies which have examined different age groups and considered different issues. These result in the construction of a profile which is taken to be applicable to all boys, irrespective of age, class and other differences.

What these studies have done, however, is to focus on girls and draw attention to them, an essential task given the obliteration of girls from so much of the education literature in the past. In effect the feminist literature has introduced the female human agent, to paraphrase Aronowitz and Giroux (1986) in an otherwise male-dominated analysis of the education system. But the feminist-inspired analyses have tended towards mono-causal accounts, and in spite of a number of statements which emphasize external structural forces, in the end these are obliterated or consumed by the patriarchy argument.

The introduction of the human agent into the analyses, as mentioned in the Introduction, was a reaction to the reproduction thesis, popularized particularly by Bowles and Gintis (1976). Some of the major criticisms levelled against them was their tendency towards an economic reductionist position. So feminist arguments against Marxist and neo-Marxist analyses have been similarly couched although writers such as MacDonald (now Arnot) (1981) have combined structural analyses with the concept of patriarchy.

Where the feminist writers have introduced patriarchy, many of the radical writers have concentrated on cultural formations and have drawn on the concept of resistance.[1]

Resistance theorists have attempted to demonstrate that the mechanisms of social and cultural reproduction are never complete and always meet with partially realized elements of opposition. . . They point not only to the role that students play in challenging the most oppressive aspects of school but also to the ways in which students actively participate through oppositional behaviour in a logic that very often consigns them to a position of class subordination and political defeat (Aronowitz and Giroux, 1986, p. 71).

59

The concept of resistance embodies notions of power. Here power is multi-dimensional. Thus:

> . . . power is exercised on and by people within different contexts that structure interacting relations of dominance and autonomy. Thus power is never unidimensional; it is exercised not only as a mode of domination, but also as an act of resistance (Aronowitz and Giroux, 1986, p. 105).

In addition the notion of resistance includes the notion of accommodation.

> To the degree that oppositional behaviour suppresses social contradictions while simultaneously merging with, rather than challenging, the logic of ideological domination, it does not fall under the category of resistance, but under its opposite – accommodation and conformism (Aronowitz and Giroux, 1986, p. 105).

The emphasis in resistance theory is on cultural formations. When applied to the schooling situation, working-class pupils, in particular, are no longer seen as passive agents willingly submitting to their future life time of dead end jobs. Rather through the process of both resistance and accommodation they participate more actively in their own life histories. These accounts, according to Aronowitz and Giroux: 'have sought to redefine the importance of mediation, power and culture in understanding the complex relations between schools and the dominant society' (op.cit., p. 96). Finally an important element of the resistance theory is that oppositional behaviour is seen to contain the elements of 'radical significance' in so far as it contains the basis for altering the course of events.

However, as Aronowitz and Giroux point out – and it is an important area of criticism of the notion of resistance – there is the possibility of confusing resistance with all forms of oppositional behaviour, and it is not always a response to domination. As an example of this latter point they refer to the much quoted article by A. McRobbie (1978) on 'Working Class Girls and the Culture of Femininity'. Although McRobbie refers to the girls' activities which include combing their hair under the desk lids, or carving their boyfriends' names on their desks as oppositional, Aronowitz and Giroux see it in terms of conformism to sexual conventions which require 'developing a sexual, and ultimately successful marriage' (p. 100). Contrary then to such behaviour constituting oppositional tactics, they see it as a form of 'sexism that characterized working-class life and mass culture in general'.

All this suggests an alternate way of analysing boys' and girls' behaviour and their perceptions of each other. Where possible these ideas will be applied to the subsequent empirical material. The taking for granted of stereotypical notions of boys will be avoided. The girls' forms of opposition, aggressive behaviour and their active participation in the everyday life of the school will be discussed instead of being overlooked. In this way the complexities of the education system becoming subsumed under the presentation of popularized stereotypical descriptions will be avoided.

Pupils' assessment of their behaviour

The data which follows is derived from interviews conducted when the pupils were twelve and then, using the same schedules, when they were fifteen. Further data is derived from interviews conducted when they were nineteen or twenty. The evidence suggests that neither girls nor boys have neat, tidy composite views of either group. Their ideas reflect the contradictions they continuously experience – at school, with their peer group and in their families. Many of their statements do reflect some of the dominant ideologies which portray specific differences between men and women. Age does play a role in the way they express themselves and also their perceptions of the world. It will be shown how difficult it is, therefore, to produce a composite global statement about what boys and girls are like and how each group reacts to the other. What follows are some of the descriptions by the pupils on their notions about each group and their behaviour.

Girls' perceptions

All were asked whether they thought it was important for girls to be pretty, to dress well, to be more obedient than boys, not aggressive, less dependent than boys, good at school work and whether they had ever wished to be the opposite sex. Similar questions were asked about the boys and in addition whether it was important for them to be good at sport. The girls were not asked any questions directly about whether they found boys' behaviour threatening, oppressive or contributory to their own level of achievement: leading questions of this nature were avoided.

The girls held conventional views about the importance of being pretty and dressing well at both interviews. Their responses were, in the main, not detailed but there was a clear indication that they thought being pretty helped in attracting boys. Just how important it was to be fashionable emerged in comments they made at different times in the interview situation. Being unfashionably dressed could make girls vulnerable to verbal abuse by others.

It should be pointed out that in spite of what they said about dressing well, the girls wore school uniform which most of them accepted without grumbling. They thought that it was a good idea, and Carol said that it proved a great equalizer. But concern with fashion was never out of sight. Of school uniform Lisa said:

> It's O.K. I suppose. It saves me a lot of money because I don't have to keep going out and keeping in fashion . . . but I think that once you get up to 3rd or 4th year you should be allowed the choice of wearing school uniform or not.

The beginning of their opposition to the restriction of the school uniform was in their efforts to be allowed to wear trousers. They started petitioning in their second year and it was several years before they won this battle.

By the age of fifteen some found school uniform 'monotonous' and would far rather have worn their own clothes. Others, such as Carol, recognized there were distinct advantages in school uniform:

> I like to keep my clothes for going out and you have got to wear clothes for school and there could be competitions trying to keep up with one another, and there might be other girls who can't afford to have nice clothes for school. I think the uniform solves it.

The form of opposition by the girls to the wearing of school uniform varied. By the second year they had not yet devised ways of adapting the uniform but they still managed to effect a change in their appearance. This was done through the use of make-up, hairstyling, shoes, and jewellery. This was particularly noticeable following the Christmas break and a period in which I had not been at school for some weeks. I was astonished at how different many of the girls looked. It seemed as though there was a complete transformation overnight: eyebrows plucked, hair dyed and streaked, eyelashes mascared, eye shadow in evidence and very high heels.

According to Carol, those who used make-up in school also smoked and swore, behaving 'big'. Carol did not disapprove of make-up but thought it should be restricted to use outside of schools. She recognized it as an attempt by the girls to make themselves look older but, as she pointed out, 'not all boys like girls wearing make-up but most of them do'. But its use and method of application is one of the indicators of style and the means of establishing the conformity of any one person to the dominant expression of the female youth sub-culture, as will be considered in Chapter 6.

By the time they were fifteen the girls had devised ways of adapting or circumventing the rules about uniform. In the summer they would wear tee shirts under the regulation blouses. On one particularly scorching hot day when I was interviewing, Mavis told me that even though the girls were forbidden to do so she herself was wearing one: 'If we have a blouse undone Mr Sands comes round and says do the blouse up. . . But I have seen the third years taking them off.' Lara in her interview as an adult, pointed out how she would 'get on the teacher's nerves' by what she wore:

> Well girls could wear trousers and they were supposed to be black. The teacher might tell you that your jacket was wrong – maybe leather and leather shouldn't be worn. And I had a leather jacket and kept wearing it. It was things like that and they used to get on the teacher's nerves. And that sort of thing went against you eventually.

She became the victim of her oppositional behaviour in that, according to her own account, she was always singled out by teachers and marginalized within the classroom situation.

There is no doubt that there was a change in attitude towards school uniform, as the older the girls got the less they liked it. They did not see it as a means of control although some would break the school rules knowing they stood to be punished for this infringement of the rules. Fashion and dressing up was something uppermost in many of the girls' minds and was closely tied in with the importance they attached to going to discos.

Did the girls see themselves as more obedient than boys? At the age of twelve a third of the girls thought they should be, several felt that obedience should apply to both girls and boys alike, and the remainder either had no opinion or rejected the idea. By the time they were fifteen a question on obedience was inappropriate, as they no longer thought of themselves in these terms.

The majority of the girls thought girls should not be aggressive. Girls 'should talk nice, be gentle and graceful and that' said Jane at twelve but Shirley acknowledged that under certain circumstances it was legitimate for them to be aggressive and fight:

> Girls shouldn't fight but if somebody like starts calling them names and telling them that they will bash them up or something like that, well it's alright for a girl to stand up for herself instead of getting other people to bash this girl up, because they have got to say what is right but not to fight over it.

By the time she was fifteen, Shirley had completely changed her mind. When she answered the question about boys and aggression she made it clear she did not like it in anyone and she now found that 'aggressive girls seemed masculine'.

Irrespective of the ideological view on aggression and fighting, it did occur regularly amongst the girls and continued throughout their years at school. Mary was highly informative, describing her own and others' violent behaviour:

> No if you really researched into what girls fight about you would be surprised. Lots of things. It is really stupid. Standing in the playground and one girl says that she can beat up another, you know, and the other girl goes 'Oh no you can't, I can fight better than you, I beat up so and so'. Then one says a really horrible thing about the girl, and she gets, oh I could kill her, and sort of wack. That is how it starts, really stupid. It was rubbish, just over Jean, and Jean couldn't really defend herself, and I couldn't stand back and watch her being beaten up, and I thought 'No it can't happen' and I said, 'You leave her alone'. It seems as if I was picking a fight but I didn't want to, and she really got me mad. The things she said about Jean, and I look on Jean as my sister and I thought if she said that to my sister I would really hit her. But she started it first because I was defending Jean. She thought, um, she is defending Jean so she is not on my side, and somebody

pushed her I think. I don't think it was worth it. It was a waste of energy, really stupid. I would never fight over a boy anyway.

Q. *But some do, don't they?*

Because they are stupid. If a girl come to fight with me over a boy I wouldn't fight her, because I am not afraid of losing my pride or anything. Some girls would go and say that she is scared because she won't fight. That is the general thing that starts up fights. One goes, 'You are scared; that's why you won't fight'. The other girl is timid really but she goes, 'I can't let her think that of me' and she tries to pluck up enough courage you know, and she just wacks her and she finds that she can fight. . . .
I don't really like fighting. I mean when I started at this school I can only remember three fights that I have had, honestly. I don't like fighting. I would rather step in and break one up.

Q. *What do boys fight about?*

Well they might have an argument about football and one thinks he knows all about football more than the other. One says 'Chivers plays for Chelsea' and the other says 'He doesn't. He plays for Tottenham' and one goes 'Arsenal is better than Tottenham'. It sort of builds up from that. It doesn't sound like that at the time but if you break it down it is what it's for. And that is it. I have never heard of a boy fighting over a girl. One thing I hate is when boys fight girls.

Q. *But do they here?*

When she gave her reply to this she switched to discussing how girls fight boys.

It's not really meant. But a taller girl hits the littler boy and his head goes through the window. Because Lorraine and I was talking and a little boy Roland, we were talking and we said 'Oh shut up' – wack and his head went through the window. He wasn't cut or anything. He just laughed.

Q. *Well that is not really a fight is it?*

No. That is the only thing that I could think of.

She went on to talk about the fights in the playground. During the period at the school I never witnessed a fight. But what is perhaps more interesting is that I never heard any of the teachers talking about fights. The question that must be asked is, how does one account for this absence? Does this represent a refusal on the part of the teachers to acknowledge that girls are violent at school? Or is their acknowledgment couched in terms of deviant behaviour? Perhaps the teachers, like the girls, hold an ideological view of girls as non-aggressive and non-violent even though examples of such behaviour are far from being rare, as Mary's comments indicate:

Q. *Does it happen when the teachers are on duty?*

Well they do it when the teachers are there usually, but it just sort of happens, an argument or something.

Q. *Do the teachers break it up quickly?*

Yes. Sometimes it is getting interesting and you don't want it to break up, and the teacher comes along and spoils it. Everybody is enjoying it. What I am talking about boys fighting, of course. In the first year there was loads, oh yes. But just over some stupid thing or another. They are all stupid.

Some of the girls volunteered information about girls still fighting at the age of fifteen. One girl simply said 'The girls fight. Miss Leyland spoke to the girls about the bad behaviour of the girls'.
    Katherine complained about a group of girls in a class below her who were verbally aggressive. She said they:

Go around in a big group and they always if they go to discos or something and somebody hasn't got the latest clothes on they say out loud comments about them and they are always ready to fight which I hate.

Carol, referring to the same group, identified them as black girls. She spoke about their verbal violence which referred to comments directed against herself. She said that they said:

nasty things that aren't always true. I think that they do it to annoy you and you will turn round and say something back to them. I usually don't take any notice and they in the end get fed up and they don't do it any more. . . .

She did not know how widespread it was but 'if there is somebody they don't like they all go out to her'. She was reluctant to claim that it was racist but said 'the names they call you will be involved with being white. Probably if they were white it wouldn't be as bad'. Although there was a sizeable number of black pupils there were few comments about ethnic differences in the course of the interviews. This was one of the few occasions on which it happened. The reversal of experience is interesting: the white girl experiencing prejudice by black girls.

Questioning them about whether girls should be independent or not was not informative at either interview. Several were not sure what was meant by this question or, if they understood, claimed they did not know the answer. However, some girls did think that girls should be independent; one of them related this to adulthood and family responsibilities. She regarded independence as an essential ingredient for running a home:

When the boys grow up, into men, well when they are at work, or anything the girls have got to stay at home by themselves with their children, if they have children. In the home they have got to be able to cope on their own, cope with accidents, all the things that crop up during the day.

She recognized that motherhood involved responsibility and the need to be able to 'cope' with everyday problems.

Being good at schoolwork was something that they thought more important at the age of twelve than they did at fifteen. But as twelve year olds what this meant was related in the main to girls' behaviour: they should behave well at school. Their replies did not relate doing well at school with academic achievement or the openings this could provide for them as adults. On the whole, school work and occupations were not directly connected although, in contrast, in answering the question two of them related this to boys and viewed attainment as important for boys because they would grow up and have responsibility for supporting a family whereas girls would become housewives: 'They should work in the home and keep the home nice because the boys have to go to work, to know everything, and keep their families.' By the age of fifteen the girls were even more casual about being good at school work. Mavis, one of the girls who avoided doing any work in class, thought that one should work just before leaving school; this might help in getting a job although she was not clear why. Jane said that girls 'should try their hardest if they can so that they can get along in life to get a job and that when they leave school' but giggled while answering these questions. It was not something that she was going to do. Carol who had had high marks up to this age, shared this sentiment and spoke about her friends who bewailed their lost opportunities. She said:

A lot of my friends that have left school and they have said to me when you leave you will wish you were back and I have said, No I won't, but they do and wish they tried harder because it is very hard to get a job without qualifications. And they say I wish I was back at school. You should make the most of it while you are there.

Only Katherine, at this age, recognized problems that girls could encounter in the future if they wanted a good job:

If you are going to do something you are going to have to do it that bit better than anybody else. . . . If the person thinks the man is more suited than you are he is going to choose him but if you have got better qualifications then it would be wrong not to choose you if you are the person for the job.

Having said this, she nevertheless said much later in the same interview that she had lost interest in her school work:

I think I would have to say that all my interests are in clothes and I like going places; I like doing new things as well as going to normal you know. Every Saturday going to discos. I like experiencing new things. If I do things I don't enjoy I lose interest. . . .

Here is a clear statement of her social life absorbing her to the detriment of her school work. The effect of her engagement with sexuality on her school work will be considered in Chapter 6.

But how did they see themselves in terms of their behaviour in the classroom? In discussing boys' antics a few acknowledged that they 'mucked' about in the classroom or were talkative. But they saw their personal preening as the type of activity that upset their teachers:

> Making-up their face while the teacher is explaining something and the teacher goes mad. Or if they sit there chattering with their friends, like I do, I know that the teacher goes mad. I know that the teachers don't like you brushing your hair in a lesson. I know a couple of times girls in our class have done that and I think, yes, it must have been Mr Sands had a go at them, said how unladylike it was. . . I think he thought it wasn't becoming to see you doing yourself up in front of everybody.

The use of a great deal of make-up was also seen as something which would upset the teachers and which they used as a means of resistance. The stereotypical view of girls as being 'good' is further jolted by some candid reports at the age of fifteen. They reported that some girls deliberately blocked the toilets with sanitary towels:

> The girls leave their sanitary pads around instead of putting them in the burner. They just leave them anywhere and put them down the toilet and they can get blocked up. They put on too much make-up and the teachers get annoyed with it.

Did any of the girls wish they were boys? At the age of twelve a quarter expressed their desire at some stage to be a boy, each offering a different reason. For Mary it was clear cut. Girls did housework and did not have freedom to go out at night or feel safe at night. She said:

> At home especially when you are a girl you are expected to stay at home and do the housework and the boys they go out. They seem to be able to go when they like because girls if they go out at school and they are out late they are liable to . . . well people come up and things like that. The boys there are sort of able to look after themselves and I don't think that is really fair.

Tricia thought that all girls went through the tomboy stage, as she herself had done and her sister currently was. She had played football with the boys at the weekend outing to Elstree, something which she said she would not be able to do in school, as they would shout at her if she asked to join in. There were too few boys on that occasion to make up a team so they allowed her to join them. She recognized that football was a dividing factor, because when she defined a tomboy it was a:

> girl who goes around playing football and climbing up a tree – what am I talking about, I did that in the forest didn't I? – and doesn't care if she gets covered in mud and my sister goes through the trouser knees like butter. Not five minutes if you get her a new dress it's gone; she's ripped the hem off – she's always tearing her clothes.

And then there was Doreen. She said that she really did want to 'play football and do things that boys do'. She said her father had wanted a son when she was born and had brought her up to do things such as paint furniture and repair broken window panes. She appeared quite concerned that she neither liked the things that the other girls did, nor was she interested in clothes. She changed considerably and by the time I interviewed her again two years later she had a boyfriend, she worked Saturdays at a boutique and she no longer helped her father. She was married soon after leaving school and had a daughter when I interviewed her a few years later.

The picture that is emerging about the girls' views on themselves does not correspond to a stereotype. They do not project an image of themselves as studious, sitting quietly and working, passive, lazy or namby-pamby as the teachers had described them. They accept that girls can be violent and aggressive, traits which they do not admire but recognize as sometimes necessary to adopt in certain situations. Their ideas change with age, and here the question of their physical maturity and involvement with boys is something that plays a role. They do see themselves as a group with a clear identity.

What did the girls think about the boys? As mentioned above, the same questions, where appropriate, were asked and in addition there was a question on the importance of sport. There were some differences in their responses between the ages of twelve and fifteen.

The girls did not like the boys to look scruffy or dirty and by the time they were fifteen some specified that they did not want to go out with boys who did not dress well.

They did have views on boys' aggression but none of them spoke of it as being directed against girls. It is important to emphasize that this might well be the outcome of the absence of older boys in the school. This cohort was the first intake in the school and at no stage were the girls confronted by any older boys within the school precincts. Only one girl compared girls with boys saying that boys were more aggressive than girls whom she thought of as quiet and obedient. She said that:

Boys are usually not very obedient because they are a bit more aggressive. When we were little my brother used to start all the arguments. I used to be sort of quiet if my mother told me to.

Aggression was not a quality that the girls admired at either age amongst boys and on the whole they thought boys should avoid being so, although Shirley, when fifteen, felt that a 'bit of aggression' was appropriate; it was 'unnatural for boys not to be aggressive, but girls if they are aggressive seem so masculine', aggression for her meaning 'being bad tempered and telling people what to do'.

Only one of the girls in answering questions about boys' behaviour in the classroom said that she found them arrogant:

Well the way they act is really different to the way in which the girls act and, how can I put it, they are so superior. They think we are boys, and they are girls and they draw the line when it comes to girls and they think that boys should do every-thing and they talk too much.

The desirability of boys being independent was recognized by the girls at the age of twelve but by the time they were fifteen they seemed less concerned with this.

In principle, at the age of twelve, the girls thought the boys should be good at schoolwork and presumably here they were referring to behaviour in the classroom as they did in relation to themselves. By the age of fifteen some expressed the conventional view that boys would have major familial responsibilities as adults and this affected the way they should work at school: 'Boys have got to work at school a bit more harder because they have got to get their good jobs when they leave school and pay for their families.' But what did the girls think about the boys' behaviour in class?

There was a range of comments which indicated that they found the boys noisy in the classroom – they 'shout a lot, are all talk and no work', lazy because 'they've got football and TV on their minds and they just play around most of the time': 'Well some boys they flick rubbers across the room with their rulers, muck about in class, tease the girls.' Indeed somebody pointed out that 'they play football all the time in class', obviously not as played in the play-ground but probably referring to playing with a ball in the class-room or using socks as a ball. At the age of fifteen Katherine said: 'I know that the boys in my class tend to talk while things are going on, teachers are trying to get things organized and that is annoying, you know.' Only one or two, like Mary, acknowledged that they too were noisy. She said: 'Well some girls talk a lot, like me for instance'. Someone else underlined the difference in the level of noise between the two groups using the term 'natter' to apply to the girls and 'shouting' to apply to the boys: 'Boys make most of the noise, the girls sort of natter a bit, but the boys shout a lot.' Jane was the only one to say that the girls did much the same as the boys in class. 'Boys may muck about more in class but so do girls'. As an adult Katherine used very similar terminology to describe her own behaviour in class.

Being good at sport was something that the girls at the age of twelve agreed was important for boys, and for Mary playing foot-ball was a clear indicator of boys' masculinity:

Well when I think of boys they are good at running and every-thing. Every time I think of boys I think that they are quite good at sport, but if a boy can't play football they just call them a poof, sort of thing.

But by the time they were fifteen they did not regard this as at all important; and did not know who played in the football team.

In general, there were some who saw boys and girls as quite different from each other in class. One of the girls attributed the differences to 'natural' reasons and these she thought also resulted in boys' recognition of girls' superiority:

Well all boys have sort of got that feeling that they have got something in them that tells them that they are boys and they should listen to what girls say. . . . They just think they are boys and boys should be boys and they don't think they should listen to girls or anybody.

When interviewed as an adult Shirley said that the presence of boys made it difficult to talk in class:

> I found it very hard to express myself at school. If I wanted to say something I found it very hard. It used to embarrass me a great deal and I think also at that age. It's a separate subject, but different schools for boys and girls. Um, at fourteen you begin to realize that boys and girls are different and they are there and saying things in front of boys is quite embarrassing.

Q. *Like what?*

> A teacher asks you a question about geography or anything like. If you had to say anything in a room of silence in a room mixed with boys and girls. I can understand why a girl of fourteen will get embarrassed. I did, I got embarrassed because there were all boys in the room.
> I didn't fancy them. It was just them being there or maybe it being fourteen, you think if I say something stupid the teacher will think I am daft. *You want the men teachers to see you as adult women and not just as school children.* The lady teachers they all seemed to look down on you, as children. I don't know it's just. . . . I couldn't seem to keep up the pace of learning and I just couldn't be bothered (my emphasis).
> I used to fancy Mr O. like mad and then one day I think he embarrassed me in front of the whole class. I can't remember what it was about. And I went off him from the word go. I didn't like him then.

Shirley's embarrassment in front of boys was linked to her 'fancy' for the geography teacher. Both aspects are associated with her developing sexual awareness – realization at fourteen that boys and girls are different. Not wanting to make a fool of herself in front of boys was not that different from wanting to appear as a young woman rather than a school girl, in front of the geography teacher. Her embarrassment, therefore, cannot be defined solely in terms of male power and boys' domination. The link and tie-in with issues surrounding sexuality are far more complicated than a simple causal connection to the mere presence of boys, and involves a number of interconnected factors, some of which will be discussed in the section on sexuality.

Boys' views

How did the boys perceive themselves and girls?

The present portrayal of boys in the literature, as discussed in Chapter 2, is one of aggression, violence and domination of the girls. This image is derived partly from observations in classrooms, partly from what girls say is the position, and partly from teachers' statements about boys. Less seems to be known about what boys themselves say or think, particularly in regard to girls.

Like the girls, the boys were asked questions on matters common to both boys and girls, some of which were gender specific. There was some difference between the boys' responses at the age of twelve and fifteen; by fifteen some of their answers had a direct relationship to adulthood.

When they were twelve only half the boys thought it important for girls to be pretty. By the age of fifteen all thought: 'it's quite essential for girls to be pretty because a lot of boys in this school like pretty girls. Some girls who aren't too pretty, [the boys] just kind of laugh at them or make remarks.' Two of them thought that a good personality was as important as looks. Overall their change between the ages of twelve and fifteen signifies the development of their interest in girls, except for Graham who had said that he was not at all interested in them – he had been labelled a 'poof' by various pupils. Adam discussed their attractiveness in terms of competitiveness between the girls saying:

> We have no one like Marilyn Monroe here, as you probably gathered. Carol I suppose is the one who is centred out from the rest of the girls in the class. A lot of them are jealous of her; it's very snidish the things they say behind her back.

His comments should be read in conjunction with what Carol herself said about the way in which a number of girls abused her.

At both ages boys thought it important for girls to dress well but Robin, at fifteen, condemned the use of too much make-up: 'because it kinds of spoils it because a lot of girls in this school wear a lot of make-up. . . . ' Like the girls, the boys found it difficult answering the question on independence particularly when applied to girls. Independence was taken to mean 'standing up for themselves' and at the age of twelve more than half the boys did not think it necessary for girls to do so. The others were ambivalent. By the age of fifteen the boys were even more ambivalent, perhaps because the notion of independence conflicted with the stereotypical view of what girls should be like. David, quiet and given to monosyllabic answers, captured this contradiction with his classical stereotypical statement: 'You always imagine a girl as being sort of soft and feminine and boys as sort of hard and that.' At both ages boys rejected signs of aggression in girls. Nor did they comment on this question.

At twelve the majority of boys thought that girls should do well in their schoolwork, but what was particularly interesting was the way in which some of them contrasted girls with boys at this stage. There was an assumption that girls behaved well in class and therefore they should do well at their schoolwork while boys were different: 'It ain't like the girls to be bad in class . . . mostly all the boys' seems to sum up this sentiment. One boy specifically related girls' schoolwork with their future role as housewives: 'Well we have some classes in cooking and the girls have got to cook when they get older and know how to add up and things.'

Although a few of the boys at the age of fifteen thought it unimportant for girls to do well at school by the age of fifteen, several who still linked classroom behaviour with schoolwork now thought that girls were cleverer than boys. As one boy said 'girls are mostly brainier than the boys – they go straight to work, they get the work done'. Robin was clearly surprised 'because they go out every night and so on'. Perhaps his view was a straightforward representation of what he had heard throughout his school days – that girls did do better than boys, that girls worked harder, and behaved better. Furthermore several boys related girls' schoolwork directly with work they would do when they finished their schooling. Two of them, both black, thought that girls stood a better chance to get work than boys. Although it was 1976 and the unemployment had not reached such high numbers as it has now, the boys were conscious of difficulties in getting jobs. One of them said quite simply 'that girls have more opportunities than boys and they lead a better, interesting life'. The boys were fully aware that girls were likely to have to work even if they married which suggests that they no longer believed that a working man could support a wife and family:

It's important for some girls to do well at school. A lot of girls are going to get married, aren't they, by the time they leave school or a few years after. They should be able to do some jobs. They ought to have some qualifications in case they have to get a job. They're bound to need a job.

As will be shown when their projections for their future is discussed in the Epilogue, many had mothers who if not actually supporting the family did contribute significantly to the family coffers.

The one exception, and his views did not coincide in the main with the rest of the class, was Adam. He had very definite views about everything. He had his future career mapped out and planned to move out of the area in which he lived, away from all the black immigrants, and set his sights high: 'I don't like the girls who are at the bottom of the class, because what is she going to do? She'll probably end up in a factory canning baked beans or something.' But his was a lone voice.

On the surface it does seem that the boys accept the stereotypical notion that girls do well at school and settle down and work. They also had realistic views about the future. They recognized that the girls would marry but would also have to work, as did their mothers.

Michael, when he was twelve, introduced a completely different perspective on girls. He had found them intrusive in his own life and said he wanted them to 'act normal' as though he was 'anyone' rather than:

> Well, pushing other girls around and laughing and being stupid.
> They start running and they run by you and they hit you and
> that. Not hit but punch and they want you to chase them and
> that.

Michael did not want to be bothered with girls at this stage of his life but some were out to get his attention. (These girls could hardly be termed passive!)

In regard to girls' behaviour in the classroom there were two opposing comments, one of girls being noisy and the other of girls being quiet:

> Girls can make as much noise as boys. Well, they talk too
> much sometimes, just sit around and talk and don't get on
> with their work. Sometimes they are just as lazy, but so are
> boys come to that.

and

> Girls can be silly – either laughing a lot or saying silly things.

The second view was expressed by some boys when they were fifteen. Elliot found some of the girls quiet:

> They always seem to be quite quiet. They don't really join in the discussion properly. They always try and be quiet, but Carol does and Katherine – they join in discussions, but the rest of the girls do nothing 'Why?' I think because when they talk they get embarrassed and they shouldn't get embarrassed because there isn't anything to get embarrassed about.

Elliot was not the only one who thought of them in this way. When Michael, as an adult, recalled some of his escapades while at school and in response to my question about what girls did in class while he and the others were playing football with a sock looked puzzled: 'I'm trying to think what they would be doing. I suppose sitting on the tables, just be sitting around'.

Were the girls just sitting around or was it that Michael was simply not conscious of what they were doing? Did the boys perceive a change in the girls' behaviour when they were fifteen, and had the girls changed? On the basis of the comments made by the girls, perhaps one or two did find themselves suddenly conscious of the boys' presence and as such remained quieter in the classroom, but others were obviously not abashed and continued to 'muck around' as much as the boys. Then there were the girls who probably just talked amongst themselves as Paul said, 'girls kind of talk between themselves'. But, as one boy said, suggesting that girls did avoid talking out loud in class: 'kind of um . . . paying attention to the class, joining in, if they [the teachers] are asking questions, [the girls] try to keep out of it.'

Some found the girls' voices irritating and it was this that Paul implied could be used by the girls to 'get at the teachers'.

> I think it's their voice. You know, some girls might have a very high voice, and it gets on the teachers' nerves. They don't actually flick and things like that, it's just the way they talk.

Discipline and control

The attention the girls gave to their appearance in class – combing their hair and so on – was another factor that Thomas commented upon, although he did say that boys did the same thing. It is difficult to conceive of girls who were embarrassed in the presence of boys publicly brushing their hair and so on.

What did the boys think about themselves? Did their views reflect the stereotypical picture of boys as represented by their teachers: 'troublesome, noisy, need keeping down, and pushing them to work'? Did they have definite ideas about the girls which involved their harassing them or generally putting them down? Did they appear to be consciously seeking the attention of the teachers? How did they see themselves in the classroom situation?

Like the girls the boys thought it important to dress well from the age of twelve onwards: ' . . . Can't go kind of tatty. Well you aint going to get . . . no one is going to pay you much attention.' The boys did, though, have to wear school uniform – navy trousers, jacket with school badge, white shirt and tie. The boys accepted and welcomed the idea of a school uniform. Graham thought it 'good in a way because it makes you feel that you belong to the school more', a view that several of them expressed. This feeling didn't alter drastically as they got older although their acceptance of it became far more pragmatic by the age of fifteen:

> You don't have to worry about what you have to wear the next day, and if there is something wrong with it and, will I look funny, you just put on your school uniform and that's it and go to school.

The boys had become more dress conscious by that age, but the wearing of a school uniform meant they were under no pressure in terms of the way they dressed.

Apart from two boys, all the others thought that being aggressive was important, even Graham who was the victim of teasing by both girls and boys. He said when he was twelve: 'If someone come up to you and keep on teasing you and they kept on and wouldn't stop, it's only natural that you get aggressive sooner or later.' He might have felt this and tried to retaliate but his behaviour never did appear aggressive. This raises the question of how they would define aggression and whether it meant physical fighting or not. In this regard the boys did not offer as much information as the girls had done. Perhaps this reflects the fact that fighting was part and parcel of everyday life and was not something that warranted particular comment.

The boys did link aggression with independence and none of them doubted the need for them to be independent at either age.

There was one boy who admitted to wishing that he had been a girl. His name was Robin. His reason for this was directly related to fashion. He said:

> About last year, because a lot of fashion came out and a lot of things were cheaper. But they looked good, like shoes and skirts and so on. And well really some of it really suits girls and it is hard to get men's fashions. Like if you want really stylish things; like, I am small build right? But big kids like Leonard it is easier for them to go into a man's shop and get real stylish stuff, but it is hard if you are small built to get clothes that look fashionable. So that is why I thought yes, it would be better to be a girl. But they have brought a lot more fashion out into our sizes now and a lot of shoes and so on, which look good, so girls have got their fashion so you have got to have boys' fashion to keep up with it.

In regard to their schoolwork, it was taken for granted that they should do well. In this they were presenting the traditional view that, as one boy said: 'When you get married, you have got papers to sign and that.' In other words they would have responsibilities as adults. Doing well at school meant literacy. Someone else spoke about it in terms of some vague notion of qualifications: 'Because there's such high unemployment rate. If you don't get a job, if you get some qualification and don't get a job you are much better off with qualifications. Something might crop up.'

However, the relationship between 'doing well at school' and getting a good job was vague. They did not have clear ideas about further or higher education. But Adam did. He had mapped out his life by the age of fifteen and was the only one to have his sights on going to college or university. School for most of them was a 'laugh' and their report on their classroom behaviour substantiates this. They reported that they were noisy, they avoided work when they could and they mucked about in the classroom: 'Well they are either flicking papers at each other or talking when the teacher says don't talk and then just having a little fight in the classroom, a friendly one.'

Alan used almost the same words three years' later when he said that the boys: 'Flick about with elastic bands'. When I reminded him that he always did that he laughed and said that 'boys did much about' but quickly accused girls of bad behaviour as well saying that 'girls come in late'. 'Boys do so many things to irritate the teachers. They generally much around and won't do work.' Disruptive behaviour seemed to be the norm in the class: 'They would get up and wander about or have a kind of little fight or talking out loudly.'

Graham was the only one to claim that the girls behaved equally badly. Elliot drew attention to the difference according to whom the teacher was. He said:

> Well . . . if we have a lady teacher we might not work so well, but if you have a new teacher you don't work very well – you are trying to see what they are like – to see if you can get away with things, you know.

He thought that women teachers and all new teachers were easy targets for their misdemeanours.

Michael recalled:

> I remember once making a paper boat sitting in the front of the class and I was going like that with it as if it was going over the waves and the whole class, well all the boys were laughing. In the end we all got sent out of the classroom except Graham. . . . We used to get on very well. I had a pair of old football socks in the locker and we used to start a fullscale football match in the classroom when the teachers weren't there.

In the course of the same interview he said how he had given up college because it was a 'drag' and 'might have reminded me of school too much'. His view of his school days was that:

> Truthfully I had a great laugh at school, you know. That was all that came out of school. I really enjoyed it . . . I enjoyed the social side of it more, with me mates and that. The lessons really were in between the breaks like. After school it was great.

As could be anticipated the majority of boys did place importance

80

on their sporting prowess. Those who did not share this view were, predictably, boys like Graham who hated sports and PE. It was not generally anticipated that the 'brainy boys' would be sportsmen, although Robin said that some were. And it was Adam who provided some insight on this. He said:

> I have achieved more this year than I have last year because I am in such a high position in the scale. I can also play around, also my squash has helped a lot. *They used to think I was a right weak, not athlete at all, but I proved them all wrong.* . . They associate me with that now in the class, as well as physics of course (my emphasis).

Adam had expressed his views about how he was one of the élite in the school because he was one of the few boys doing physics at O level. However, he was conscious of the isolation and the divide this created between himself and the other boys and being good at sports was an indicator that he was like all of them and not a homosexual. (This aspect will be discussed more fully in Chapter 6.)

The behaviour of the boys in class was, according to their accounts, noisy, active and oblivious of certain aspects of discipline. This was not confined to the schoolroom. As will be recalled members of the class went on weekend excursions to Elstree. Although Mr Sands had commended them for being 'responsible', Thomas gave a different account of their first visit. When interviewed as an adult, he looked back on those visits nostalgically with great pleasure. He told how the boys had gone 'scrumping [stealing] apples at a neighbouring farm'. He said that Fisher decided to run straight through the fence. The local farmer was incensed by the boys and called the police and the teachers were then questioned about the pupils. Thomas said that the staff pointed out that all the pupils had been on a nature ramble but Thomas said this was not the case:

> We hadn't. I mean none of us could fill our worksheets in. I mean when we went on that trip we had to take two suitcases. But there was only one pair of jeans and shirts in the one; the rest of all bottles of cider and cans of beer.

Whether on this occasion the boys had been drinking is unlikely, but drinking did become a feature of these visits, according to several comments. The boys were fitting into the mould of the male drinking culture quite easily. Thomas reported how:

> Fisher got pissed out of his mind and stripped off and went dancing in and out of the girls' changing rooms and then we had to try and sober him up. Michael was punching him trying to sober him up and by then a couple of the girls were running around hysterical and it ended up with him being sick all over Michael and we had to sling him out and wash him off.

This particular event does seem to capture one of the elements of masculine culture and the one that would have been dominant amongst that group at the time: learning to drink and coping with drunkenness both comprise an important part of working-class male culture. Here these boys at the age of fifteen were slotting into this particular image.

Thomas claimed that the teachers never knew about this, but then said realistically that 'No teacher is going to turn round and say, oh yes, the class I took out there was all pissed out of their minds'. However, by the fourth year they had been banned from going on these outings.

Now for some details relating to truancy. One of the observable measures of the success of disciplinary instruments is the reduction in the rate of absenteeism. By removing themselves from school completely or for some of the lessons the pupils effectively remove themselves from the constant surveillance of the school. They are outside the bounds of control. As is known truancy has been of concern since the nineteenth century (Humphries, 1981) and both girls and boys have truanted. Whether the rates are different is not known although Davies (1984) cites some evidence pointing out that in one study:

> Sex differences in behaviour were not so acute as might appear from punishment books. Likewise in a study of third year boys and girls in three English comprehensive schools Bellaby (1974) claimed hostility to school to be a predominantly working-class affair, and that it occurred about as frequently among girls as boys . . . more (girls) reported having stayed out of a lesson than boys (p. 135).

At Berkeley both groups reported school avoidance although I had not asked direct questions about truanting as, at the time, had overlooked this question. What information did emerge was volunteered by the pupils themselves during the course of interviews either at school or as adults.

Mavis, at the age of fifteen, was quite open about her truanting. She complained that it was more difficult for her to do so than her boyfriend who attended a different local school. She said that: 'He don't hardly go to school, but swimming and all that and don't get caught . . . he could just stay away and they take it like that.' Not so Mavis. She hated participating in games and sports and so avoided school on a Friday so that she could miss PE and sports. She needed her mother's collusion in this regard because her mother had to sign a note covering Mavis' absence, and this the mother did not always do.

Several others did admit to missing school but were hesitant to go into details. Shirley remembered that she had been an habitual truanter: 'I carried on for quite some time truanting and when I did stop it was too late. When it was time to put your head down and start studying for exams. Then I stopped but that was a bit too late.' Her truanting was 'opportunistic', a term used by Humphries (1983).[2] She visited her aunt and did so quite manipulatively: it was as much a means of avoiding school as resisting her mother:

It was one up on me mum, if you know what I mean. Being as there are so many sisters as my mum has got they can't wait to talk about one another behind their backs and that sort of thing. So when I played truant it was one up on me mum. . .

She also would go sun bathing during the summer days with another girl from the same class. Although her father 'did find out about it and it caused trouble' she continued nevertheless.

Another example of opportunistic truanting was reported by Thomas. He and his friends would cycle for miles and miles often on a school day. He said they had to be careful not to bump into teachers:

You had to be careful because you'd go out in school uniform and then you'd have to get another set of clothes somewhere so that you could make a miraculous change. We used to do miles and miles on bikes. Stopped by police a few times. It was all great fun.

He saw this as something that the girls missed out on because:

As soon as they get to a certain age they sort of dedicate their life to looking good for the boys. I think an awful lot of the boys look at them and think 'nice', and then just carry on with what they are doing.

This type of truancy provided the basis for establishing friendship networks within the class. Earlier in the same interview Thomas described how Graham was always an outsider because he was:

different. That's what segregated him because he wouldn't do the things that we would do. We sort of cast him aside. . . You would never have got him sort of off down the High Road in the middle of a lesson that he didn't like. . . It just seemed the thing to do.

Co-Education

Given all these differences how did the Berkeley pupils view co-education? Both boys and girls were unequivocally in favour of co-education on the basis of the advantages they got in social interaction. Lisa was an exception. For her co-education meant control over coloured girls whom she claimed were too domineering in single sex schools: 'When I went to a girls' only school you found the coloured girls were always trying to be bigger than the white girls, but if you are in a mixed school the boys sort of push them down.' For the rest the girls found it an advantage to have boys around: they quite simply found it more interesting, reflecting their developing interest in the opposite sex. Typical of the comments made as twelve year olds were:

When you are in a girls' school it gets boring and you get fed up with seeing each other and fight.
You can mix more with boys and that.
You get to know nice boys and that. You wouldn't meet any boys and be keen on boys.
If it was a girls' school it would get a bit boring all the time; just girls in the playground and girls doing this and that, all the time.

Nor did they alter their opinions as fifteen year olds.

The boys were somewhat more effusive in their preference for mixed school. At the age of twelve Graham felt that the presence of girls mediated the treatment of teachers; they were likely to be 'harder on boys than boys and girls'. For many of the boys the advantages of co-education were in terms of overcoming boredom and widening their horizons. The presence of the girls resulted in social mixing as a norm, and enabled them to develop along other lines: 'I think what people talk about. Boys will be talking about girls all the time, but when you get boys and girls – you just don't talk about each other. You talk about different things.'

By the age of fifteen many of the boys viewed social interaction with the girls in a positive light:

Kind of get on better together.
Because if it was an all boys' school you wouldn't know how to get on with girls.
I think if you were in an all boys' school it would be a bit boring. Some of the girls are alright . . . if there are girls in the school it can make it more livelier and that, and it can be more fun.

Fisher was quite explicit about his preference for having girls around:

If I was in an all boys' school I would hate it. Now and again if you have got any problems and you look round and see a girl sitting there . . . it just takes your mind off it, well in my eyes it does.

No doubt he was into fantasizing about girls.

There is little doubt that both girls and boys regarded co-education as advantageous at both twelve and fifteen. None of the girls spoke about the presence of boys as oppressive except for Shirley who referred to it on one occasion when she said that she had found herself embarrassed to talk in class. None of the girls expressed any desire about attending single-sex schools or classes but then no direct questions on this were put to them. Given the methodology and the nature of the questions it is hypothetically possible that had the questions been more pointed or direct the girls may have spoken about the oppressive presence of boys. Whatever the case may have been, the point that can be drawn is that some girls might experience boys' presence oppressive at some times; but there is a large body of girls who do actively enjoy having boys in the same school as themselves.

Views on teachers

There was no consensus amongst the pupils about the control teachers exerted or whether this was mediated by gender. They were asked discrete questions about their general likes and dislikes of both female and male teachers, followed by a direct question on whether they thought one or other group was better able to control a class.

The pupils' likes and dislikes appeared to be directly related to the personality of the individual teacher and as such were not affected by the gender of the teachers. For example, at the age of twelve, half the girls expressed their preference for Mrs Ivory because of their familiarity with her – they 'knew her'. The others preferred Mr Sands because he could 'take a joke better than some teachers' or was seen to 'be strict but fun at the same time'. At that age the boys were less explicit about their likes or dislikes.

Dislikes by the girls were also not gender specific. Two men were disliked because they were seen to belittle the pupils, treat children as though they were ignorant, and behaved in a 'haughty' fashion. One of the girls said:

Oh I can't stand him. He never gives you a chance to explain. He is right all the time, and he can't be because he would be inhuman. He is not right all the time. He just thinks because he is a teacher and he is older than us that he is right.

Doreen, as an adult, surprised me by expressing her intense dislike for Mrs Ivory because of the effective way she could marginalize individuals. She said that she could not discuss this while she was still at school and said:

She made us come out in the front if you don't really understand something. But when you do go out there she usually tells you to sit down and you should know. I know sometimes she explains things, but not all the time.

On the whole the boys were very easy going about their likes and dislikes of individual teachers. Elliot, at the age of fifteen, recalled how he had enjoyed Mr Sands because he used 'to tell us these stories and things like that – adventure stories about ghosts and things like that', but he no longer had any favourites. At the age of fifteen Simon was the most explicit about his dislikes, and rather condescending about his tolerance of the bulk of the teachers. He said how originally he had regarded them as little 'gods' but he now felt they were not a 'bad bunch'. However, there were several he could not tolerate:

I don't particularly like one or two. Mr Wallace is a pompous idiot. He is a drunken twit. I would use stronger language but I disallowed myself that since the first year. I haven't sworn since the first year which is good. I do occasionally when I am riled and very worked up. But he is a twit is Mr Wallace. I don't know why they employed him at this school. He is mad. He's not really a teacher; he has not got the ability to control a class. I don't know where he had got his training. I would fail him if I was his master. Definitely. There are one or two teachers [who] like too much power such as Mr Baker. He is alright these days but he did go on a bit in the second year. . . They are sort of teachers in their own right and you get older and you can sort of understand them. They are not gods. I used to treat them like gods but they are not gods anymore. They are just ordinary people.

In spite of these views several did regard the gender of the teacher as important in terms of classroom control, and these views solidified the older they got. At the age of twelve there was an equal distribution between those who thought there was no difference and those who thought that men were more effective teachers. Katherine was the most vociferous about the advantage of having male teachers. Following her discussion on co-education she volunteered that one of the benefits of this was having men teachers because they 'have different approaches to things'. She said:

I think that men teachers are far more able to take sort of chances like try something different because you know I think they take more responsibility onto their shoulders. I think that women teachers probably don't like to do anything too much out of the ordinary just in case it doesn't work you know and they're not quite able to control it. I think. Look at drama. Like Mr Sands takes us and we do drama and he's able to control it you know because he . . . men teachers always seem to have more control over a class. I mean like if a woman teacher might have the class quiet but if something was to happen then that started the class going then I think that a man teacher would be sort of able to control it better than a woman teacher could.

Q. *So in fact you have found that the men teachers can control classes better?*

I started to realise this in my junior school. Some of the women teachers you know who were just out of college they used to be put straight into the classroom and the children would play them up an awful lot and not pay attention. I think that women teachers find it very hard to be sort of strict with them unless they have had some sort of experience in another classroom. I think that men teachers adapt more easily to this sort of situation.

This represents a straightforward stereotypical view of women and women teachers. However, the ambivalence about this view was expressed by Elliot who said at the age of fifteen that it was impossible to define what the ingredients were that enabled a teacher to maintain control of a class. He said: 'A teacher can keep the class quiet really without saying anything, you know. You first see a teacher, you know whether he is strict or not. I don't know what it is but you can tell.' And Simon categorically said that women teachers were stricter than men teachers. He said: 'There was one teacher we had, she was very strict. They put her into the worst class in the school and that class stood to attention every time when she came in. She was the strictest person I have ever met.' Simon was no supporter of equality for women. Elsewhere he had told me that 'women would never be equal to men' although he was not opposed to their getting equal pay. He simply viewed women teachers within the context of the school itself. Just as he disliked some men teachers for their inability to control a class so he recognized that this could occur amongst some women; there was one young woman teacher who was going to leave because she could not control a class. But his view was a minority one.

Thomas, at the age of fifteen, recalled that he had originally held male teachers in awe. At junior school he had never had a male teacher. And when he first came into contact with them at secondary school he was overawed by this:

> I mean when I was at junior school . . . we never had male teachers before, you know, so they were sort of looked upon as not knowing what they were going to do. So you sort of treated them a bit carefully until you got to know them . . . and then you get the sort of feeling of things and then you can stretch the rules a bit and see how far you can stretch them until you get caught or if you don't get caught you just keep doing it.

According to Thomas the power of male teachers diminished as the boys got more familiar with the rules and how to manipulate or resist them. In spite of this, and contrary to the evidence given above, the stereotypical view held about women teachers strengthened the older the boys got. They began to describe women teachers as 'soft' and unable to control class. David summed this up:

> A lot of women teachers in this school are easy and you can get away with things, like the French teacher and the geography teacher. They are kind of soft like. So you can get off doing work, skive from work and so on. But with men teachers you have got to work.

He held this view even though when pressed on the subject he said that he had lessons with only two women teachers and one of these had no problems with classroom control. She was a 'good teacher'. But he was able to justify his views by claiming that it was necessary to have male teachers in such subjects as engineering and science because if they were taught by women then: 'The majority of people studying for them exams, would kind of take it a bit more easy. It would . . . there would be a lot more shouting in class, a lot more talking, not much concentration.' Of course, such sentiments were not borne out by experience. The success of pupils has never been equated with the gender of teachers.

Conclusion

The pupils were not directly questioned in terms of what messages the girls received from the boys, nor whether they found the boys' behaviour oppressive or not. It was concerned to establish both girls' and boys' views on themselves and whether their views reflected the dominant stereotypical portrayal of girls as hard working, quiet, settling down, being no bother, and boys as the trouble makers, demanders of attention, needing discipline and so on. Linked to this line of enquiry were questions relating to the importance they attached to each group's achievement in their schoolwork. Questions were asked of them to identify those aspects of each group's behaviour which they regarded as troublesome in the classroom. Their desire to be the opposite gender was also explored. The data proved very interesting and also uncovered aspects which the original research design had not anticipated.

Beginning with the girls' responses, there are aspects of their perceptions which are congruent with stereotypical views and others which diverge from this quite dramatically. The former is revealed in the comments they make, particularly about their appearance. They are very conscious of their dress. They are competitive with other girls, and through their dress they establish their own standing amongst the other girls, and further they dress to attract the attention of the boys. When they are younger they do see themselves as more obedient and less independent than the boys, but as they grow older these views seem to alter and although some continue to express this viewpoint others recognize that girls behave disruptively.

Although not all admitted to behaving out of character, it was as young adults recalling their school days that others admitted to their misdemeanours which they did not admit to when originally interviewed.

The violent and aggressive form of girls' behaviour is important to recognize. Violence amongst girls is largely ignored in the education literature and it is only in terms of deviancy that girls' aggression is referred to. In these circumstances it is only girls who have been *defined* as deviant who are spoken of in terms of aggression, otherwise it is assumed not to exist amongst ordinary girls. Lynn Davies (1984) had been concerned to 'sort out the actual nature and comparative extent of boys' and girls' deviance in a particular school setting'. She pointed out that girls are not supposed to be violent or aggressive or tough so when they are their behaviour stands out and they are labelled accordingly. But once this happens then there is no problem recognizing just how difficult they can be. She found that:

The majority of both pupils and teachers, male and female, saw girls as being 'more trouble', girls received more suspensions. Pupils were twice as likely to see girls rather than boys breaking rules; only one teacher, a female RE teacher, saw boys as 'probably worse' in behaviour. (p. 7)

While this may be so, it is only under certain circumstances that it is recognized as such. The question that needs to be posed is how does one account for the differences in perception about the girls' behaviour? In my study deviant behaviour was not identified as such and nobody was asked to label either group as more problematic than the other. The girls tended to represent themselves in conformity with a stereotypical portrayal but it was in the course of replying to other questions and issues, or in their recall of their school days that their disruptive or violent behaviour was referred to. The girls did not automatically recognize these aspects of their behaviour as inconsistent with their being feminine. As for actual violence, playground fights were not everyday occurrences and from what the girls said there were a number who did not fight. But the girls did not label those who fought as deviant. As for verbal abuse this was not unusual. It occurred all the time – the teachers employed this consistently in the classroom – and the form it took amongst girls was accepted by them as part of their everyday lives. The girls, therefore, both conform to the stereotypical notion of appropriate behaviour but violence of some form or other is present amongst them. They do not see themselves as passive, quiet, compliant members of the school. Far from it.

Teachers, as shown in the previous chapter, did not equate girls' disruptive behaviour with that of the boys, at least when the girls were younger. Girls, in fact, were not as physically disruptive as the boys in the class and consequently their disruptive behaviour could be overlooked or ignored.

The fact that girls' violent behaviour was not a topic of discussion in the staffroom reflects the staff's inability to recognize behaviour which contravenes stereotypical thought. Pupils, on the other hand, accept such forms of behaviour and take it for granted. Furthermore, recognition of behaviour which threatens to question accepted wisdom of how people should behave is difficult to handle and teachers have enough to cope with in their everyday school lives.

Following the question on the importance of girls doing well at school, it was apparent that this was closely associated with good behaviour in the classroom and not, in the main, with academic attainment. Achievement in this sense was something rather vague and unconnected with definite pathways that could be pursued. This reflects the girls' almost automatic acceptance of a life dominated by domestic duties and work which did not require high levels of skill or training. This will be discussed in Chapter 9.

The girls were given a chance to express their desire to have been a boy. At the age of 12, three girls did so and although the details varied, their wishes were associated with activities conventionally restricted to boys. By the time they were fifteen this was no longer the case. The girls' female identity had been firmly established (indeed Tricia had had a baby by that age).

The profile that exists in the education literature about boys is largely about counter-school boys and deviants with assertive, aggressive behaviour oppressive of girls and women teachers. Little is written about the ordinary boy who goes through school doing minimal work, but not necessarily domineering or sexually harassing.

The profile that emerges about boys from this study is very different. Clearly they were interested in girls. They did attach more importance to girls' appearance when they were fifteen years old than they did when they were younger. They liked pretty girls and they liked them to dress well. This reflects their growing interest in girls and is coupled with their own sexual identity.

They seemed to hold stereotypical views on what comprises appropriate behaviour amongst girls as reflected in their comments on the girls' independence and aggression. Independence did not seem to conform with femininity and yet at the same time the boys' comments on the girls' behaviour in class and how they thought it important for girls to do well reflects the problems that stereotypical views can generate. The boys had no illusions that girls would work both after school and as married women, and some even regarded the girls as having better chances than themselves for getting interesting jobs. Here the reference point for many of them was work for men in factories or as storemen. In spite of this they, like the girls, associated being good at schoolwork with good behaviour. They thought girls did settle down and work and some even expressed the view that girls were cleverer than boys. This would appear to be an important point that needs further investigation. It contrasts directly with the expressed view referred to above that girls are a 'faceless' bunch.

Perhaps this notion is partly applicable in reference to classroom behaviour and may reflect those boys who seem to spend the bulk of their time in class playing around, 'mucking about' playing football with socks and so on. They seemed to have been so engrossed with their own activities and enjoyment of themselves that there was no room for them to be concerned with those outside their circle. They might well appreciate the presence of girls but then they would get on with their own activities. They not only ignored girls but other boys who did not participate in these activities. And the ones singled out for this type of marginalization were the ones who did well at their schoolwork. Furthermore, boys were conscious of some girls who were very talkative. This also does not conform with the stereotypical picture referred to above. Nor does it follow that boys can both treat girls as a 'faceless bunch' and sexually harass them.

The picture of boys sexually harassing girls all the time needs much further investigation. The observations referred to here and in the previous chapters were obtained when the boys were in the first two years of high school. The comments derived from interviews were obtained from the same boys when they were older but were not backed up by observations. The girls did not complain then or subsequently of sexual harassment. This does not mean that it did not occur but that if and when it did it was only part of a number of different experiences at school.

The boys did not hold out high hopes for themselves. Schoolwork was seen by many as relatively unimportant or even an interference in the course of their pursuit of pleasure. Although the second set of interviews was conducted in 1976 the writing was already on the wall. Unemployment was beginning amongst their parents and the boys anticipated difficulties getting jobs. But there was still a vague notion that qualifications helped though they did not seem to know what these were.

While girls and boys may hold stereotypical views about themselves and each other this only encompasses a part of their understanding of themselves. Their ideas reflect confusions and contradictions and some of these will be discussed in the next chapter. What is important is that girls' self image is complex.

The pupils' internalization of stereotypical views about gender differences is applied also to their teachers. This is exemplified in their statements on their assessment of their teachers. Although they may have liked or disliked individual teachers irrespective of gender, when it came to assessing the teachers' ability to control the pupils they tended to fall into a stereotypical view, particularly with the boys as 15 year olds. Their view corresponded with that of Mr Jason who unequivocally felt that men teachers were better able to control a classroom, even though empirical evidence contradicted this view. The girls acknowledge that they reject certain rules, and do not behave in conformity with what is expected. But their resistance is part of their culture and the fact that they resist just as the boys do needs full recognition.

PART TWO

SEXUALITY

Introduction

One of the causal factors in the low level of 'achievement' in academic terms, and this applies to boys as well as to girls, appears to be the effect of erupting sexuality on their lives (Wolpe, 1977). Girls' developing gender identity and accompanying sexual awareness during adolescence seem to have an adverse effect on their commitment to studying, an element which has been largely ignored or glossed over in recent mainstream educational literature.

Wood (1984) commented on the dearth of material on sexuality in the schools when writing about his research in a school 'sin bin', a unit for 'disruptives'. He said:

> The whole sexy atmosphere of the period [of his research] led me to reflect on the absence of any real work on sex *as it manifests itself in schools*. Even good, recent feminist work (e.g. Deem, 1980; Spender and Sarah, 1980) has not really covered this significant gap. I mean, particularly, how sexuality manifests itself in school as an axis of power relations and as a locus of social orderings. (1984, p. 56)

There has, however, been an ever growing literature on specific aspects of sexuality in schools which focuses on the girls' experiences. The work has represented a 'locus of social orderings' in one crucial aspect which is also linked to what is considered the 'axis of power' as the following brief comments will demonstrate. Common to these studies, in spite of differences in theoretical approaches, is the view that girls, on the whole, are disadvantaged in relation to boys, on the whole, through their experiences in school which are structured or directed by boys. This has led to a linear type of analysis in which the axis of power relations is seen to reside in boys, with an underlying theme of the oppression located in some form of sexuality. An examination of two particular studies illustrates this point.

Mahony's (1985) overall concern was with the effects of co-education on girls. On the basis of her own and other findings she concluded that all girls suffer from some form of harassment at school, and that they are all 'equally vulnerable to similar treatment'. She characterized various aspects of girls' experience at school concluding that boys have a built-in advantage over girls because of their gender. The basis of her argument is an assertion that, through patriarchy, all men dominate women and benefit from this. Neither the existence of patriarchy, nor the format it takes is questioned. It is a simple form of domination which affects all social relations. She says:

> Once it is acknowledged that there is not necessarily any connection between patriarchy and particular kinds of economic systems, a new material base for patriarchy has to be found. . . Educational analysis is incomplete without an understanding of patriarchy (p. 69).

Patriarchy provides 'an account for the oppression of women by men and the oppression of girls by boys in school'.

The material basis for all this, according to Mahony, is to be found particularly through men's control via women's sexuality which in turn is controlled through a 'particular form of heterosexuality' (p. 70). She claims that she rejects an essentialism, arguing that the 'construction of male sexuality as well as being a material force in the oppression of women, also has a history'. She quotes the work of Jack Litewka (1977) whom she says maintains that male sexuality is organized around three basic notions: 'objectification, fixation and conquest'. From an early age boys learn to objectify girls; men learn 'to fixate on portions of the female anatomy' and, finally, 'conquering is a highly valued skill in our society'. All of this, she says, constitutes masculinity and emerges amongst teenage boys in an exaggerated form.

She substitutes one set of linear arguments, that is economic determinism, for another, ignoring the complexities of the issues with which she is dealing. Sexuality is reduced to three elements and sexuality in schools is to be understood as an 'exaggerated' male dominated form although exactly what it is is never specified. Girls are portrayed as the victims of boys' domination. Schooling is reduced to a set of relationships structured through sexuality of the exaggerated male form. Nothing else seems to count. The argument appears to be that if girls were removed from co-education schools to single-sex schools they would somehow or other achieve a desired level of education which is never stated nor analysed.

Lees' (1986) study, on the other hand, emphasizes the social construction of sexuality. In her detailed study she also focuses on the experiential and wishes to establish the constricting effect sexuality has on girls' lives. Lees' major concern in her study was to: 'raise questions about the way individual experience is socially constructed – and, in particular, since it is so crucial to a girl's identity, sexual experience' (p. 13).

She warns about the dangers of using patriarchy as an explanatory tool:

> Generalizations about patriarchal power and the control by men of women's sexuality and labour are frequently cited in the feminist literature but little attempt has been made to *describe how power is exercised in the sexual domain and to examine the mechanisms* – both material and ideological – that underlie this dominance. . . The underlying premise of this approach is that there is more than one root – that anatomy is destiny – of women's subordination (my emphasis) (p. 13).

Unlike Mahony, Lees sees a place for ideology in understanding these processes:

> The idea that sexuality is socially constructed implies that our individual experience is a product of ideologies, social practices and social structures. . . Though the mere fact of being a girl seems to a great extent to determine the way girls experience life, their class and race also contribute to their social 'subordination' (p. 13).

She argues that 'we need to examine the implicit assumptions that underlie the constraints' that operate in girls' lives. It is girls' reputations which she regards as a means which steers girls' ' "acceptable" forms of sexuality and social behaviour'. It is the process of labelling which operates as a form of social control. ' . . . girls are seen primarily in terms of their sexual reputation'.

Now, although Lees claims a role for ideology in terms of individuals' experiences she does not pursue this line of analysis. Other structural factors such as class and race are also mentioned but these do not enter as major elements in the course of her analysis. Her aim is to 'describe how power is exercised' and the mechanisms of this operation. She does this very successfully and we gain a great deal of insight from her study. But the effect of this labelling process in relation to other facets of girls' lives is not established. It is taken for granted that labelling restricts girls' chances without establishing the basis for this. The form of ideologies and different aspects of the culture are not analysed. In the end there is a similar linear analysis to the one that Mahony provides because it is male power which is at the root of it all.

Both analyses examine sexuality through the experiental. While their interpretations are different their conclusions converge largely because sexuality is dealt with in terms of power relations reflecting unquestioningly male domination. In this way complex relationships are reduced to a linear dimension of girls responding to boys' behaviour, and this, in turn, determining the outcome of their education.

Instead of this type of analysis, the following section is concerned with understanding the different facets of sexuality in a secondary school, including those which reflect some of the structural forms of control that exist and operate external to individual interactions, experiences and interpersonal relationships. For the purposes of this analysis it is not relevant to examine critically the different accounts of what constitutes human sexuality.[1] So whether psychoanalytical analysis is preferential to behaviourism is not an issue here. The discussion is concerned with the ways in which sexuality are dealt with and controlled within the education system, how the processes of sexual contact occur, how teachers and pupils react to these, and, in the final analysis the role sexuality plays in the course of being educated. Sex and sexuality are important parts of adolescence and the final form adolescents' gender identity takes and, as such, need to be considered in full when education experience is considered.

The different factors of sex and sexuality will be considered within a structured context of the school. The ideology on sex and sex education, and its relation to moral order, structure the official way in which sex and sexuality are handled within a school. In spite of these discourses and the tendency for teachers to accept these seemingly unquestioningly, sexual issues are ever present but not necessarily recognized as such by teachers. They appear in the course of applying disciplinary procedures, they exist in social interactions between teachers and pupils and pupils and pupils, and yet teachers may, for a variety of reasons, overlook or ignore indicators of sex and sexuality amongst their pupils.

Girls and boys, as already established, are not passive actors in the classroom or in the school in general. They act as already constituted gendered subjects which has direct consequences on overt forms of behaviour which are far more complex than straightforward situations of domination and submission. The parameters of what constitutes socially acceptable forms of behaviour of a sexual, non-erotic nature, reflect family and peer group culture.

The following chapters examine sexuality within a school, demonstrating how this impinges on all spheres of school life, at times operating as a form of social control. The first chapter examines the way in which sexuality is officially dealt with in the school. The next chapter presents details of the intrusion of teachers' sexuality into the control of pupils, as well as their ability to shrug off aspects of their pupils' sexuality on the basis of the pupils' age and the nature of these sexual manifestations. The third chapter presents the pupils' perceptions of certain aspects of sexuality including their experiences.

Overall these chapters present details, where it occurs, of the sexual nature of the interaction between pupils and teachers within the confines of the school which itself is a highly structured organization.

CHAPTER FOUR

Sexuality and moral order

Control over pupils and teachers is contained in forms other than the disciplinary practices referred to in the first two chapters. These controls, like the disciplinary practices, operate through 'normalizing judgments' which define what constitutes 'good' and 'bad' behaviour. These norms are the orthodoxies of the moral code and as such prescribe social forms of behaviour.

The education system is charged with teaching pupils these orthodoxies. However, because the moral code is closely identified with sexuality, when the moral code is translated into concrete parts of the curriculum, it is taught under the heading of sex education. Sexuality as a phenomenon becomes contained within this context. Other forms of sexuality may therefore be ignored or overlooked in the school unless they are seen as some form of deviance or 'abnormal' behaviour.

This chapter will contextualize the provision of sex education. An examination of this as well as the nature of the discourse of individuals in the pastoral care system will provide the means of analysing some of the specific effects that the handling of sexual issues within the educational context has on gender differences. Whatever the discourses on sex education are, there is a consensus about girls' sexuality which is that it is directly related to marriage and motherhood and, as such, permeates all aspects of discourses on sex education and informs the way in which female sexuality is conceptualized.

Moral order and moral codes

What constitutes moral order has been the subject of discussion by philosophers through the ages and the content of the discourse has reflected the historical moment. At the risk of bringing down the wrath of philosophers, suffice it to say that moral codes prescribe acceptable forms of behaviour applicable to all aspects of life thereby exerting a form of control over individuals and thus they contain the fundamental prescriptions of moral order.

There can be no doubt that each succeeding generation must learn the moral codes of the society. With the decline of the power and influence of the Church, which in former ages was responsible for this training (Althusser, 1971, David, 1980) and the supposed disintegration of family life as constituted by the nuclear family (Wolpe, 1983, Denscombe, 1984), the education system has been charged with the responsibility of teaching the moral codes which reflect the Christian Church's construction of morality, to each new generation.

Irrespective of what comprises moral behaviour, moral codes in the education system will, in general, according to Peters (1963) be: 'as much concerned with the promotion of good activities as it will be with the maintenance of rules for social conduct with what ought to be as well as with what men ought to do' (p. 53).

In addition to stipulating what ought to be done, moral codes create social consensus and in the course of their dissemination they provide for: 'the preparation of individuals for participating in social life and acceptance of social rules: in short the problems of role allocation and socialization' (Halsey, 1963, p. 35). So moral codes create the blueprint for the approved form of social behaviour.

Some philosophers and social scientists share the view that moral actions are the outcome of conscious, rational choices made by individuals, although this may include a number of unconscious elements which have been internalized over the years as a result of the socialization process. Niblett (1963) referring to a conference of a 'small mixed band of educationists' including philosophers said: 'all agreed that actions that are moral imply choices that are conscious, however many the unconscious elements in the situation; there can be no morality without rational and personal decisions' (p. 28).

How moral codes are acquired and at what stage of children's development this occurs has more recently been the subject for a great deal of examination. Particularly influential in this area of enquiry has been an American, Kohlberg (1963), who identifies six stages of development of moral behaviour amongst children. His work has provided one of the main bases for a number of empirical studies particularly by social psychologists. Such data is considered invaluable amongst educationists concerned with ensuring that children learn to behave correctly.

The study of moral education is relatively recent (Wright, 1976) and has not yet emerged as a distinctive discipline with its own subject base taught in teacher-training colleges. But what comprises moral education? There is no part of the school curriculum labelled as such, no doubt because of the highly abstract nature of the components of moral behaviour.

However much moral education may be discussed in abstract terms and irrespective of the techniques developed to measure various indices of moral behaviour, in popular culture moral behaviour is inextricably linked to sexual behaviour. Behaving morally often is synonymous with adopting a sexual code of conduct that is acceptable and which reflects the Church's view on marriage, fidelity and monogamy. There is, therefore, a tendency to 'equate the whole idea of morality with the morality of sexual behaviour' (Eppel, 1963).[1] Although Eppel made this point in 1963 there has been no significant change since then.

Where moral education is translated in concrete terms into a recognizable part of the curriculum, it emerges as sex education; elsewhere it is included under headings such as Life Skills and so on which cover less well defined or obvious moral forms of behaviour. But its inclusion heralds problems and difficulties, not least because sex and sexuality, according to Weeks (1985), comprise a 'contested zone' and have been ' . . . a moral and political battlefield over the past 200 years' which has been 'punctuated by a series of panics around sexuality' which he suggests has 'grown out of or merged into a generalised social anxiety'. Notwithstanding the development of study by sexologists of the physical act of sexual intercourse, or the analyses derived from Freud's work, issues surrounding sex and sexuality are highly volatile, as Weeks suggests, and they are no less so when incorporated into a school syllabus.

As will be shown below sex education has been predominantly concerned with physical aspects of reproduction within marriage, and with what has been defined as the abnormal which in males takes the form of VD and in females illegitimate births, or pregnancies.[2]

This element of the curriculum has differential effects on girls and boys because of the differences in the way in which female and male sexuality are conceptualized. Since the nineteenth century female sexuality has always been located within marriage and male's in the gratification of a 'natural' urge. In spite of the advances in knowledge which questions this double standard, girls' sexuality is still not seen in the same way as boys' in ideological terms. There continues to be a denial of girls' libido, and a direct equation of sex with marriage for girls. In the course of presenting this view in sex education, there is a specific control over girls which does not apply to the same extent to boys because of this. It is taken as morally reprehensible for girls to have sexual intercourse, but acceptable for boys to be sexually experienced, now with the cautionary note of taking various precautions because of the risk of contracting AIDS. The labelling of teenage girls (Lees, 1986) indicates the strong pressure of the peer group in this regard. She, as others have done, referred to pejorative terms which are applied to girls but boys, on the other hand, are congratulated (Willis, 1977). In addition, as will be demonstrated below, there is a class-based dimension to this form of control with more control being exerted over working-class girls than over middle-class girls.

Sex education in schools[3]

In 1959 sexual immorality was commented on by the Crowther Report which spoke of 'the disappearance of the code of practice about sexual experience'. Amongst other things it called for chastity before marriage and fidelity in marriage, reflecting the 'battle for chastity' that has prevailed since the fourth century A.D. when Cassian held forth on this topic (Foucault, 1985).

With the endorsement of the Crowther Report's call for chastity before and fidelity in marriage, sex education was equated with teaching biological reproduction, which is in conformity with the ideology that sexual intercourse should be directly related to procreation. The Church of England Board of Education (1962) on sex education accordingly specified that the emphasis should be on preparation for marriage and that physical, spiritual and moral elements should be included. Teaching could take place in 'homecraft, physical education, social studies and religious education', and schools should aim to answer questions and provide information relating it at all times to marriage; parents should also be involved. These recommendations do appear to be the ones that have been consistently pursued. Where schools do provide some form of sex education, what is taught is determined by its location in the curriculum. If in homecraft (which usually devotes some time to child-rearing practices reinforcing the notion of motherhood) and biology, the focus is likely to be on biological reproduction; in Religious Instruction (RI) and social studies family centred issues would be covered. Little or no provision is made for dealing with emotional elements of sex and sexuality.

This particular focus of sex education is legitimized further by the perceived absence of morality. So there appears an urgent need for schools to counter the prevailing immorality through adequate education. This view is constantly reinforced by some claims that parents are to blame for this absence because of their poor child-rearing practices. For example Chandler (1980) linked teenage pregnancies to the emotional instability of girls who became pregnant because 'that is what lost, emotionally neglected and generally uncared for girls are doing these days' (p. 113). And, as will be discussed below, it is implied that this failure is not so prevalent in middle-class homes.

Just as there is a definition of 'good' sexual behaviour, so there is a discussion on bad sexual practices which represent loss or absence of morality. Both aspects comprise integral parts of 'normalizing judgments'. The bad practices are identified through particular indicators which include illegitimacy rates, teenage pregnancies, and the incidence of sexually transmitted diseases. This was seen as a heritage of Victorian attitudes to morality almost twenty-five years ago when it was argued that it was:

given a fresh impetus by the form in which current statistics or venereal disease and illegitimacy among teenagers has been presented. These are indeed grave and serious problems, but one notices a tendency to equate relations between the sexes with promiscuity, and premarital conception with general immorality (E. M. Eppel, P. 116).

Going back to the 1950s, the Crowther Report (1959) produced statistics which claimed that 'one girl in 50 might expect to give birth to a child conceived before she was 17'. While these figures declined in succeeding years, particularly after 1967, the rate of abortions replaced illegitimacy rates as an indicator of sexual immorality.

Such discussions – although of a general nature – often mask two factors, the first being the class based nature and the second the gender specific nature of some of the discourses. Middle-class children are not seen as in need of sex education to the same extent that working-class children are. The underlying idea is that middle-class families are of an educational level which will make sexual information available to their offspring. In fact Dallas (1972) claimed that middle-class adolescent girls were unlikely to become pregnant unlike working-class girls who wanted, 'something of their own and reflect the likelihood of having been "unwanted herself" and brought up by parents unaware of the needs of children for understanding communication and genuine friendship' (p. 25). She did not stop to consider whether middle-class girls were more likely to obtain abortions than girls from less financially advantaged homes. She suggests that middle-class girls are better brought up, learn skills and benefit through parental roles and 'constant reference books', facilities which she assumes are the prerogatives of middle-class families. She did not discount, totally, the possibility that middle-class girls could fall victim to their own desires when she cautioned that:

> Intelligent girls from good homes . . . have never realised how quickly the point of no return can be reached (p. 19).

Her views had, in fact, been substantiated by Schofield (1973), who found that girls who had taken GCE examinations were less likely to have had sex education than others. Given that more middle-class girls take GCE examinations than working-class girls, the latter are more likely to have more sex education than their more privileged peers in the course of doing home economics (HE). This is not to discount the fact that girls doing biology are likely to encounter sex education although in terms of physiological reproduction.

There is a remarkable absence of any clear demarcation in terms of differences in relation to male and female sexuality when the indices of 'bad' behaviour are presented. This may be due to the general nature of the discourse which does not take account of different perceptions about male and female sexuality. However, the ultimate visible evidence of premarital sexuality may be pregnancy. It is the girls who are held responsible for this and not their male partners. This has a long history and the consistency of this orthodoxy is apparent in the ways in which female deviancy is defined and treated. Shacklady Smith (1978) referred to the tendency of official agencies to ignore female delinquency. Where it was acknowledged, the offences became 'sexualised' thus equating female deviancy with sexual promiscuity. Indeed girls who are sexually experienced stand the risk of being defined as in need of care, as Eaton (1986) found in her research:

> Adolescent girls who come before the court are more likely than their male counterparts to be questioned about their sexual activity, more likely to lose their liberty for activities which would not be against the law if committed by an adult. The courts appear to be concerned with enforcing a specific gender-role on those young women who engage in unfeminine behaviour since such behaviour poses a threat to their future role within the domestic sphere. (p. 25)

Sex education at Berkeley

Given the link between sex education and moral questions, its inclusion at Berkeley was not likely to be straightforward. The Longford Report on Pornography had come out in 1972. It reflected the moral conservatives' reaffirmation of family life and contrary to what had become recognized as a necessary part of the curriculum, condemned what it saw as the reprehensible inclusion of 'the more personally relevant sex-education, access to birth-control facilities, information and advice on abortion, a sensible attitude to VD', according to Weeks, (1981). The report was clear 'that a sound sex education could not come from the amoral instructions of the school but only from the familial framework' (Weeks, 1981, p. 255). Notwithstanding this attempt to remove sex education from the curriculum, the provision of sex education in Berkeley was going ahead.

The LEA adviser, Miss Jack, was given the task of introducing sex education to both the parents and the pupils. This was in conformity with equating sex education with health by the head, as will be discussed below. Miss Jack must have been aware of the criticism levelled at schools by the Longford Report as well as the unease that could exist amongst parents in regard to the provision of sex education.

In line with the then current school policy of informing parents on curriculum content it was decided that Miss Jack should address a parents' evening devoted entirely to this topic. The provision of sex education could be a tendentious subject. Although this was the 1970s, there was still a need to justify to the parents the inclusion of sex instruction in the formal syllabus, reflecting the prevailing conservatism, contrary to the popularly held beliefs that there was a rampant promiscuity before marriage.

She advised the parents that her lessons would deal with sources of infection, changes in the child's bodily development caused by the effect of the pituitary gland (which was directly related to the process of reproduction), the menstrual cycle and puberty, and finally child care and nutrition. In other words, she was going to deal with the biological aspects of reproduction and how to care for children in the home. To make the first point quite explicit she levelled a general criticism against parents who fail to tell their children the truth about 'where babies come from'. She said:

It is surprising that babies still come in the doctor's black bag, or they are bought in shops or found under the gooseberry bushes!

In her experience she had said that children were not fooled and quoted one 10 year old who had said 'Shall I tell my mother where babies come from, because she said a stork brought me? So I don't think she knows'.

At the same time she warned against parents going into too much detail. There was a limit to what they should tell their children and at what age:

In response to a boy's request to his mother about where he had come from he was given a lengthy explanation about sex and how he was born. The boy said 'yes, it is all very interesting but Jimmy next door says that he comes from Liverpool'.

Her message was unambiguous: parents should give only basic facts on biological reproduction. She was opposed to dealing with questions of 'human relationships' until pupils were much older and recommended that this should be during their fourth year at school. What she meant by human relationships was not spelt out but presumably she was referring to sexual and emotional relationships. She concluded her talk by saying:

I don't think it should be treated in isolation. It should be part of the syllabus and it should be progressive in the fact that I haven't gone into much detail. But later on they will go into more detail on the reproductive system. Perhaps when they get into more senior classes one will bring in subjects like population, particularly in terms of the humanities and this brings us onto should we control this.

For her, the legitimate academic criteria for discussing sex in the classroom was to inform pupils about the issues of biological reproduction and the consequences this could have in demographic terms. Her hidden agenda was locating sexual intercourse within the family and the specific role of women in child care. Child care, when it was taught, did not question men's role in the family. And the discussion of sexual relationships as such were to be avoided if possible.

What was even more telling than that evening's meeting was Miss Jack's private views which she volunteered to me following a lesson. She said: 'What I really think sex education is all about is to get the boys and girls to play their correct roles'. These were quite straightforward. They meant, as far as she was concerned, that 'the boys open the doors for me when I go through from room to room or carry my bag for me and so on'. Sex education was a means of ensuring the perpetuation of a set of rites and rituals reflecting the appropriate behaviour of men and women, within the traditional gender boundaries with the male acting as the protector. For Miss Jack this was what mattered, the demarcation of boundaries of acceptable social forms of behaviour between men and women, and nothing directly to do with sexuality itself. The reinforcement of normative behaviour would ensure adequate control over the adult population, particularly women.

Miss Jack's representation of what she planned to do reflected some of the contradictions between providing necessary guidance for 'abnormal' behaviour in the course of preventing illegitimacy and at the same time upholding family values. On the one hand she confirmed family values but she also planned to introduce the children to contraception. Perhaps she held similar views to Dallas (1972) about the need to educate the working classes! Miss Jack was quite prepared to provide an accurate description of biological differences between males and females, particularly regarding genitalia, and elaborate on contraception, but she was reluctant to deal with sexual relationships as such. Sexual relationships were referred to obliquely and only in the context of monogamous marriage, a position which, as already pointed out, linked biological reproduction to child care and nutrition.

Miss Jack's presentation to the parents was consistent with the official views on what should be taught in sex education classes. The traditional orthodoxy on this topic was reflected in her emphasis on biological reproduction. This reinforces the traditional ideology which locates female sexuality strictly within the context of family life, thus excluding any discussion on female sexuality outside this context.

Furthermore, formally, Miss Jack's position reflects the points made above that sexuality and related issues could only be dealt with in conventional pedagogic terms of imparting knowledge; sex, like all forms of education, had to be concerned with knowledge and facts, the actual biological way in which reproduction occurs. Any considered position involving emotional relationships could not be included within a school curriculum directly. Sexuality and its potential effect on adolescents in this crucial stage of development was significantly overlooked. Just as the discourse on sexuality in adult society is in terms of morals, so it is to be with adolescents.

How effective were these and subsequent sex education classes on the pupils, particularly the girls? The pupils' perceptions, although limited, will be discussed in Chapter 6. However, it is difficult to establish the effective transmission and reinforcement of an already extant ideology on women's sexuality and its relationship to motherhood and family responsibilities. It is obvious that the teaching of sex education ignores the existence of women's libido, their sexual gratification outside of marriage.

Without having studied the provision of sex education for the pupils all the way through their secondary schooling at Berkeley, it is impossible to assess whether the girls did receive more sex education because of their gender and their class backgrounds. The Berkeley group on the whole did not follow GCE examinations and are more likely to have done home economics all the way through school, thus ensuring a surfeit of sex education. Indeed one of the girls complained about how often they were given advice about contraception! This seems to confirm Schofield's findings (1973). Furthermore, the beliefs expressed by Dallas (1972) who regarded it as less important to provide middle-class girls with sex education than their working-class peer group may also be reflected here. The overall control over working-class girls and their sexuality could, therefore, be greater than that of middle-class girls.

The identification at Berkeley of sex education with sex in marriage conformed with the prevailing official policy. The question that arises is whether there has been any significant change in the nature of the discourse since then. There was a marked shift in official thinking in 1977 when the DES appeared to have recognized the contradictions and confusions surrounding the teaching of sex education. They said:

> There is growing consensus that whatever the phrase 'sex education' may mean, it is certainly inextricably bound up with the physical, emotional and mental development of children, especially in adolescence, and for many with their not too far distant prospect of parenthood. (pp. 114–115, DES 1977)

They followed this with a bold statement which raised the question of enjoyment involved in sexual relations: 'As integrity and respect for truth are basic in this, as in all teaching, it is dishonest and futile to hide, at the proper time, that sexual intercourse should be highly enjoyable' (p. 17).

It is highly unlikely that this recommendation has been taken up in general by schools although this is not to suggest that these issues are never addressed. Where this has occurred it would reflect the commitment of the headteacher and the availability of a member of staff able and willing to do such teaching. Understandably headteachers are often afraid of permitting the introduction of controversial material into the classroom, particularly given the directives either of their LEAs or the DES, and the possibility of protest by parents.

Notwithstanding the recommendation by the DES, the terms of the discourse on sex education have not significantly altered over the years. In contrast to the 1977 document, the DES in 1981 set out an unambiguous proviso that parents should be informed of the ways and the context in which sex education is provided in schools, at the same time as recommending the provision of sex education. In 1986 the guidelines for teaching sex education reiterated the need to locate it within a moral framework. The HMI discussion document, *Health Education from 5–16* (1986), stipulated that when taught in primary schools it should be 'presented in the context of family life, of loving relationships and of respect for others: in short in a moral framework' (p. 5). As for teaching at secondary level, although it should contain 'factual information about the physical aspects of sex', these should not be 'more important than a consideration of the qualities of relationships in family life and values. . . ' (p. 5).

While all these aims are not to be disparaged, it is the limitation of the aims that is in question. Official discourse has not moved from family orientation since the 1950s. These issues were again raised during the debate on the third reading of the Education Bill in the House of Lords in June 1986. The clause that was being debated, according to a report in the *Times Educational Supplement* (6 June 1986):

> enjoins governors, LEAs, and heads to take such steps as are reasonably practical to secure that, where sex education is given to registered pupils at a school, it is given in such a manner as to encourage those pupils *to have due regard to moral considerations and the value of family life* (my emphasis).

Moral considerations are equated with marital sexual intercourse and sex education is entreated to reinforce views about monogamy and family life. Lord Denning in the same debate (*TES*, 1986) asserted that marriage was under attack as an institution because of freely available divorce and an absence of stigma of illegitimacy.

Such debates ignore empirical evidence which does not support their ideological position. A study by Dr Bury (1984) on teenagers' sexual practices, indicated that:

> Teenagers are more likely to have sex at an earlier age, but they are no more promiscuous than their parents were twenty years ago. . .
> Their relationships are still dominated by fidelity, romance and even marriage. . . Far from being an epidemic of teenage pregnancies, the numbers have fallen. . .

Most importantly Dr Bury's report refutes the notion that if we talk about sex to teenagers they are more likely to indulge. The reverse is the case, 'the evidence is that the more we talk about sex, the less likely they are to have sex at an early age' (*Guardian*, 28 June 1984).

Irrespective of such evidence, the views expressed in the Lords' debate prevail.

The present day panic over the spread of AIDS is likely to affect sexual practices, but whatever changes may occur the control over women's sexuality through its identification with family life will continue.

Yet the extent to which sex education is generally available and its effect is not fully known. From the responses of 500 headteachers Jackson (1978) found that 85 per cent claimed that their pupils were:

> given information on VD but only ten per cent of schools gave information on contraception and the majority thought this should not be included in sex education. This somewhat contradicts Reid's (1982) conclusion which he reached after reviewing the National Child Development Study (1974) and Farrell's study (1978). He concluded that there had been a substantial increase in the amount of 'basic sex education' provided. He did not comment on the protests that organized parents could make about any provision.[4]

How effective has the teaching of sex education been? Schofield (1973) concluded after interviewing 376 young people that its effects were minimal and hardly altered their attitudes towards sex. Furthermore, there seems little doubt that the sexual experience of individuals is never dealt with. Jackson (1978) said that there was little or no provision made for dealing with emotional elements of sex and sexuality, and that, although it was inadequate for both boys and girls, it was 'particularly misleading regarding female sexuality and is therefore less potentially meaningful for girls' (p. 346). And, of course, homosexuality and lesbianism are generally avoided and attempts to introduce such elements into sex education are likely to be met by strong protests as occurred in Haringey, London, in 1986 when a Parents' Rights Group was set up to oppose the Council's decision merely to introduce positive views into their Equal Opportunities programme on lesbian and gay issues. The opposition to the Haringey council's efforts received national press converage.

Pastoral staff's view on sexuality amongst pupils

At Berkeley the pastoral staff met regularly to discuss specific problems. On one occasion Mr Trim convened a special meeting to discuss sex and health matters which he specifically related to moral issues. 'Another big thing', he said as he introduced the topic, 'is the whole area of relationship between pastoral and health education and general morality of life.' Although he did not define what he meant by the 'general morality of life', the unspoken agenda was sexual issues.

His main concern appeared to be to alert the staff to the potential dangers for boys who could contract VD and girls who could become pregnant. He pointed out that in his last school such matters were tackled in a series of lectures with fourth year pupils and he now wanted his staff's opinion about when they thought a similar programme should be adopted. It was not at all clear why he should have raised the question at this stage when he had only first and second year pupils. Perhaps it provided him with an opportunity of expressing his views on sex education and sexuality within the school.

He located sex instruction within the realm of health education and here he drew a distinction between health problems associated with sexual intercourse and those with smoking or drinking, the last two which he regarded as 'harmless areas'. But having said this he was keen to promote his image as an enlightened and modern head by saying that he wanted to bring out into the open all these issues so they were not like 'something as a hole in the corner'. His views were not questioned by three of the four teachers, although the fourth suggested that the school doctor's advice should be sought.

The extent of his enlightenment did not go beyond accepting in principle the provision of sex education in the school. But the focus was to be on the health hazards of sexual intercourse – VD or pregnancy. Personal relationships and emotional and sexual issues were not to be included. Sex instruction could then be conducted by the specialist who would formally deal with the various biological aspects. Defining the problems in this way provides an obvious example of 'forms of knowledge facilitating the production of categories or parameters for differentiating "abnormal" from the "normal"' (Urwin, 1985). Abnormal forms were evidenced in the 'health' hazard, although how pregnancy constitutes a health hazard indicates the tendency to confuse a physical condition with a moral question.

The scene was set for the pastoral staff to conceptualize sexual issues in these terms. The effect of this delineation was to compartmentalize sex education as the provenance of a health educator or sex expert, and 'abnormal' forms for the pastoral staff. Teachers like Miss Leyland, who went to listen to Dr Hemming (a well known educationist) speak at the local teachers' centre, did not oppose such views.

Dr Hemming addressed the question of pupils' sexuality. He stressed the need for schools to recognize the 'normality' of developing sexuality amongst its teenage pupils, particularly in a society which he classified as 'post-prudish' where 'sex is writ large everywhere'. He said both young men and women were fully conscious of sex, and recommended that there should be the 'development of the full sexual capability we want the young woman to obtain before she marries so that she can create from the start a profound relationship with a young man and therefore put into the background warmth and mutual trust'. He advocated 'real passionate love in each home which would provide the right environment for growing children'. The need to accept adolescent sexuality was an imperative in order for the development of women's sexual capability.

He spoke about the 'thorny path' he was treading and the apprehension society had in accepting adolescent sexuality, particularly as adolescents were 'ready for sexual experiences before they left school', although he was not advocating that they should necessarily experience it. He felt that schools tended to overlook this whole area. Schools prepare children for most situations except sexual ones. 'Only in the sexual relationships do we say put it aside, and then present them with a big challenge, which is marriage'. He also argued for a distinction to be made between the physical and the emotional aspects of sexuality and recommended working 'through the basic emotions of sexuality before you reach the ultimate test'. He said, 'If parents won't accept the sexuality of the adolescent, what they reap is deceit'. He did not set out how this change in attitude could be achieved. It should be left to the individual teacher to do so.

Accepting Dr Hemming's views that pupils were likely to be 'fully conscious of sex' I wondered if the pastoral staff had any distinctive views on the question of sex and sexuality.

After I had established a good working relationship with most members of staff, I asked for a meeting with the four pastoral teachers. I wanted to explore their perceptions of their pupils' sexuality, if possible. I thought I could lead into the subject through asking them their views on the peer group culture. To introduce this I commented on the overriding problems that appeared to affect the school: discipline and control. I then said that I was very conscious of massive changes that had taken place amongst the girls in terms of their personal appearance over a period of only a few months. At the age of twelve, their eyebrows were plucked, their hair dyed, their heels were higher, and they were using eye shadow. I then raised the question of what constituted popularity and referred to Bob Evans whom the girls consistently spoke about and who appeared to be a leader. This led the teachers onto a discussion of boyfriends. He was the first boy whom the teachers realized had a 'regular girlfriend' signified by a ring that he had given to his girlfriend.

Then they turned their attention to another boy whom they said was at the root of so much trouble because 'girls kept falling out with each other' because of him. He had acquired a new girlfriend, Tricia who was then subjected to:

a lot of lip from other girls including Jane who really fancied him. As a result Tricia stayed away from school and her mother became concerned about it and I found out about it and this came out. She was frightened to come to school because Jane was apparently going to beat her up.

Miss Leyland resolved the problem through discussions with Jane and her parents in which Jane was threatened with suspension if 'there was any fighting in the playground'. Apparently the threat worked and equilibrium was restored.

The teachers did not find Jane's threatening behaviour towards Tricia extraordinary in any way, and presumably it was something they encountered from time to time. As with other examples of girls' violence, the situation was not commented upon. Their main concern was with Tricia's school attendance and the cause of her absence and not with the emerging sexuality amongst the girls or their violence.

Their comments led Mr Sands to describe certain of the rituals that were observed by the pupils. He said that the pupils did not sit next to someone of the opposite sex because to do so indicated that the person was your boyfriend or girlfriend 'and so there is a presumption . . . that if you go and sit next to a girl, or if you associate with a girl, that is your girlfriend'.

Mrs White said:

It seems to me that pressures on say, the girls, if they fancy a boy, is not to sit next to him. Not to make it a sort of pact comes from the other girls in the group. Therefore at this age in particular they are more susceptible to the pressures from their own sex, than the pressure within them to sit next to the boy they fancy.

Mr Sands tried to account for this ritual in terms of biological factors. He drew a contrast between what he observed and how his mother had described her school days. He said when she was a child – and presumably this was during the 1920s – boys and girls sat next to each other in the classroom 'and thought nothing of it', but this he attributed to the later physical development. He accounted for the difference on the grounds that the pupils matured earlier now than ever before. In other words he was acknowledging the emerging sexuality but it was seen as affecting them in ways which did not directly impinge on the school's main task of teaching and controlling.

These rituals referred in the main to personal relationships of a sexual nature. As pointed out in Chapter 2, girls and boys did sit next to each other and did work together in classroom situations, the difference being that it was in the context of classroom work that this occurred and therefore was not to be confused with boy/girl relationships. The exception was Bob Evans. He ignored this convention by working closely with his girlfriend in the same class. This exception indicates the possibility of conventions being flouted by individuals who enjoy positions of power or strength or confidence within the peer group and who can afford to ignore cultural taboos when it suits them. (For an elaboration of this point see Chapter 5.)

Notwithstanding these rituals, boys did speak and boast about their girlfriends and this occurred outside the bounds of the school situation. Mr Sands said:

At the social club [run by staff members in the evenings] they like to say that I have got a girlfriend and it is so and so and they wouldn't dream of carrying it out in the classroom.

Although they boasted, this did not mean that they actually spent time with the girlfriend during the course of the evening. He described how, at the disco:

A gang of boys go round and then at the end of the evening or sometime they will get together and dance with a girl. They will separate again, and they will go to each side of the room and they will talk about it, but they won't keep sort of holding hands or clinging relationships together for very long.

He thought the boys stayed together in gangs in order to cope with their *lack of confidence*. 'They are very unsure of themselves and so it is much safer to stay in gangs.' At the end of the evening they walked home together in groups and tended not to pair off.

Significantly Mr Sands only reported on boys' behaviour. He did not discuss the girls at all. Disco dancing in the 1970s was characterized by formation dancing and the girls would line up together linking arms and gyrating to the music. The boys would sometimes line up opposite them but overall the girls seemed to dance more than the boys and were much better dancers than the boys.

Another area of interest and one which I asked directly about was whether the girls had crushes. Underlying this question were the observations (see Chapter 5) on how some girls behaved in the presence of some male teachers: they simpered, smiled and behaved in a generally coquettish fashion. Nobody responded in terms of girls having crushes on any particular male teacher. There was an overall denial of sexuality amongst the girls and their crushes were likened, by Mr Sands, to their reactions to pop stars:

> They are not yet ready to have a relationship with a boy, but none the less the sexual feelings are there, and they transfer them onto somebody, a pop star or somebody who is distant enough so they can fantasize about them and yet see that the person is real.

The boys, on the other hand, did not frequently have crushes, according to the teachers, and there was general agreement that when this occurred it was 'embarrassing' as much for the teacher as for the boy concerned. And yet, having said this they referred to the new young woman art teacher who was not only popular with the girls, but also with the boys in her tutor group. This led them on to discuss the behaviour of older boys:

> You will hear boys when they get older . . . passing remarks about new teachers. It happens all the time. They come in and say have you seen so and so, have you watched her go up the stairs? And they would know all about this new one.

To a certain extent my question and the responses reveal a number of points. The first is my automatic assumption that all such 'crushes' would be heterosexual in nature. Girls' 'crushes' on women teachers is a topic that has been discussed since the nineteenth century and seen as morally reprehensible because of the 'danger'

119

of lesbianism, as A. Farraday points out (1985).[5] Because heterosexuality is taken as the norm neither I nor the teachers questioned the 'popularity' of the new young art teacher. Could the girl pupils have had a 'crush' on her?

The second point, and this is embedded in the comments of the teachers about the boys' behaviour, is that it was legitimate for older boys to comment on women teachers. None of the teachers recognized the possibility that women teachers could find such behaviour oppressive or denigrating. It was assumed to be normal and acceptable.

The third aspect is that although girls' crushes are seen to be childish, boys' crushes are not. Where it occurs with boys, the situation is deemed embarrassing for the teacher concerned because underlying this is a sexual/erotic content which is not seen to be present amongst girls.

Finally these comments do support conventional wisdom on co-education schools. As Farraday pointed out, the debates on co-education schools centred on the 'naturalness' of putting the two groups together: once boys and girls are in this setting then the natural turn of events will follow.

Conclusion

Although teachers are not charged directly with teaching moral codes, there is little doubt that schools continuously demarcate and delineate what constitutes moral codes. Where it is part of the official curriculum, moral behaviour is related directly to sex and sex education, and the problems which may arise such as sexually transmitted diseases and unwanted pregnancies.

The discourses reveal the tendency to treat the school population as homogeneous and not divided on the basis of gender, so chastity and fidelity in marriage are represented as applying equally to boys and girls. But in terms of our culture, boys are not expected to be chaste or practise fidelity; quite the contrary. Their masculinity is often equated with successful sexual exploits, and failure to appear heterosexually adroit threatens their claim to masculinity (Willis, 1977, Plummer, 1975, Brake, 1980). Boys are expected to be sexually experienced, unlike girls.

This is reinforced in the provision of sex education which is likely to concentrate on the reproductive elements from a biological perspective, ignoring almost completely the emotional and physical elements of sexual intercourse. Relating sex education to reproduction provides the link to family organization and it is at this point that the direct repercussions on girls occur. In ideological terms, girls' sexuality being directly related to having children within marriage extends an ideological control over them. This particular message occurs throughout the curriculum, directly and indirectly.

However, this reinforcing of the notion that the main function in life for girls is as wife and mother is not effected without problems. There are a number of contradictory messages which the girls receive. Sexuality as portrayed in the media and popular culture emphasizes youth, beauty and the need for girls to be available. But at the same it is only 'bad girls [who] like sex':

> Television, film and our mothers all reinforce the notion that only bad girls like sex. . . The training we received as girls encourages us to renounce acting on our own behalf and for our own pleasure. Our . . . desires threatened Mom and Dad, and they told us how dangerous sex was, especially curiosity or experimentation (Webster, P. quoted by B. R. Rich, p. 528).

So their flight into sexuality as teenagers, (as will be discussed in Chapter 6) is of a temporary and transitory nature. This has to be discarded when they become fully responsible adult women fulfilling their roles as mothers and wives. Sexuality amongst mothers is not acceptable. The mother is represented in non-erotic terms. She is the 'missis' of the family (Willis, 1977) not to be confused with an object of desire.

Heterosexuality is the norm, and teachers presume that boyfriend and girlfriend liaisons will occur at school. But this is outside the bounds of teachers' responsibilities, which, in the main, do not include concern with the sexuality of their pupils, particularly at the junior level of secondary school. In this way sex and sexuality may be largely ignored and teachers are spared the uncomfortable need of having to deal formally with adolescent sexual desires. Formal concern is with the provision of sex education and 'deviant' forms as defined in terms of health issues.

CHAPTER FIVE

Sexuality in the school

Teachers take for granted that there is a 'normal' progression amongst their pupils in regard to sexual interests. As discussed in the previous chapter, sexual issues may be covered officially by the provision of sex education. The schools tend to limit their surveillance of sexuality amongst their pupils to the 'health' aspects through the pastoral system. In 'vague' educational courses such as 'social education', 'political education', 'learning to live' (J. Wilson, 1979), personal relationships which include sexual questions may be included in passing. But recognition and acceptance that sexuality plays a very important part in the lives of adolescents is not apparent in spite of the continuous eruption of aspects of sexuality within the school. Sexuality surfaces directly from time to time but the tendency is to thrust it aside as a 'natural' part of children's development provided it does not interfere with the main goals of the school.

This chapter will identify some of the everyday incidents which are directly sexual and how the staff reacted to these. To begin with there will be an examination of the unintended use by teachers of their own sexuality in the course of maintaining classroom control. There follows a discussion on what constitutes social scripting, a way of understanding the social form of sexual behaviour, with examples drawn from the classroom situation. This will be followed by a description of incidents within the school and specific events outside the constraining force of the school which illustrate the ever present sexuality and how the teachers, in particular, accounted for and dealt with this. All this data will then be related to the possible consequences these situations might have on girls' and boys' development.

Teachers and disciplinary control

When disciplinary issues are related to gender differences, it is often the male teacher who emphasizes the advantages of certain qualities of masculinity in the course of maintaining classroom control; women teachers tend to be reticent about this. Whitbread (1980) says that there is a commonly held belief that women are 'soft' and unable to control classes; they need a man around to back up their authority. She claimed then that this inevitably meant a recourse to physical force or a threat of its use. She says: 'It follows that the successful control of experienced female teachers is often discounted because it does not look like the paralysed silence of the disciplinarians' (p. 92). On the surface this does not seem to tie in with issues of sexuality but being male or female is linked to and identified with various aspects of sexuality. Gender identity involves the resolution of the individual's sexuality in a specific, gender defined manner.

Mr Jason, the science teacher, had no doubt that size and stature helped enormously. He said that men of large stature and with big voices had distinct advantages. 'Perhaps a woman teacher in very "mod gear" with a high-pitched voice starts off with a disadvantage. She is less able to maintain discipline.' And, he said, women science teachers were even further disadvantaged because these subjects were associated with the male teacher. 'They may have to try that much harder to get the class to listen. It might occur in maths as well.' The only woman teacher he knew who had had no problems had a 'sergeant-major manner' while the others were 'almost trampled upon'. In essence what he was saying was that women teachers who appeared feminine were unlikely to be able to control the classroom.

None of the women teachers at the time of the first part of the study said that they thought they had a more difficult time in controlling a class because they were women. It was during a follow up interview in 1982 with Miss Cray that the topic arose. She said that while studying for a higher degree she had read an earlier publication of mine (1977) in which issues relating to the emerging sexuality in the school had been discussed. Because she was familiar with the school and the incidents referred to she said she was particularly interested in the topic and found that she was alerted to aspects relating to sexuality that she had never previously thought about.

As was discussed in Chapter 1, she was one of the teachers who fell into the liberal camp when it came to expressing a view on the nature of discipline. In an interview with her in 1982, having identified boys as constituting the major problem in terms of classroom control, she described how physically strong male teachers would not have problems in controlling a classroom:

> There is some way in which, when I go into a classroom and relate to the boys, like most people I am seeing the boys as the greatest threat to classroom discipline, for all sorts of reasons. This is the way I perceive it . . . I might be wrong. When I see a bloke going in there and especially if he is the sort of physical, sports playing and so on type, there is the element of – when it gets down to it – I am bigger and tougher than you are anyway . . . If you have actually got a teacher, a male teacher who appears to be reasonably fit and strong and athletic, then I think he probably tends to relate on that sort of level. . . .

His masculine qualities were effective in controlling girls in the following way:

> and when it comes down to it . . . he relates to the girls, very much that I am halfway between the older boyfriend and caring father, depending on which way he comes over. I mean in some cases, it's sort of, you will do this for me won't you? It's established on that sort of adoration. Not that I am saying that it is conscious.

This is a straightforward description of how a man could employ his sexuality in the course of obtaining the cooperation of the girls:

> There are quite a few male teachers who are successful with getting classes to respect and to admire them. It is often the case. I can think of one person who was at my present school. He is the absolute archetype – your blond, 6'2" sports master, a really beautiful looking bloke. All of the boys in his form admired him because he was the kind of good-looking athletic bloke they wanted to become and he was twice as big as most of them anyway. Even though he was the mildest, kindest

person, nobody dared say anything. He didn't ever have to threaten them. There was this kind of assumption there all the time. All the girls were in love with him, because he was everybody's idea of the perfect dreamboat who would take them to the altar one day. I mean, he had it both ways, in that sense.

Being beautiful and masculine had double advantages: he could control both boys and girls, the former because they could identify with the teacher and the latter because they could fantasize about him.

This leaves the question of how women control the classroom. In considering the question Miss Cray directed her comments to the control of boys only; girls were excluded from this discussion:

How does a woman compensate for not being a dashing blonde type? The way in which I feel myself reacting with classes, and the way in which an awful lot of women do, as far as the boys are concerned, I think is in a way in which *you use the same techniques when you were a little girl, smiling and being nice to your father*. One of the sort of reasons, I think, is to get boys to develop protectiveness towards you, so that they are not going to mess around in your classroom because 'poor miss, we feel sorry for her, we feel protective, we don't want to make your life a misery'. There is almost getting your role reversed – getting them to act the older person and you act as if they have got to take care of you (my emphasis).

Miss Cray provided a concrete example of this when she referred to the reunion held earlier that year with some teachers and pupils five years after the last interviews had been conducted in the school:

I mean I can think of boys coming up at the 'do' and looking down and saying 'There, there, miss. How are you?' I am the sort that kids will come up to and put their arms around my shoulders. For a lad to come up to a woman who is shorter than him and put his arm around her shoulder, the implication is that I am taking care of you, alright?

According to Miss Cray it was the little girl role, the presentation of herself as a defenceless woman that procured the boys' co-operation.

Miss Cray extended her comments on the role of sexuality beyond the question of discipline into a more general area. She said:

> There is a fairly direct sexuality that operates, and it's not just me. I have attempted to talk about it with other people, with other women friends. There is some sort of direct level of sexuality between a woman teacher and boys as pupils and there is some kind of appeal that is used in discipline. I don't know exactly how it works. . . I have also been in situations where it almost started to get out of hand, to get suggestive remarks. That sort of thing. I think that was one of the things that started getting me aware of the fact that it was going on at all.

She was discussing sexuality in quite different terms from much of the feminist literature, referred to in the general Introduction, which has concentrated on the oppressive and aggressive element.

In contrast with the male teacher exploiting his masculinity, she introduced the possibility of women teachers exploiting their femininity. She is the only one to have raised this question. Furthermore she was the only teacher to have directly and consciously discussed classroom control in terms of sexuality. She saw it as affecting male and female teachers with a distinct connection with adult sexual roles. Male teachers, according to her, could invoke their masculinity to effect control while women could use their femininity for similar ends.

One other woman teacher did discuss this question indirectly in the course of talking about her own subject area, home economics. Mrs Francis was in her early thirties. She was conventionally pretty and dressed fashionably. She expressed her amazement at her success with older boys who normally constituted a major disciplinary problem in her last school. She found that they attended her cookery classes without any difficulty, enjoyed cooking and caused no problem at all. Amongst the regular attenders were 'boys involved with courts, and someone who had bashed up a chap from another school crippling him'. These boys were not only deviants, but one, at least was known for his violence. In passing she casually referred to their sexual behaviour. She said 'these boys made you aware of what you looked like . . . they used to make comments you know'. She did not find their comments offensive, on the contrary, she reacted in a traditionally feminine manner, accepting their comments as complimentary and gratifying. The boys were expressing their approval of her as a woman, not a teacher. And this she did not find offensive.

She described how what had begun as a single afternoon's activity with the acknowledged villains of the school had developed into a regular event:

> They were keen. They really loved it. Nobody had been there all that week and I would get a message in the morning that there were only two people and in the afternoon they would all be rolling up. . . They all used to come and they all took great pride in taking these white aprons home that I had, and they used to wash them and we used to make bread and the fuss they made. They used to go all round the PE staff and stop people and say 'have one of my buns'. They thought it was fantastic. They used to have me in fits of laughter. It was a smashing atmosphere. There just wasn't any discipline problem at all. They had broken things in school. They had caused a lot of problems and here they didn't because it was something they really enjoyed. It was the only thing that was relevant to them in that year.

It is not surprising that Mrs Francis was perplexed by her success which, on the surface, would seem highly unlikely amongst deviant and difficult young men. Their behaviour was quite at odds with their aggressive masculine sexuality which appears to be their trademark. How then can their activity be reconciled with their image? There are several possible explanations. The first is that where the boys' masculinity is unquestioned they can afford to flout conventions and behave in a contrary and contradictory manner. Once their reputations had been established the boys could pursue those activities which otherwise could be associated with cissies or 'poofs'. They might well have enjoyed activities which had some concrete achievement at the end. It was instant gratification. Lastly, one cannot discount the erotic enjoyment the boys may have had out of being in Mrs Francis' class because of her physical attractiveness and sexuality. The lads may have had a straightforward desire to please her!

The focus has been on how to control boys. Neither Mrs Francis nor Miss Cray seems to have taken account of how girls were to be controlled. In her opening remarks Miss Cray defined boys as constituting the problem and yet when she described how her blond, 6'2" 'beautiful bloke' operated, he was able to control the girls as well as the boys. It must follow that girls also required disciplining but either she failed to see this as a problem, or she could not account for the way in which she controlled the girls. This fell outside the bounds of employing her own sexuality and, presumably, she would invoke other instruments of discipline which are taken for granted and would have been outside the framework of this particular discussion.

The question of sexuality and how it enters into the field of control is complex and one that needs far more detailed examination. The preceding discussion has provided concrete examples of the often unconscious use by teachers of aspects of sexuality in the course of maintaining classroom control. The more obvious external representations of masculine traits – build, stature and external appearances of masculinity – may be seen as comprising advantages that men have over women teachers. The usual reference to gender differences is in terms of stereotypical notions of masculine or feminine qualities with the assumption that women teachers of feminine appearance are less able to control classes than men. This is obviously incorrect; if women teachers were unable to control the classrooms the education system would collapse because they outnumber men teachers.[1] This belief also fails to recognize the possible and, as demonstrated, unconscious employment by some women teachers of their femininity to achieve similar ends as their male colleagues. This is not only contrary to popular belief but also adds a further dimension to the discussion on gender differences. Women teachers are active and not always the passive victims of male aggression and male sexual advances. Control through sexuality, while not generally acknowledged or recognized by teachers, is not restricted to male teachers.

When sexuality amongst teachers has on some occasions been discussed the focus has been on the experiential relation to women teachers as victims of oppressive behaviour from the boys and/or some male teachers. For example, Jones (1985) researched 'into male violence in one secondary school'. She recorded a staff meeting on discipline problems where:

One feminist teacher raised the issue of sexual harassment arguing that it must be central to discussions on discipline.

> She spoke as if the harassment was experienced by girls from boys, by women from boys and by all girls/women from male staff. All the men – including normally sympathetic men – became defensive and aggressive claiming that she was exaggerating (p. 32).

She detailed the content of the ensuing arguments, concluding that the men ignored the 'fact that violence came from all the boys and adult men regardless of ethnic or cultural background' (p. 32).

Whilst not denying the negative and at times frightening experience of girls and women, this characterization of all girls and all women experiencing this, negates the diverse and complex nature of sexual issues and the way in which these are reflected in the course of everyday interaction.

Pupils participate actively in the classroom: the sexual connotations of the boys' behaviour is more immediately identifiable than that of the girls. The boys might act as protectors of some of the women teachers or simply set out to please them. This adds a further dimension to the rather one-sided view of boys as aggressive and sexually oppressive actors within the classroom situation. Also there seems little doubt that there are sexual connotations in the girls' reactions, although these may not be immediately recognizable and would require further study. Sexuality spills over into the classroom and is one of the factors involved in the interchange between teachers and pupils.

When discussing the sexuality of pupils, age is obviously an important factor. It is at the senior level that it becomes more difficult to ignore some aspects of sexuality, particularly with the female pupils. Mr Trim elaborated on this aspect during one of the many interviews I had with him. The topic under discussion was potential problems with older girls. He said that as the girls got older there was 'less of a gap in ages' between the staff and the senior girls, not in chronological terms but in respect of the physical development of the girls. He spoke about the 'interplay that goes on with young members of staff and older pupils' and said this was desirable because 'it keeps staff young and gives impetus to the pupils, whether it is girls to men or vice versa'.

The bonus, according to Mr Trim, for men teachers was the young women in their charge. Presumably the mild flirtation between the male teachers and the older girls was good for both of them. He suggested that this would help keep the girls interested in school and prevent them from going 'wild' in the course of seeking pleasure outside of the school. Here he suggested that the problems were particularly acute with 'West Indian' girls. In this way he saw the men teachers as providing the object of girls' sexuality which he regarded as contributing to their loss of interest in their schoolwork which occurred from the fourth year onwards.

Sexuality amongst the boys did not concern Mr Trim. There was no suggestion that women teachers could be given an 'impetus' by the boys or vice versa. The benefits of this type of interplay were seen only in terms of male teachers to female pupils. Issues such as boys directing sexually offensive remarks towards women teachers were not referred to. His reference point was entirely male teacher–female pupil, reflecting a male oriented view which fails to recognize women's sexuality and desires. He had, in passing, recognized the possibility of adolescent girls going 'wild', but presumably this was restricted purely to the pupils, and particularly ethnic minorities. His women teachers could not be included in such categories. His denial of adult female sexuality conforms with the dominant ideologies on women's sexuality. Furthermore, his views do reflect the power relations involved in sexual encounters with men having greater power in this regard. It is not possible to establish whether Mr Trim reflected the views of the majority of his staff or, even, of the teaching profession. Such issues should be investigated.

Sexuality in interpersonal situations

What now follows is the description of sexual encounters between pupils and teachers, and pupils and pupils. This will include details on two specific incidents, the first a 'touching up' by some boys of one particular girl and the second a school outing.

There are as many theoretical positions accounting for what constitutes human sexuality as in other facets of the social sciences. The immediate concern is not an interpretation of the understanding of sexuality but rather a phenomenological account of its appearance within the school. The description of these apparent and sexually oriented forms of behaviour will be in terms of representing 'social scripting' as defined by Simon and Gagnon (1971). This type of analysis, as Plummer (1982) points out, 'is an enterprise [which] has only begun in recent years, and even then has primarily been restricted to areas of the unconventional' (p. 229). He says that the underlying organizing principle whereby meanings are established is through the operation of 'social scripts' which, he claims, are 'the sources of our various constructions of sexuality', and which involve the 'life-long learning processes' derived from cultural categories. Social scripting appears to be an integral part of the cognitive phases of development. Miller and Fowlkes (1980) have summed up the work of Simon and Gagnon in the following way:

> Rather they view sexual behaviour as social behaviour, entered into and endowed with meaning by social actors whose interpersonal relationships are bound together by common and shared understandings and communications that are the product of their common and shared social and cultural worlds. Sexual behaviour is above all learned behaviour; sexual conduct is 'neither fixed by nature or [sic] by the organs themselves'. Social scripts organize an understanding of the particular in social activity. A sexual situation exists when the actors involved are responding to a socially constructed definition of what is sexual with strategies for doing the sexual (p. 262).

They rightly emphasize Simon and Gagnon's notion of the social construction of sexual behaviour, particularly given the tendency to attribute various forms of sexual behaviour to an essentialism and a naturalism. These two writers rejected the notion of:

> ... the masked expression of a primordial drive. The individual can learn sexual behaviour as he or she learns other behaviour and through scripts that in this case give the self, other person and situations erotic abilities or content (p. 74, 1971).

Consequently, if sexual behaviour is learned within a cultural milieu and this milieu differentiates between boys and girls, then it follows that there will be marked differences in the sexual behaviour of boys and girls.

As for the shared set of meanings relating to various aspects of this behaviour, these are the outcome of the way in which the construction of the behaviour occurs and again each group will have its own specific sets of meanings: girls will interpret certain behaviour in a way particular to girls; similarly boys will share sets of meanings. These meanings are, therefore, culturally specific.

It is interesting to note that there is some convergence between this position and that adopted by Lees (1986) in her study on sexuality amongst sixteen-year-old adolescent girls. Her concern is with debunking the essentialism and the accompanying double standards that have dogged so many discussions on sexuality. She sees these different standards being deeply 'embedded in language and conceptions of masculine and feminine' but which are seldom questioned by girls. Masculine and feminine behaviour are 'subjected to different social rules and operate within different norms'. Although she talks about the social construction of sexuality she does not refer to Simon and Gagnon's work. This might be because of her reliance on exploring 'the way girls describe their experience in order to throw light on the way individual experience is socially constructed'. Her foci are different because of her reliance on the role of the stated experience by the individual as a means of understanding the social formations.

Employing the concept of 'social scripting' provides a useful base for presenting the processes involved and the emerging shared meanings of these situations. No mention has been made of ideologies and the transmission of these. Underlying the discussion has been an acceptance that within the culture are a set of ideologies on sexual relationships. These ideologies are the base for the development of the 'social scripting' processes. Without their existence there could be no social scripts at all.

The observations confirmed the 'social scripting' of many aspects of classroom interaction in Berkeley. It was possible to identify a set of patterns of behaviour which were defining the appropriate way girls and boys should behave in relation to social-sexual behaviour; they provided them with their 'social scripts'. It was embedded in language, but also included style and body gestures. Many of the activities appeared as rehearsals or practices not only for the actors but also for the audience. The girls and boys were all participating or watching how to behave in appropriate gender specific ways.

Take the example of how some girls behaved towards some male teachers. They used body language and expressions that can be described as coquettish with the young 'dishy' male teachers. It appeared incongruous with their own stage of physical development and was an obvious mimicking of women's behaviour on television, in films, and magazines in the course of presenting themselves as desirable and attracting men's attention and favours.

Those girls who practiced this were participating in learning the scripts relating to adult sexual behaviour, and, at the same time, providing the others with a role model.

This occurred in Mr Sands' class. He was young and stylishly dressed. I had noted in my diary that 'he has an easy going manner, succeeds through a series of jokes and gets the kids entirely involved in the lesson. Is not a stickler for quietness yet keeps firm control over the class.'

He was popular amongst the girls and it was unmistakable how several responded to him in a very specific manner, particularly the more articulate and high achieving girls. When they brought work to the desk for his comments it was accompanied by smiles, giggles, fluttering of the eyelashes. He was an object of their fantasies, and they played these out within the classroom situation.

This type of behaviour did not occur in all classes. The same girls did not behave like this with Mr David who was of a similar age to their fathers. Mr David's manner in the classroom was totally different. He was a strict disciplinarian, and effectively distanced himself from the pupils. With him some of the girls adopted a far more demure, little girl, manner. The flirtation apparent in Mr Sands' class disappeared in Mr David's class.

Mr Sands, as discussed in the previous chapter, never acknowledged his popularity amongst the girls nor defined it in terms of schoolgirl crushes; perhaps it would have been difficult for him to publicly admit to this.

The active, albeit unconscious, orchestrating of 'social scripting' was conducted by Mr Sands very effectively. He instructed the girls how to behave in a gender appropriate way. On one occasion he needed books that Mr Warne had. He calculatingly asked Carol to run his errand. He did not select a boy to do this because he was going to use Carol's prettiness and coquettish behaviour to diffuse Mr Warne's irritation at the disruption. 'Charm him, use a lovely voice, say "thank you sir", and smile at him when you ask for the books.' Significantly, Carol was the stereotypical pretty girl – long blonde hair, blue eyes and always ready to cooperate and help. (She subsequently became a fashion model and was held up as the success story of her year – brought back to the school to talk about her career. This reinforces the notion that a woman may be successful if she is attractive, as defined in terms of the popular media.)

This advice may have been given in a flippant, jocular manner, but the underlying message was there waiting for the girls to decode it. Females could obtain what they wanted from males if they were charming, smiled, spoke carefully and presented themselves as pleasing people. And the males were being taught what to expect from females. Such incidents occur all the time in the course of life in school. Both girls and boys are constantly being given the scripts for gender appropriate behaviour.

Obviously there are a number of other examples which demonstrate the way in which girls and boys familiarize themselves with social scripting relating to sexual encounters. The school situation provides them with the stage for such a rehearsal. In doing so they are conforming to the present day cultural formations which define gender appropriate behaviour. Girls in the course of the unfolding adolescent years practise and reinforce such types of behaviour with which they are already familiar. Similarly boys are involved in the learning process. They are being taught what they may expect from girls, particularly if they are in positions of power and authority. Both girls and boys are learning the appropriate behaviour and how to achieve this in heterosexual relations.

Teachers' views on sexuality in two particular situations

I now want to discuss two specific incidents which highlight the staff's attitude towards the latent sexuality amongst the pupils in their first and second years at school. As will be seen there are several distinct, not necessarily exclusive interpretations which the staff may give to such incidents. The first is that blatant acts of sexuality may be construed as breaching the rule of discipline and order, a position which the head adopted. The second is that any surfacing of incidents reflects the 'natural' development and as such should be taken as a 'normal' part of the pupils' maturation, unconnected to the learning process. The third, linked to this, is that sexual activity amongst young adolescents is far closer to the play of children and removed from adult sexual activities. The fourth position relates to the prescription which events occurring on the school premises have. If they occur on the school premises their decoding is closely related to what is seen as the main purpose of schooling, and that is learning, and not necessarily part of a broader social environment. When they occur outside the school boundaries and hence are removed from the prescriptions of disciplined school behaviour, they are accorded different meanings. Finally, there is a tendency to apportion blame to girls even if they are the victims of boys' aggression.

The 'touching up' incident

The head received a complaint from Tricia's mother that she was too frightened to come to school because she had been 'touched up' in the corridor. The head's response was to hold two special assemblies the following morning separating the boys from the girls. All members of staff were instructed to attend, the men at the head's assembly, and the women at the girls' assembly which was to be conducted by Miss Leyland. The boys remained in the school hall and the girls were sent to the dining hall.

The head reported the following to me:

> Basically the boys had been touching up the girls as you might say; it's something that's catching on. The boys are doing it for the hell of it. In some cases some girls may have egged them on; it's all a bit exciting, a bit of fun. There's no vicious-ness with it and it's probably an aspect of puberty. But Tricia was so upset that she came home crying and didn't come to school in the mornings without her mother. As a result of hearing about it and confirming that the boys had been run-ning into the girls' toilet I saw the boys myself and got Lorraine to see all the girls. I told the boys that any future occasions when boys interfered with girls in any way or went into the girls' toilets would warrant their immediate suspension. I wouldn't agree to their return until I had been assured of a complete backing of their parents, so they might well be suspended until their parents came up and this would be followed with an interview with parents and the child con-cerned. They were all very subdued. If you let them get away with it it mushrooms out of all recognition. More and more boys would do it; some girls will egg them on and some would be frightened.
> Kids expect to be told off, reprimanded for it. Apart from be-ing initially surprised if they are not told off they think what the hell.

He summed up the situation in the following way:

135

This affects the whole development and goes back to expectations. If you don't give them a yardstick they don't know how to behave. I don't think that what we might think is moral attitude is inborn. It's all part of education, and part of education is to set certain standards for the kids. This standard of common respect and respect for others. In the last resort where you get violations of a person which is what this is beginning to be, you have to clamp down. This isn't a vicious thing and you can't stop them anyway. If a boy is setting about a girl in an indecent way – having been warned, they know the consequences and this teaches them what life really is.

This statement is particularly interesting because it represents Mr Trim's view of his pupils' sexuality. In the first place when it occurs amongst twelve year olds it is not serious in itself – it is 'exciting' and 'fun'. Although it may be part of puberty, it is nevertheless defined in terms of games and not really part of sexuality.

He was conscious of some of the contradictions of the situation as his statement reveals. On the one hand he blamed the girls because they 'egg the boys on'. He fell into the same trap that has been present for a long time and that is blaming girls or women for sexual harassment or assaults they suffer at the hands of boys or men. But he could not leave it at that, recognizing that such behaviour may upset some girls. So in order to resolve this contradiction he emphasized the element which related to control. He could not entirely ignore the sexual connotations. But his frame of reference was moral order and control which while it covered sexuality obliquely, was more concerned with overall behaviour and discipline in a general and undefined way. The 'touching up' could 'violate' a person and as such could not be tolerated. It was not the overt sexual connotation with which he was concerned. Rather he needed to assert his authority at all times over the pupils particularly in regard to the correct form of behaviour.

The situation provided Mr Trim with the scenario whereby he could flex his disciplinary muscles and inform the boys in no uncertain tones about his expectations. Any breach of discipline and order would be met with immediate retaliation. In this case 'touching up' or going into the girls' lavatories would be followed by instant suspension of the guilty party. Both these activities were defined as morally reprehensible behaviour.

He, like the other teachers, did not attach importance to the act itself. Rather it was represented as a breach of a code of behaviour which he wished to establish in the school. Indeed when Mr Trim referred to this incident at the pastoral meeting mentioned above, he did so in conjunction with another incident which I had not yet heard about.

He compared this 'touching up' with the boys 'peeing in the bins'. He must again have reprimanded them severely for he said 'I enjoyed myself on that occasion'. Nobody asked why and one can only speculate that he enjoyed the power and control he had over the boys and the ability to abuse them verbally:

Peeing in the bins is very different from touching up the girls.
I was very livid. To me, though, it was fair to put it on the basis
that they wouldn't expect their own mums to clear up somebody else's pee.

Presumably he rated such action as worse than the 'touching up' incident because, while the latter did represent a breach of good behaviour, its relationship to 'natural' development and its link to childishness mitigated the severity of the act. However, the comment about mums not cleaning up 'somebody else's pee' is interesting. There was no suggestion that boys would clear up their own mess: it was taken for granted that such activities were the responsibilities of mothers. This suggests that misbehaviour on the part of children reflects the way they have been brought up by their mothers. If boys misbehave then their mothers are responsible and must accept the consequences of their son's misbehaviour. Therefore mothers could expect to clear up their own son's mess, even if it was their pee, but would not be expected to be responsible for other boys' misdemeanours. 'Touching up' the girls represented 'normal' behaviour in Mr Trim's eyes, peeing in the bins was dirty and messy.

How did the staff react to the 'touching up' incident? Unlike Mr Trim, the teachers who commented on it did not discuss it in terms of disciplinary problems except for one woman who, at the pastoral meeting already referred to, likened the incident to theft, regarding both actions as a violation of the individual. The senior teachers, including Mr David, agreed with Mr Trim's handling and did not comment further on the event. The others were vociferous in their disapproval. Mr Warne was incensed by Mr Trim's reactions because he felt that Mr Trim had blown it out of all proportion. He said he would like to resign from the school on the spot. He said that Mr Trim had used terms like 'dirty, disgusting and filthy' in reference to the 'touching up' ' and had warned the boys that if it occurred again he would immediately suspend the culprits from school and would only consider having them reinstated if he was convinced by their parents that they were fundamentally 'decent' and had only temporarily 'gone off the rails'.

Mr Warne regarded such incidents as ' "normal" and as such should not be defined in terms of "dirty, disgusting or filthy" '. He was not the only one to hold these views. Mr Sands, referring to this incident at the pastoral meeting devoted to the discussion on sexuality, said: 'Our reaction should just show disapproval. Touching up girls is very normal. I did it early. We have to think of it in the context of kids today and what they are learning today.'

Miss Leyland treated the whole incident in a low key manner. She regarded it all as 'normal' and in response to my questioning passed it off casually saying that she had treated the matter very lightly and had glossed over it during her assembly. For her it represented childish play having nothing to do with sexuality. Mrs White thoroughly approved of the way in which Miss Leyland handled the situation saying that she had introduced a degree of levity into the discussion. Mrs White, it should be emphasized, went further, by apportioning blame to the girls. She suggested that the girls behaved in a provocative manner, citing as an example girls walking out of the toilet area exposing their bosoms. She had warned them that they were courting the sort of behaviour which was the cause of complaint against some of the boys. She thought that girls who acted provocatively had to anticipate a particular response from boys and men. (Would Mrs White's ideas have been altered by the campaigns against violence by men that occurred later in the 1970s?)

In fact during the mid-morning break the overwhelming reaction was that the situation had been exaggerated and it could all have been dealt with in a discussion with the children concerned. The conversation then turned to the behaviour of the school's caretaker.

He was said to spend an inordinate amount of time 'cleaning' the girls' lavatories, at a period when they were likely to be in use. He was suspected of 'chatting up' some of the girls, questioning them on where they lived, what they did when they left school and so on. The staff were worried about the implications of the drift of his questions. They already had doubts about his honesty, and he was generally considered lazy and uncooperative. All these factors contributed to the generally disparaging remarks that were made about him and the consensus was that he should be given the sack. It was not simply his acknowledged sexual interest in the girls which led them to this view, but a combination of negative aspects.

The 'touching up' incident illustrates how social scripting occurs. In this case boys are learning aggressive forms of social behaviour in terms of relating to girls. This is precisely the type of incident which could constitute a topic for discussion in sex education. In this way the exploratory nature of mixed gender sexual contacts could be discussed and the oppressive nature of the boys' behaviour analysed.

Summer day trip

In the introduction to this chapter I pointed out that teachers are primarily concerned with teaching, with imparting information to their pupils. Because of this there does appear to be a blindness to some of those elements within the pupils' own lives which have a crucial effect on their achievement at school. This blindness is confined, though, to their surveillance of the pupils *within* the confines of the school building itself. The surveillance takes a totally different form, and may even disappear, once teachers and pupils are removed from the restricted, prescribed atmosphere of the physical environment within the school's walls. On various outings the staff/pupil relationships underwent changes. The teachers would relax their vigilance and treat the outing as a welcome break for themselves, a welcome break from the repetitive daily routine of containing, restraining and teaching the children. In the course of this their concern with the pupils was less structured, and even seemed to verge on a 'let them get on with their own business' attitude. Outings were like miniature holidays and the staff were out to enjoy themselves every bit as much as the pupils were.

During the summer, a day trip to Boulogne was organized in which almost 150 twelve-year-old pupils and all but two members of staff participated. The visit to Boulogne never materialized, as a mine, a relic from World War II, was discovered in Folkestone harbour and the train was diverted to Dover. We spent most of the day in the train shuttling back and forth but finally arrived at Dover where the children were sent off on their own to look at the Castle and the staff flopped into the nearest restaurant to eat and drink until it was time to return to London.

The pupils, always quick to read the hidden agenda, soon realized that vigilance and surveillance were not the order of the day. They were to be on holiday every bit as much as the teachers and this became abundantly clear as the day wore on. They were not supervised during their stay in Dover. Although they were told to visit the Castle they were under no compunction to do so. The reassembly took place and everybody boarded the train for London.

The train provided the setting for a great deal of movement between the children. Some of the girls constantly moved in and out of the compartments, with many sitting on boys' laps, giggling, blushing, and cuddling. There was little sign of embarrassment or inhibition in doing so in the presence of their teachers and head. What was not possible or permissible within the school suddenly became quite legitimate. Mr Sands' comments about the 'pressure on girls not to . . . sit next to the boys' no longer applied. Their school rituals were no longer operative. They were outside the bounds of ritual behaviour prescribed within the school.

I had found the uninhibited behaviour of the pupils quite startling, as well as the staff's lack of concern for their role as supervisors. Quite obviously the staff had looked forward to this outing: their conversation focused on previous trips to Boulogne and their visits to French restaurants. The Dover trip had not come up to expectations but it provided them with a welcome break. None of the teachers commented on the pupils' behaviour either that day or subsequently. They shared the pupils' feelings of festivity with all barriers down.

At the pastoral meeting devoted to the discussion of pupils' relationships, I referred to this event. I recalled my surprise at the pupils' behaviour and how different from a normal school day it was. I mentioned that the pupils I was studying had quite often crossed the gender barrier and worked together within the classroom situation without the apparent incursion of sexuality.

The immediate response from Miss Miller was to recognize the absence of restraint and surveillance:

It's bred in them, OK? When you are in school we have got these lessons to do, etc. etc., but then specifically we told them they were going off on an outing to Boulogne. I think it was that rather than the walls and the school set up. I think it was because *they were different that day* (my emphasis).

But this did not account for the display of sexuality. What she was also suggesting was that the sexuality was natural, 'inbred', something that would emerge when the restraint of the school walls and lessons was removed. The urge was there but the school through its routine lessons repressed it. Someone else suggested that the possibility of pupils mixing outside their usual classroom groups also opened up the way to a greater ease.

Mr Sands' explanation was that this outing was a one-day phenomenon, similar to an office staff party where:

> All sorts of things occur and then the following day people
> arrive and they just carry on as if nothing had happened. And
> I think that the kids are reflecting perhaps what they have not
> consciously thought about, but sub-consciously absorbed.

Because it was outside the norm, the unusual could occur and the unusual was not necessarily so outside the constraints of the routine, whether in school or office. 'Normal' behaviour could occur only when the constraints of the structure of the institution, be it school or office, were removed or absent.

Both these incidents reflect certain ways in which the staff deal with emerging sexuality within the school. There is the tendency to label as childish those events which occur in the lower levels of secondary school. Neither the girls, on the whole, nor the boys have matured fully. Because the boys are likely to lag far behind the girls in terms of physical maturing it is even easier to dismiss such situations as 'touching up' as childish while at the same time acknowledging that there is an element of 'natural' development involved.

Conclusion

In this chapter three distinct aspects of sexuality amongst school children have been discussed, all of which reflect the extent of the presence of sexuality within the school boundaries. The first relates to the interpersonal relationships between staff and pupils in which teachers unconsciously employ sexual ploys in order to aid them in the control over pupils. The perception of such situations by teachers usually reflects the cultural specificities of gender differences. Male symbolic strength is contrasted with female frailty and there is an assumption that men are better able to control classes by virtue of being male, stronger and more in command of the situation. The less obvious employment by women of their femininity as a means of control is not generally recognized.

These beliefs are not empirically verified. In the course of observations in the classroom the wide differences between teachers and their ability to control the classroom was related to a number of factors which included experience, confidence and ability together with the judicial use of the various instruments of discipline at their disposal. Some teachers could control a class and others could not. In addition to the instruments of discipline described in Chapter 2, it was seen how aspects of masculinity or femininity could be drawn on in the course of maintaining classroom control. But gender was not the decisive factor as some male teachers prefer to believe.

The pupils would not consciously recognize what was happening in the classroom. But this constitutes part of the 'social scripting' which became more obvious in the second section of the chapter which focused on the ordinary social interactions within the classroom which mirrored many of the social situations common amongst adults. As this covers a period in individuals' lives in which their gender identity is being strengthened, such situations must carry a certain weight. As Simon and Gagnon (1971) said of this period:

> The beginning of adolescence marks the time when society, as such, first acknowledges the sexual capacity of the individual. His or her training in the postures and the relation of the sexual experience will now begin to accelerate. Most important, the adolescent will start to view others in his or her immediate environment in particular peers, but also some adults, as sexual actors and will find confirmation of this view in the definitions of others towards these actors (p. 75).[2]

The third section illustrated the overt forms of sexual interplay that occur. One of the main points that I wish to draw out in this section is the tendency to ignore issues relating to sexuality in the school. Where such obvious incidents as the 'touching up' occur there are two possible scenarios. The first is to react to the incident as a symbolic breakdown of discipline, as Mr Trim did. The second is to ignore the whole incident because it is a perfectly 'normal' event reflecting the 'natural' development amongst children and as such should be given freedom to develop and grow. Either view is likely to imply that sexual issues are not important and should not be part of the agenda in the secondary school.

Whatever the situation, learning what constitutes the social forms of behaviour associated with masculinity and femininity are complex. These are integral parts of the learning process which commence with the acquisition of language and continue throughout life. During school hours there are a variety of situations which relate to this, and in which girls and boys participate actively. They are watching, doing and learning, and all this is related to the broader social context in which they live. Their own peer culture observes certain rituals and establishes the parameters of behaviour, all of which has an impact on the way in which they receive their education.

CHAPTER SIX

Sex and everyday life

It has been shown how control of pupils' sexuality is subsumed under the guise of teaching moral order through the provision of some form of sex education. For the rest, pupils' sexuality may be disregarded except when it becomes apparent as a problem – either girls becoming pregnant or boys being infected with some sexually transmitted disease. Sexuality does not impinge on the daily life as far as the teachers are concerned.

Pupils in secondary school have moved out of, or are in the process of moving out of, childish behaviour. Girls in particular are increasingly aware of the form adult gender identity takes. This corresponds with their bodily changes and their developing physical maturity. Their interest and self-involvement appears to have a deleterious effect on their schoolwork; there is a negative correlation between this heightened interest and the attention to their schoolwork.

This chapter is largely descriptive. It will explore pupils' perceptions of various aspects of their sexuality. Details will be given about their views on friends of the opposite sex, the role of style in their lives, their views about pre-marital sex and homosexuality. Some of the data was unsolicited and was given spontaneously during the course of interviews while still at school. Those who were interviewed when they were adult talked more freely about some of these topics than they had as pupils. It should be emphasized that the data spans a period between the ages of twelve and fifteen, but also includes some recall by the respondents when they were young adults. It is obvious, from their responses, that changes in attitude reflect their age.

What this chapter will set out to demonstrate is that their emerging sexuality engulfs girls and boys in the course of their quest for identity. It will demonstrate the active participating of the girls in their peer culture, the conflicts they have to face, and points to the precedence of their interest in boys over their commitment to school work.

The general Introduction referred to the particular emphasis given to sexuality when it is discussed in relation to the educational scene and girls; the girls are portrayed as the victims of male tyranny (Jones, 1985, Spender, 1980, Lees, 1986). This particular emphasis has been determined by the way in which the problem is formulated and that is as determined by male behaviour. There is very little about girls' views on boyfriends. The much quoted article by McRobbie (1978) on fourteen- to sixteen-year-old girls who attended a youth club is an exception.

There has been, as pointed out in the general Introduction, a different area of study outside of education which has concentrated on youth culture. As is well known it was the spectacular elements of male sub-cultural groups which were examined. Female sub-cultural groups and ordinary boys and young men were overlooked.

This chapter seeks to redress this omission. This cohort was not composed of members of a spectacular youth group of that period. But their style and actions did relate some 'opposition to dominant values and institutions'. Their views on boy/girlfriends reflect the continuing process of 'scripted' behaviour discussed in the previous chapter. As for their views on sex and sexual encounters, their diffident and tentative views reflect adolescence in which the gender identities are being overtly related to sexuality. There are examples of a puritanism, bravado, and diffidence towards sex, and none of the boys exhibited the blatant and aggressive sexuality of which they are so often accused. Even though they were unlikely to be frank and open in their responses to me, nevertheless some of their detailed discussions as young adults highlighted the difficulties that they did experience in terms of girls. Growing up is a painful, difficult, and tentative period.

Girls: their boyfriends, their style and sex

Boyfriends
How interested were the girls in boys? At the first set of interviews all the girls acknowledged their interest in boys, sometimes quite

naively. Shirley, who at the age of twelve said she did not have a boyfriend but wanted one, regarded boys as playmates. She said 'the boy round my way and his sister and his friends and we all play together like hide-and-seek and things like that'. Mavis, although difficult to interview, said she had a boyfriend at twelve and by the age of fifteen spoke about the problems she encountered because her parents were Greek Orthodox. This meant she had to keep her friendships secret and meet the boys 'at their homes or something like that'.

With the passage of time, as adults, some interviewees added new information. At the age of thirteen Carol did not know if she was really interested in boys. When nearly sixteen she said that she had had boyfriends who were from other schools and was also just friendly with some of the boys in her school. But as an adult she admitted to a school girl crush on Jason which had begun in the first year and continued through to the fourth year. In neither interview at school had she spoken about this. Quite simply she said he could not stand her because she 'was clever and didn't dress up'.

Their interest in boys could lead to physical scuffles:

> Usually when a girl is going out with a certain boy and another girl gets jealous and she starts . . . perhaps she spreads tales about her . . . she might make up a few stories or something and the other girl gets a bit angry with her and she wants to have a fight with her. . . This is how it starts.

According to Tricia the fights involved 'pulling of hair and would take place in the toilets, in the playground, out of school and at the disco and social club'. This rivalry continued into the senior years. Shirley for one, at the age of fifteen, said that she was friendly with a lot of boys although she did not have any particular boyfriend at the time. She said that this caused friction with other girls who were jealous because she was friendly with so many boys. She claimed that some of these girls wanted to fight with her and she said they 'walked around school as if they own the place'.

As the girls got older their interests moved away from boys in their school. Doreen said:

> Most of the girls were going out with fellers from other schools, mainly from the schools round here. Carol was going out with a boy called Ian and that was the main subject

because he was good looking and that and he came from a different school. Jane was always talking about her feller because he was married. She seemed much older than us anyway. Lara went out with a married man. She was always talking about him. Mavis was going out with a boy from another school as well.

Shirley offered some explanation for this:

Well the boys in school don't seem very important, you know. We see them every day. They just seem . . . you know what I mean. But the other boys out of school we don't see them very often. A boy in another school you admire and you talk about him.

Of course, it should be remembered that there were no older boys at the school. There might have been a difference had this been the case. There also was a difference in maturity. As the girls got older the differences were more marked. The girls appeared more heavily involved with boyfriends than the boys with girls at the same age. Lara attributed this difference to the boys' comparative physical immaturity and shortage of money:

Because they hadn't grown up mentally really. I believe that girls are far advanced in comparison with boys. In terms of everything. I mean the girls of say, in 1976, were at least sixteen um . . . they were going out with blokes who had money and were working, but the boys couldn't do that could they. The boy of sixteen then had no money. They were still school kids and still a lot of them looked like it too. Although the girls tend to have gone ahead in that way. In mental and physical terms you know . . . the boys of their own age were very immature and still interested in playing football in their lunch break and the girls really wanted to go down the local or whatever. They were still – I don't know – but the boys were that step behind that way.

Interest in boys was there from the beginning of their high school days. What were the qualities the boys had that attracted the girls, particularly as twelve year olds? Shirley had the answers:

The one with fashionable clothes, smoked behind the toilet with his bovver boots on and was a toughie. Toughie . . . the one who click their fingers and the girl will come towards him, that sort of thing. A smoothie, a cool, a boy.

Bobby was constantly referred to by the girls as one of the most popular boys. Bobby was the cause of fights amongst the girls. Tricia had fancied him and the outcome of the jealousy was discussed at one of the pastoral meetings (see Chapter 4). Tricia said her best friend went out with Bobby at the time so that put an end to her being able to go out with him! She did not talk about the fights that Miss Leyland had referred to.

What made Bobby so popular? I was told that he was good looking, 'flash', a term which one girl defined as 'coming in on his bike, and goes whizzing around the playground and he is always wanting a fight'. Someone else said his attraction lay in the way in which he behaved: 'He seems to get on with all the girls. He makes a fuss of them and if he sees you he will come up and talk to you . . . and he has got a sense of humour'. (Here is another example of a boy flouting the conventions, like the boys discussed in relation to Mrs Francis and the cookery lessons in Chapter 5.) Instead of ignoring the girls, Bobby could act quite contrary to that convention. He had established his masculinity and could, therefore, set his own parameters of behaviour.

None of the girls mentioned love except for Katherine who said that there was no such thing as love at the age of twelve, just attraction. But their interest in the boys was there and it did have an effect on their schoolwork. Katherine recalled:

Well I messed about a lot. I don't know; we used to muck about and talk in class and it didn't seem that important to do homework and if it was late, it was late. You know. It was when I first started going out.

Style
Style and presentation of self obviously played an important part in the pupils' lives. Mention has already been made of the extensive use of girls at the age of twelve and thirteen of make-up, hair styling, footwear and so on to present themselves in a more feminine fashion at school. The pressure to conform if you wanted to be successful

only emerged in Carol's recall about why she failed to attract Jason. She said how unsophisticated she was and how different her dress was in comparison with her peer group and the girls who gained Jason's admiration. He liked:

> the girl who used to hate school uniform. She never would wear her school uniform. She used to like to smoke, and wear a lot of make-up and I think that that appealed to him more. Perhaps she was more grown-up than me. I was a bit immature. Not so much immature but because I wasn't trying to be like five years older than I actually was. I think that perhaps that's it. I am not sure.

She, on the other hand, was a conformist. She described herself as a demure, neat, good school girl:

> Because I used to have a briefcase, I used to wear white socks and I used to have pony tails, and I didn't smoke and I didn't swear. He didn't like me. The boys you used to like never used to like you, which I seemed to find happened not only to me but to my friends.

While she hankered after the boys like Jason, she was not successful in gaining his favour: she was unsophisticated. And her failure in this regard was compounded by her obvious cleverness. Being clever in schools such as this was not seen as an advantage. She was not likely to get the boy she was interested in. She was handicapped by her conformity to both school values and the appropriate form of dress. The two aspects – cleverness and style – militated against her. She recognized what comprised the signifiers of that particular sub-cultural group but did not personally adopt them. As such she paid the penalty of falling outside the peer group's accepted code of dress and behaviour.

In the course of asking the pupils whether they liked the school uniform or not (see Chapter 2) there was no indication that they differentiated and labelled people according to the way in which they dressed in the school uniform. None of them admitted to hating school uniform. Consequently there was no indication of this process of differentiation and labelling related to this. This information only emerged in the adult interviews.

Had Carol dressed in a way that would have caught Jason's

attention then she would have found herself labelled as tough. Being tough reflected style of dress, and various forms of resistance. Shirley captured this image:

If you were prepared to do anything. If you went into the toilets at the lunch break and smoked behind the teachers' back. If you were tough, if you had fashionable clothes and latest fashionable hairstyle and you went round in a little gang. Also if you were allowed out at night late. I think that was classed as being quite a tough girl.

Clothes played a very important part in their lives, and the older they got the more important it seemed to be. Katherine summed up their involvement in clothes and dressing up when she recalled her school days:

We had Saturday jobs. We used to get five or six pounds and we used to say what can we buy with this. And it was probably in your pockets for five minutes. I don't know about the others, but I loved buying clothes. Going out, especially when going round with a crowd, if there is a couple of girls in it always the sense of competition, who is going to go out looking the best this week. Um, I suppose that is where it comes from.

As an adult she recognized that she was competitive with her other girlfriends and attributed this to her teenage period.

There was one exception to this absorption with appearance. Doreen, at the age of twelve, described herself as boring, particularly to the other girls, because she did not have any interest in clothes:

I don't like pretty dresses and things – I haven't got a lot and when girls say they have got this and that I think, Oh gawd, why talk about things like that when you can talk about football and things like that and what you made.

She felt quite marginalized from the other girls, even her best friend Barbara:

I think it's when I come to school and Barbara starts talking about who's got a new pair of shoes and she describes her shoes to the other girls and the other girls start saying that they have just bought a new pair of shoes then I just don't know what to say. I just say 'Ah, yes, well Pip [the rabbit] had babies'. Yes, and they think, 'Oh yes', and I must be boring because I don't know what to talk about. What I do, I don't think most of the girls find interesting.

By the age of fifteen she had undergone a metamorphosis. She was beginning to lose interest in her animals and the work in the shed, spending her spare time watching television or going out. She, like so many other girls, had a Saturday job working in a boutique. At the time of her interview she spoke about having broken up with Thomas (she was the exception of having a boyfriend from the same class) and was now going out with some other young man.

How did boys behave towards girls?

As pointed out in Chapter 4, there were very definite boundaries about what constituted the acceptable way in which boys and girls behaved towards each other in school. There was a narrow boundary which distinguished between working together legitimately and sitting with someone you fancied. This applied not only to the classroom but also in the dining hall.

What seems linked to this taboo is the convention by boys to feign lack of interest in girls, at least publicly. Carol recalled that boys seemed to *have* to behave badly towards girls in public in front of other boys and gave the following example about someone she had liked at school:

I thought he was really nice looking. He seemed like a really nice boy when I was on my own and I talked to him. But you know what they are like when they are at that age, I suppose. When they are with their friends, if they are with a girl they are either really nasty to her, and really like putting her down, in front of her friends, or just completely ignore her. A lot of the boys used to be like that all the time.

Again this description is at odds with the image of boys behaving in a sexually aggressive manner. The public avoidance of girls may be due to several factors. It could be coupled with their relatively

151

lower level of maturity at the same age, their involvement with boys' only groups (remember Michael's comment in Chapter 3 pleading for girls to behave 'normal' and leave him alone), and their own embarrassment. Whatever the reasons, there appears to be a lesser investment by the boys in girlfriends in early and middle adolescence than vice versa. Katherine said that, 'I think when a girl starts going out with a boy it takes up the whole of her'. She had no doubt about this.

Where they went with their boyfriends

But what constituted 'going out with a boy'? Although that expression refers to having a sexual relationship at an older age, when they were twelve and fifteen this was not the case.

There was a range of answers to this. Katherine recalled that when she was fifteen she would 'go to the pictures with him; I thought it was a big night out, and hanging around waiting for boys for ages'. Where to meet boyfriends and where to go with them constituted a problem for at least one of the girls, who at the age of fifteen said that she had had a few boyfriends but they always split up 'because there's nowhere to go. Sometimes they come round to my house, go out to the park or something'. But in the main she went out to discos with her girlfriend or went with her parents to a club where she worked as well. Lara said that together with her boyfriend and a girlfriend 'sometimes in the evening we would meet and we'd go out. We'd go to Leicester Square and Piccadilly, you know. Various places. We just used to go out. Sometimes drinking, pictures, discos anything', and usually in the West End.

Doreen recalled that when she was fifteen they would be 'going to the pictures, or going roller skating, or ice skating or just going out'. And going out often occurred in pairs.

> John might suggest that we go to the pictures and I'd say what shall we see and he says so and so, and I would say so and so wanted to see that and she would want to come but she won't want to come right with three, so she will bring whoever she will want to bring.

Discos did not constitute the highlight of Doreen's week as they did for other girls. But she went to them nevertheless. She recalled how discos were an obvious topic of conversation amongst the girls particularly, as she said:

That was the big thing because you are not allowed in under twenty-one. That was a terrific giggle to get in when you are only - what fifteen. They used to say that. They used to talk about places, and what happened and that sort of thing.

For these girls discos enabled them to act older than they were: they tried to get into places where there was an age barrier not necessarily to obtain drink but simply to beat the ban. Discos provided something to look forward to. It was one form of resistance open to them. There was no feeling of revulsion as described by Amanda McLoughlin (1984) who called the waiting men 'sinister predators'. Discos were enjoyable and the girls spent a great deal of time in planning what they would wear to the disco and discussing who they had danced with or spoken to when there. On several occasions the impression given in the course of the interview was that disco attendance was frequent, although in reality this was not the case. They would go mainly over the weekends, and possibly one night during the week at school.

Sex: sex education and talk about sex

Direct questions on sex education and sexuality were not posed in the interviews held at school. As an adult Lara told me, if I had asked them such questions they 'would probably all have giggled and laughed at that time anyway'. But some information was given spontaneously, and in the last round of interviews I was able to ask some direct questions.

Katherine, for one, had views on the Design for Living class which was compulsory and which they had on Friday afternoons in the third and fourth years. She said at the age of fifteen:

Well, it's intended to tell us more about life in general but so far it hasn't really achieved anything. As far as I'm concerned it hasn't achieved anything. At the beginning of term we started to do contraception again. That must have been the third time. It just wasn't interesting any more because we've been over it so many times. It does get a bit boring. But we did have a doctor come in to show us different methods. That was the best thing.

Her comments are interesting. Not only does she express a feeling of ennui about the area of contraception but, perhaps more importantly, it corroborates the point made in Chapter 4 that the bulk of sex education was devoted to reproduction and contraception, and confirms the importance attached by Mr Trim to the teaching of contraception in sex education classes.

The teachers' concern with the 'health' hazard of sex is illustrated by Lara's account of Mrs White's method of dealing with the evidence that one of the girl's had had some sexual encounters:

> Liz was all tears and had all love bites all up her face, all over her neck and where he hadn't shaved she had scratches and all sorts of things. Mrs White rushed her off to hospital – a test for VD. You know all this sort of caper went on but that was one particular person. 90 per cent of the girls I would say weren't even dreaming of such things or weren't even allowed out.

Lara's comments reveal certain inconsistencies. Although the girls were young and naive, and not engaged in actual sexual encounters, sex was a topic of continual interest but one which could cause embarrassment and confusion. Talk started in their first year at school. According to Lara sex talk 'started with the very first sex lesson. From then on it was always a subject to be spoke about'.

Some of the group revealed the embarrassment they had experienced at that time in regard to both the discussions by the girls and with what was seen as an infringement of privacy by the teachers. Shirley, for example, said she could not remember whether they spoke a lot about sex at school but felt that she had discussed it although she had learned 'a lot more when I left school because when we did talk about sex it wasn't into much detail and I think you didn't listen very much at school either because you were a bit embarrassed'. Lara spoke about what she regarded as interference by their form tutor, Mrs Francis, who raised personal issues with girls when they were older:

> If she knew a girl was with a boyfriend she'd ask questions about contraception and that. I don't know. I just didn't like her the way she carried on. She used to tell us things like 'I've got a coil, what are you going to use then?' I thought it was plain nosey.

Shirley also recalled how Mrs Francis had spoken conspiratorially with the girls trying to establish a bond on the basis of being females. A large supply of sanitary towels in her cupboard was something that Shirley recalled with some distaste.

The toilets were the venue for talk on sex. Doreen claimed to have walked off when such talk took place. She said:

> If you go in the toilets there is a rule out there the last two toilets they used to sit down on the floor and sit there and smoke. Yes, it must have been in the toilets that the talk happened. They used to bring their own toothbrushes and brush their teeth and they used to chew polo and chewing gum. That's what they used to chew in the class after they had been down to the toilets. They come back and they have got a sweet in their mouth.

Lara confirmed this and indeed Carol had said that she and Katherine 'used to stand there and pretend not to listen'. Carol said:

> I mean I was so green . . . I knew June always knew what it was all about. I don't know if she ever slept with anyone or not at this particular time. But she and Lara used to talk about it in the toilets. We used to stand there and pretend not to listen.

The naivety of some of the girls was apparent not only from what Shirley said but was also backed up by another comment of Carol's. She said, in looking back, that 'the crowd of girls I went around with compared . . . well at that time we were very inexperienced, we were in awe of something like that', referring to sexual experience. She could not recollect past events all that clearly, but said that 'all the girls I go around with now have all had relationships of one form or another'. Lara seemed to sum up the progression. She said:

> As you are getting older really it creeps up on you doesn't it . . . it doesn't all of a sudden hit you, does it? You don't suddenly think: Right, I'm going to run out now because I am sixteen or whatever. I don't know. It very much depends on the individual.

For others, the discussions were private and restricted to two close friends. Carol said that she and Katherine 'would talk about sex between ourselves'. At school she adopted a moral position

155

about virginity and believed that sex should only occur in marriage. 'I always said I am not having sex until I get married and that's that, that's final.' Katherine thought more or less the same way. Carol remembered how she and another friend would discuss sex during their German lessons. This was made possible because the lesson was held in a small room with the teacher on the outside in the bigger room:

> It was like a small classroom inside a classroom. We would go in there and while we were writing out the German we would talk about it and I can always remember her saying 'I don't know how these girls can have sex before marriage. I think it is so wrong. It's just not right' and I'd say 'No, I don't know how they can'.

But she revised her ideas when a friend of hers at the time they were about sixteen told her how she had slept with her boyfriend and was really happy about it. Carol thought that 'because it wasn't a bad thing for her it didn't seem so bad to me'. When she was going out with a boyfriend at the age of seventeen her mother advised her to go to the family planning clinic which shocked her.

It was in the toilets that reputations were constructed by the girls themselves. This suggests that the girls played an active part in this labelling process, a point which is not made clear by Lees (1986). Reputations constituted an endless source of debate and discussion and all seem to devolve around sexual encounters. Carol, drawing on her memory, said that 'the girls in my class, we never talked about sex, as much as who was doing it and who wasn't if you see what I mean'.

Lara, an active contributor to the toilet discussions, said that reputations did not necessarily reflect reality. It was not possible to know what 'is true and what is false'. She said that she did not believe:

> half of what I heard anyway. We were all smoking. It surprised me because the ones who did end up pregnant were the ones who tended not to speak about it anyway. The quieter ones were getting on with it and not talking about it; the ones who were, probably weren't doing anything at all you know.

She should know because she seems to have enjoyed promoting a false image of herself. In her senior year she and Jane were:

the only two people in a photography class in my year and me
and Jane used to be in the dark room with Harrison [a teacher]
on his own, and the things that were said were unbelievable.
You can imagine, him in there alone with the two of us, and
us with our carrier bags bringing in cans of beer. Everybody
accused us of sleeping with him really, but it was never never
true, and he enjoyed the fact that he was being accused. He
was just laughing about it. It didn't worry him at all.

This is pertinent to the question of senior girls and the male
teachers. Bearing in mind what Mr Trim said about the 'impetus'
that senior girls could give to the younger male teachers (Chapter
5), what evidence was there of this, if any? The above account by
Lara indicates a collusion between the three actors involved in the
photographic classes, in which the girls were as much involved as
the teacher. Were there other incidents?

Lara was the only one to volunteer information of this nature.
She claimed that she used to go drinking with some of the staff.
She also referred to a school trip to Paris and in passing said that
Mr Burns used to get drunk and 'and everything'. She said how
much she enjoyed these sessions. It was this that prompted her to
divulge information about the photographic class. It was at this
point in the interview that I asked whether it was usual for the men
teachers to 'chat up' the girls. She denied this and said:

I don't believe they do really; I believe they are a bit more
cautious than that. I mean they are probably friendly with
you but there is a line isn't there to draw? Mr Harrison's wife
was pregnant and she had one other baby about a year old I
suppose. I mean he enjoyed being friendly and he didn't like
treating people like kids at that stage. When they had to be
treated like kids he did. I think he just enjoyed getting on with
them. So did Mr Burns. He was another one who I know has
moved schools because of an affair with a girl at school as
well.

Her interpretation was that Mr Harrison was treating her and Jane
as adults, and not school children, a fact which she clearly appreciated and of which she approved. As for Mr Burns, her claim that
he had admitted having affairs with girls sounded somewhat
incredible. But there was no way of checking on such information.
Mr Burns was Deputy Head and subsequently became a headteacher in another school.

Doreen raised the question of teachers and their sexuality in her comments on teachers who were disliked. In the course of expressing her dislike for Mrs Ivory she said:

> She was all over Mr Sands and all that. We were always talking about that. When we went to Holland. . . Everybody knew that they were carrying on. Like school kids talking. She was always drunk in Holland and Elstree as well.[1]

Conclusion

Freud alerted social scientists to the presence of sexuality from the earliest age and stressed its importance in people's lives. But, as set out in the previous chapter, the tendency in schools is to pretend it does not really exist even though it is visible in so many different facets. In spite of this attempt to obliterate it, girls are preoccupied with issues relating to sexuality and their emergent adult female identity which includes how to present themselves as feminine, sexually desirable people.

It is not something that is relegated to girltalk in the privacy of their homes. At school they talk about their boyfriends, they fight over their boyfriends, they talk about sex in the toilets where they are relatively free from adult scrutiny, they talk about it in the classroom, they flirt with their teachers, they construct the reputations of their peer group.

The question is to what extent does this intrude into the official aims of education; does it diminish girls' overall commitment to an education? Obviously this is impossible to establish because of the inherent difficulties in trying to quantify such effects, as well as the problems associated with isolating the role of developing sexuality from all the other factors which militate against girls obtaining a high level of education. But there is no doubt that an inverted relationship exists between commitment to school and their emerging sexuality. Going out, having a laugh, enjoying oneself was high on their list of priorities.

Take the experience of two of the brightest girls, Katherine and Carol. At the beginning of their secondary school career both girls achieved a very high standard of work. They were on a par with Adam, the only one of the group to have gone on to a university. By the time they had reached the end of their fourth year – O level stage – their downhill slide was evident. Katherine had no doubt what the cause of hers was when I interviewed her when she was twenty years old:

> I think when a girl starts going out with a boy it takes up the whole of her. I think that is one of the reasons why things start going downhill around that age we are talking about because I think that you get crushes on boys. Once you get a crush on a boy it takes over everything. Everything centres around them. You think about it most of the time. The boys don't seem to act in the same way. Oh I don't know, but they don't seem to get so dependent on girls until later on, much later on.

Carol could not account for it beyond saying that she just 'slackened off'. She did not associate her move downwards with her sexual interests although when she did talk about this it was evident that it did occupy her mind quite considerably. When interviewed as a school girl she had not spoken about her 'goody-goody' behaviour or her neat appearance as having affected her. Her crush on Jason had gone unrequited all that time; she may have been praised by her teachers but she did not enjoy peer group approbation or rewards for being good at schoolwork and well behaved.

She, like the other girls, was involved in learning gender appropriate forms of behaviour. Style of dressing, going out with boys, discussing all this with her girlfriends constituted part of the learning process of how to be feminine. When Carol spoke about her pony tails, her briefcase, and her socks, her image was one of innocence, demureness and childishness. But she was learning that this did not comply with the peer group's adolescent image of what constituted a sexually attractive girl. She recognized what the correct mode of dress was for group membership but did not apply it to herself.

This description of the girls' interests and attitudes challenges the view that the girls are exploited by boys or men, and experience their encounters in this way. While there were no older boys at Berkeley, and this is recognized as an important factor, nevertheless the girls' involvement with boyfriends, their desire to go to discos – discos were the highlight of the week for many of them – and their preoccupation with their appearance are all signifiers of the role heterosexuality plays in their lives. This involvement did affect those girls who were committed to their schoolwork in the first few years of secondary schooling. For the rest, their increasing interest in boys added another dimension to their lives. For someone like Doreen it was an important part of her life. She no longer saw herself as boring: she began actively to enjoy herself which did not seem the case when she was younger.

Boys

The comments made at the beginning of this chapter apply here. But in addition it should be noted that the type of information boys would give a female researcher is likely to differ from that given to a male researcher. The conversations I had did not, in any way, resemble those that Wood (1984) had with the group he studied as part of a project in a centre for 'disruptives' – a 'sinbin' – in a London secondary school. Amongst other things Wood reported on some boys' fantasies about raping one particular young woman when he interviewed them.

Apart from the gender of the researcher, there is another factor that should be taken into account. The group Wood was studying was a specific one. They had been defined as constituting a 'problem' in the school and had established themselves as non-conformists. As such they are not representative of the boys in that school. This then raises questions about how far their beliefs, wishes and desires are present amongst those who have not been labelled. There is the danger that the fantasies that the boys indulged in concerning the rape of one of the young women is seen as something that all adolescent boys may have.[2] Just as these are specific members of a group who may well suffer from various disturbances and difficulties, so too with the data of Willis' study with his 'lads'. These lads had attained some notoriety in their school in regard to their general behaviour and had reputations for being sexually athletic.

The boys in the present study comprised what can only be termed an ordinary group of boys none of whom had achieved any degree of notoriety within the school. They were not part of a spectacular youth group; they were not known for their deviance; they seemed to be ordinary teenagers.

Boys and their girlfriends

Boys at the age of twelve tended to acknowledge grudgingly or with a giggle that they were interested in girls. Elliot seemed to represent a number of boys' views when he said 'I'm not ready for it yet'. Only Adam and Fisher admitted to having had girlfriends and it was Adam who claimed that he had given up his girlfriend when he was twelve because 'she expected me to take her out everyday of the week'. It is difficult to know whether this was a boast or not.

By the age of fifteen the situation had changed. Thomas had just recently split from Doreen; Fisher said that he had had girlfriends since the age of five; Elliot was now much more interested in girls and admitted to spending a great deal of time in talking about them. He said 'We used to be shy, but as we got older, we just know more about girls'. Not all of them had Adam's self-confidence.

Their inexperience in how to approach girls and how to talk to a girl they fancied was expressed by Robin when he said:

A lot of boys are now talking about the girls. Like walk around and see well . . you walk around and see a nice girl and kind of try to pick her up or just start making remarks. A lot of them don't take notice.

Elliot in his adult interview went into lengthy details about the strategies he employed but this occurred *after* he had left school because, as he told me when he was twenty, 'I really only started having girlfriends about when I went to College'. Although he was very popular, with boys as well as with girls, he emphasized how shy he was about dating a girl. He recalled that:

At school I was very very very very shy – all those very shys. But you see I had to hide it. They used to say Elliot, Elliot this girl likes you and I say oh Jesus, she doesn't like me does she? But I didn't use to show it. Butterflies in my stomach, my heart used to go faster, and I thought, gee this isn't like me, you know. And if I used to like someone I wouldn't tell anyone my secret ambitions. Oh isn't she lovely, cor I could spend the rest of my life with her, you know. All that baby stuff right up to the age of sixteen, I suppose and all that – then I went to college.

This aspect of the fear and trepidation ordinary boys experience in the course of growing up and getting girlfriends should not be overlooked. Their lack of experience and their ineptitude may well account for their tendency to spend more time with each other while pretending disinterest in girls.

However, once they have learnt to make the approach, the boys may then adopt various strategies to keep some control over the situation. Elliot gave an account of his first date with a new girlfriend. It deals with his approach and illustrates the girl's vulnerability at the same time:

> I know if I'm going to get a girl, you know I don't care if it takes ten years, I know I'm going to get her, so in a way I planned it. First of all I started talking to her and get on her good side. Then I asked her all the things that interested her, then I'd give her a little test. These are what I call my little tests. We were on a bus and I said to her one day, give me a ring, and she said OK and she gave me a ring. And I tried to get onto her good side. Then I look for little things like if she is looking at me then I know I have got a point. It's a point on the board. One day it was just after Christmas, or just before, it was freezing cold and I said to her let's go down the market, you know, Petticoat Lane. I said meet me at the bus stop. The next day it was snowing like anything. The snow was quite high and I said, Jesus man I'm not coming out in the snow. I'm going back to bed. So I went back to bed and I was supposed to meet her at nine. And at ten o'clock I thought would she still be at the bus stop and I thought I'd better go just in case. And I got there about eleven o'clock and I saw the girl still standing at the bus stop. I knew that she liked me then, obviously, if she waits two hours in the freezing cold. And we went to Petticoat Lane and got off the bus and I was so cold I said to myself let's go into a Wimpey Bar and forget the whole thing. Don't let's go down Petticoat Market. I was cold and I'd only stood there for twenty minutes. So she must have been frozen. We spent the rest of the day going to Wimpey Bars.

Adam was the only one who described the kind of girl who interested him. At the age of fifteen he said that he had found that girls could be disruptive to his studies which he had prioritized.

> I haven't had a girlfriend for about a year now because they can't understand why I should work so hard for nothing,

although it is for exams. I want my qualifications badly, because the only place you are going to get in this world is if you have qualifications. They are intelligent, pretty people. . . *My work is my centre of attraction at the moment and if I put too much emphasis on a girlfriend like I normally do, then my work will suffer.* This is it (my emphasis).

He added somewhat wistfully, 'I have yet to find one who has got the same drive for work as I have'. He acknowledged that he had been interested in Katherine, that she was 'very good, and she is friendly with everyone' whereas he said Carol was not so popular with the other boys, but did not give any reason. (Carol recalled that Adam switched his attention from Katherine to herself all the way through school.) He said about Katherine that 'She has got the intellectual capacity, she has got the whole works. I like Katherine. She is very popular with me. We get on alright, but that is as far as it goes'. He said their friendship dissolved into nothing because she 'didn't want to have a boyfriend who is also a work mate which is good. I can understand that'.

Katherine provided some insight into why she had not wanted to date him. When she was fifteen she had commented, in passing, how unrelaxed and serious Adam was, lacking in fun and too devoted to schoolwork. She thought he was beginning to change and fit in more with the class:

He used to be taken up all the time with school work and he used to be a bit boring because it was always work, work and he was never able to relax and be able to talk about something else. But now . . . I think he has realized where he was going wrong and he goes out more with people from school. He goes ice skating on Saturday. Well he is just more like us. . .

He did not fit in, in her eyes, because his dedication to schoolwork left him little time to join in the fun with the others.

Elliot was convinced that girls and boys were different and it was in regard to their views on love:

I reserve the word love for maybe the person I am going to marry. Somebody like that. . . But I always say I really fancy that girl, that means I am infatuated with her for the five

163

minutes I have seen her or the ten minutes I have seen her and won't ever see her again. You know I might see her on the bus and think she is lovely and then the bus goes off and I go my way.

As noted in the previous section, Lara drew attention to the age differences which affected girls and boys at school. She spoke about the girls who went out with 'blokes who had money', who were older than the boys at school who never had any cash. This introduces the role of money into the social interaction between girls and boys and how the ritual of boys paying the bill effectively makes the girls dependent on the boys. Several of the boys make it quite clear that having a girlfriend also required them to pay for any outings. Elliot described how he took an evening job while he was at college. He worked from six to ten (acknowledging that it was massive exploitation of the youth) in order 'to take Sharon out. I would never let her pay for nothing. I wouldn't ask her to pay for anything. *I'd like to show off*'. Fisher felt it was his duty to meet the expenses for a night out. He said that he would pay for the girls and if they insisted on paying their way he would slip the money into their purses. This might well have provided him with the legitimate excuse for going out with more than one girl at a time while expecting fidelity from his girlfriends. Did his paying for everything give him the feeling of propriety over them? Did it establish power over the girls? The answer is in the affirmative and is a rehearsal for adulthood when the men, as wage earners, control the purse strings.

Style
As may be recalled, the boys said in response to direct questions that it was important for them to dress well. They also seemed to accept the wearing of school uniform with equanimity. What did not emerge from those responses was the way in which style and dress could become a basis for differentiating between the boys who worked hard and were clever, dressed in a particularly neat fashion so distinguishing them from the dominant peer group.

The norm appears to have been a casual and 'scruffy' appearance. The signifier of boys who were pro-school culture was their level of neatness. Such boys were likely to be jeered at, by both girls and boys alike and labelled 'cissy' or 'mother's boy'. Doreen presented the clearest picture of this when she said in a disparaging way how she disliked Adam because he 'was too formal with the teachers, always smart and tidy'. Nor did Graham escape her criticism when she was describing the kind of boys she disliked. He was similar to the boys:

> who came in pressed trousers every day, a nice neat shirt, white shirt and his little glasses and every day he comes to school with his perfect briefcase, and studied every day and never said a swear word. I think that is the type of nancy boy as opposed to the tough boy. And I think that that is what the boys mean most of the time.

Dress, however, was only part of the process of differentiation.

Sex and discussions about it

Understandably, the boys were far more reticent about discussing anything to do with sex with me. None of their comments reflected the rampant sexual aggression that has been attributed to boys. In the course of talking about girlfriends they would make some statement about the nature of co-education and what this meant in terms of relations with girls.

Thomas had said that if girls were not present in school 'you wouldn't be thinking about them so much. You would talk about them'. But then he contradicted this immediately afterwards by saying that 'If they are there you sort of treat them as friends because you get to know them whereas if they weren't there it would be different'. Clearly he both welcomed and was disturbed by their presence.

Michael on the other hand thought that you learnt to get on with girls because of their presence although he added: 'I don't know what it would be like if it was a one sex school. But you know', he added philosophically, 'when you are in a class with a lot of girls . . . you just learn to how to get on with girls'. But he thought there was no easy formula for this. 'You can't actually learn anything about girls. You don't take lessons. You could do so but I don't think it would do you any good'. It was the experience of being with girls that was important.

Adam was the only boy who openly talked about sexual intercourse when interviewed at the age of fifteen. He condemned boys of his age who were sexually experienced and was morally indignant about them:

We know who the boys are who lose their virginity. Usually they are very insecure – I am using Mrs Francis' words from Design and Modern Living class. They can't sort of, they have no work aspects at all. They have failed their qualifications and they don't know what to do. They just want to prove that they love the girls in the only way they can which I suppose is the only way open to them.

Adam's views reflect his puritanism and opposition to rampant sexual encounters. He equated this with stupidity. It was a reversal of the counter school position of equating homosexuality with school attainment. He said that boys who were failures in school had to prove themselves in the only way open to them, that is that they could perform sexually. He could then turn the tables on the boys who pilloried him for his cleverness and express his disapproval of them. On the other hand, as will be discussed below, he was very perturbed at being labelled 'gay' because he was clever and 'one of the élite'.

Some of the boys recalled how they talked about sex while at school. Some of the comments confirmed what so many commentators have said, namely that the major source of information about sex is derived from the peer group. The mechanics of biological reproduction and birth control may have been learnt through sex education in the school, but the intimate details were picked up from the peer group.

Oh, you learn it all from your mates. You get the basic from school and then the rest . . . you know there is a big group and you are talking. Like one of you might have read a book or something. It might not be true, but that is how you learn.

But there was more talk than action. Sex, according to Thomas, was spoken about jocularly and involved the reputation of girls. 'Well it was just sort of joking about most of the time. It was never really sort of serious'. But the jokes were made at the expense of girls. 'It was always mucking about saying this and that about different girls'. Presumably the conversation embraced their fantasies.

The reputations of girls were tenuous but there were different meanings given to the term 'slag'. 'Slags', according to Michael, referred to a range of different things:

If she told us and the boys [about her exploits]. I think being tough, used to say we slept with her. I don't think they referred to her as that. . . Also if the girls had been with more than one boy we would say they were slags or if they were very flirtatious.

During the school interviews Adam was the only one to refer to 'slags'. He said 'I don't like loud-mouthed slags you get in the school'. He distinguished between 'slags' and somebody like Tricia who had been pregnant at fourteen and had had a baby at fifteen:

For instance, you know that there are two girls in this school that are already pregnant. One has had a baby. She wasn't loudmouthed. She was very attracted to this boy and we don't blame them. She is not centred out from the rest of the class and put down in one of those sort of low chairs. . . She's not yet back but she will be treated exactly as she was a couple of years ago.

It is not clear why he did not condemn Tricia. Perhaps it was because she was settled with the father of the child:

There are one or two girls in this school who are – what do you call them – school girl prostitutes. They go to bed with other boys. There are only about four that I know in the school that do. They are very loudmouthed about it. We know who they are, we know who they go to bed with. We are not particularly bothered. One of these days they will make a mistake – they'll find out when they are married with sixteen kids in a back room of a Chinese restaurant somewhere with a load of nappies on the line – and it will be their fault. They just want the experience – they want it to be known that they know and they want to get themselves like older women. . . . The family planning lady came around about three months ago with a load of contraceptives and of course one or two went missing and you can draw your own conclusion as to where they went.

Like some girls, some boys also developed reputations, but the major difference was that boys stood to gain from having a reputation of being sexually active, while, as pointed out, it could be harmful to girls. Boys' sexuality is equated with masculinity whereas girls' femininity resides in their outward appearance and behaviour which specifically excludes sexual experience thus reflecting the double standards which have operated in society for well over a hundred years.

It is clear that boys' reputations did not necessarily confirm their experience. Elliot pointed out that boasting characterized much of the discussion that went on at school:

> Well you believe some and wouldn't believe others you know. And you think, oh yes, he might have done it, you know. It depended on the person. I mean there were loads of that sort of talk when you are kids

but he quickly put himself outside of this when he added, 'it just sort of goes over your head.'

Michael questioned whether any of the boys had indeed had sexual intercourse while still at school irrespective of all the talk:

> I don't think that any of them had been with a girl at all when we were at school. The most was a grope at the back of the classroom. That's all it got to. Thinking back on it, it's nothing like that at all. I think that in a way the boys were closer to each other than any girls at the time.

What he was suggesting was something quite different and contrary to the stereotypical view of boys' rampant sexuality in adolescence. But then he pointed out something else confirming what Eliot had suggested.

> Maybe we were *frightened* to go with a girl anyway. It wasn't so much we used to boast – what you have done with this girl the other night – but it was more the case of what five of you have done (my emphasis).

Because of the identity of masculinity with sexuality, there is a pressure on boys to try and prove that they are men, that they are sexually experienced. This coupled with their difficulties in getting girlfriends must generate a great deal of tension and may account for some of their aggression. Concurrent with this was the boys' concern with each other and within their groups, friendships which excluded girls. Overall the girls appeared to be far more interested in their friendships and relationships with the boys than the reverse.

Homosexuality and the classroom

I never asked the pupils any direct questions about homosexuality when they were at school, but the topic arose in the course of the last set of interviews and there were some interesting comments which revealed differences between the boys' and girls' recollections about Graham, the one boy who had been identified as a 'poof'[3].

In the previous chapter, reference was made to pupils adhering to certain rituals relating to gender appropriate forms of behaviour. Graham, who was uniformly disliked, flouted many of these rituals. He did not conform to the dominant peer group culture – he hated football and P.E. and did all he could to avoid these classes. He could not 'talk about anything', and never watched the very popular TV programme 'Top of the Pops'. He was interested in Victoriana and Beethoven. The teachers, as well as the pupils, singled him out. Although nobody actually said that they thought Graham was a homosexual, there was an unspoken insinuation, as well as a worry on the part of the teachers so that Mrs White referred him to Child Guidance. She did so because she said she was worried about his inability to fit in with the rest of the class and did not share the interests they had – his involvement in collecting Victoriana was seen as abnormal! She did not openly say that she thought he was homosexual and, as such, should have psychotherapy but it was implicit. Homosexuality must have appeared to her to be abnormal.

Graham's marginalization continued into the second year. Mrs Ivory became aware of a 'fuss' over Graham and asked a number of the boys what it was all about. He had apparently been verbally abused, and was accused of being a 'poof'.

When pressed, the boys said that Graham was feminine and dirty; feminine because he sat with girls at dinner-time, and dirty because he claimed to masturbate. The boys were hesitant about telling Mrs Ivory this and after some cajoling said that Graham had told them that if 'he didn't make it in bed that night, then he wouldn't make it at school the next day', referring to his schoolwork performance.

Graham was in a catch-22 situation. His masturbation was considered disgusting even though the protestors were probably engaging in the same activity. He was already damned in their eyes because of his general behaviour so there was nothing that he could do to establish himself in the class.

It is possible to identify two types of homosexual labels. The one refers to sexual behaviour and the other to identifying cleverness with absence of masculinity and hence with homosexuality. At first, this distinction is blurred. It begins with being labelled a 'mother's boy' or a 'cissy'. Boys labelled in this way are marginalized and the older they get the stronger the acts of marginalization. But also the older they become, the clearer the division between sexuality and other factors. In Graham's case, he was initially called a 'cissy' and a 'mother's boy' but subsequently labelled as 'poofter'. Adam was also called a 'poofter' because he worked too hard, got good marks, and did not join in with the others in their 'mucking about' in the classroom or playing truant from school.

Shirley was one of those who referred to Graham as a 'cissy'. She was quite explicit about this when she said:

> I don't remember thinking he was gay. I thought he was a bit of a mum's boy and that sort of thing . . . people were just seeing a 'nancy boy' who have to be round their mum all the time. I know Graham was quite a clever boy and because he was keen on studying and because he didn't go around in bovver boots the boys used to see him as cissy. I don't really think it entered the boys' heads that they would sleep with other boys. I don't think you see it as that when you are younger. But when you get older when, if someone turned round to me and said – do you think Graham sleeps with men now – I wouldn't know.

Katherine on the other hand saw him in terms of being an outsider. She recognized that in his failure to play football or fight he was different to the others. She thought that the boys were protective towards him if he was attached outside the group but that when they reached fourteen or fifteen she said that:

> Everything is really clear cut. You are gay or you are not. But I mean, I think people accepted that he wasn't tremendous. He was gay and they just took him for that. I think the girls took it as that. I think the boys took the most exception to it. But maybe it is my imagination.

She introduced another dimension to the situation, and that is the discomfort the other boys experienced in his presence. 'Taking the mickey out of Graham' was the way in which Doreen described the treatment meted out to him in some lessons and the way in which three of the girls would 'stick up for him', a move which he quietly rejected telling them he could cope with it.

The boys were more explicit when interviewed as adults. Thomas said that Graham had been very different from Adam, who because he was seen as being clever had been charged with being homosexual. The difference lay in Graham's inability to join in with them in anything that was fun. He said, 'We never communicated with him, you never got through to him', unlike Adam:

> Adam would talk and join in sort of football and cross-country running and that, sort of anything we did in the sixth form, five aside games and that. You could get him into that. But you'd never get Graham into that. If you mentioned it he would go and hide.

Thomas said they suspected that Graham was gay and then recalled that earlier:

> Everybody used to take the mickey, you know, when we were younger. It was never sort of . . . you know, you would take the mick about it, but we never really thought it was serious. . . I mean he never sort of showed anything you know, that he was after anyone. *It was just that he was different*. That's what segregated him because he wouldn't do the things that we would do. We sort of cast him aside (my emphasis).

Michael said that he never recalled ever saying a word to Graham at school. He simply regarded him as an outsider. But his total rejection of Graham was combined with Graham's level of attainment. He coupled Graham with Adam:

> When it comes down to it it wasn't just Graham. Adam was an outsider as well. But I don't know. *I think it was because they were brainy at school; they studied. Whereas everyone else wouldn't.* You might work in the lesson but that's as far as it went. . . . They weren't in on the laughs and that, or in the circle and that. I don't know why. I think that that's all it was, thinking back, because they studied and that and did the work (my emphasis).

Doreen shared the same sort of dislike for Adam. Here it was his style that counted. 'He was too formal with the teachers, always smart and tidy and he should be'.

Graham's only acknowledgment of the fact that he was the butt of verbal aggression was in his response to the direct question on whether or not he thought boys should be aggressive (see Chapter 3). He felt that it was legitimate to be aggressive if one was continuously teased. But he never admitted to a feeling of alienation and marginalization.

Adam, on the other hand, was very conscious of his marginalization. He expressed his anger and hurt at the situation. He referred to himself as one of the élite and said there were only a few of them in the school:[4] 'I have no friends at this school and I am not particularly bothered because when I go to college then I will find people of my own intelligence, my own intellect, then I can mix better.'

The élite competed with each other:

> Well in a classroom there is very much attention put onto the marks . . . if anybody got a bad mark, you know, bang, all down to the bottom of the class and if one of the élite says something bad, then you have had it you know. We sort of pass snide comments like 'revise properly did you?' or 'is your pen leaking?' or something. They understand and they take it as a hint and they don't like it. . . . It leads to a mental blow.

He said he felt isolated. The 'élite' did not provide support for one another. It seemed that their relationship was one of intense competition. Adam's sense of isolation was common to all of them and arose from a lack of understanding by the rest of the boys:

> I am to some extent [isolated] but only because other people don't understand. Everybody in this A stream is to a certain extent isolated. But we can mix with other people if we want to. And they think that everyone in this élite part of the world is homosexual, which is stupid because we all have our own social life, we have all got girlfriends, we all go out, we go to discos, and things, but they just don't understand. They don't want to understand, so why should we bother. The thicks just class the middle as homosexual as well. It's the middle people who really put the knife in.

But later in the interview he expressed his anger and frustration when talking about his perception of aggression in girls. After having said that girls should not be aggressive he followed on with:

> I am getting to the point where the next person who calls me a homosexual will get a set of broken teeth, a back broken and two broken arms. But I don't think it will ever come to that. You know, I had a chat with Mrs Francis about it. She understands how I feel.
>
> I don't particularly like it. Everybody who calls me a homosexual is inferior, is a twit, you know, is stupid. There is absolutely no background to it at all. They know that I have girlfriends and whenever they see me with a girlfriend then they treat me absolutely equal to them. They sort of think I am one of the lads. But whenever I am seen in class and doing my physics I am the exact opposite, you know, which is mad.

Adam was talking about the difficulties that boys (and girls) experience when they do well in a school in which the dominant ethos is one of counter-school culture. Going against the main drift results in the marginalization of the pupil concerned. Willis (1977) accounted for this phenomenon in terms of shop floor culture. But it is not shop floor culture which can be seen to operate amongst the Berkeley pupils (as will become clear in Chapter 10). The developing gender identity is tied in with a complex set of processes in which peer group culture plays an important part. Adam had established his bona fide masculinity and yet this was not sufficient to win him full membership (even had he wanted it) of the dominant group in the school. He was marginalized because he was going outside the group's accepted rituals of what constituted their understandable world. In their world schoolwork did not rank high. They had no examples amongst their parents of advanced level of attainment in school. Those who did do well at school could not participate fully in the various activities which the peer culture had defined as legitimate and desirable. It was not possible to study for O level examinations and play football, or go out for bicycle rides or skip classes or do no homework. To take O level examinations meant working both at school and outside of school hours. It precluded pupils from having a laugh and having fun with their schoolmates. These were not activities which the peer culture prioritized.

Conclusion

The boys' interest in sexuality was present from an early age. While the link between sexuality and masculinity is taken for granted, the need to establish masculinity is part of the peer group culture and exists even in the lower forms. Failure to appear masculine and to comply with group norms resulted in marginalization. Initially masculinity could be linked to such activities as playing football so boys like Graham who hated football and P.E. were very soon labelled pejoratively.

In comparison with the girls, the physical manifestations of boys' sexuality is delayed. This may account for the perpetuation of the boys engaging in childish and boy-only activities. While they may have been interested in girls, this did not dominate their lives. Michael, for example, appeared more involved with male friends and group activity than with girls. Like the others, he had fun, both inside and outside the classroom, with his mates – playing football, riding a bicycle in summer, skating down the High Road – and his activities were exclusively male.

Whether their continued involvement in their own male culture was a direct outcome of their interest, or slower physical development or fear of how to handle the social side of establishing a relationship with the opposite sex, or a combination of all these factors cannot be determined and needs further investigation.

Irrespective of whether they had girlfriends, there is pressure on boys to prove themselves manly and, as discussed above, manliness is not associated with mental activities. In the lower levels of the school, boys who are clever and whose style of dress reflects this may be dismissed by their peer group as 'mother's boy'. This continues all the way through school and attempts by Adam, for example, to escape such labelling indicates how difficult it is for boys to escape such marginalization.

However much they may participate in peer group activities as Adam did, boys who do not conform to peer group norms may be only partially accepted. Their masculinity has to be confirmed and one way is through the promotion of an image of rampant, aggressive sexuality with a James Bond syndrome of numerous sexual encounters. But the comments made by the boys reveal just how flimsy such reputations were and how difficult to achieve while still at school.

As with the literature on youth culture which has focused on the spectacular, so the limited data on adolescent boys in schools has promoted the stereotypical image of flexing biceps, aggressive behaviour, and a great deal of sexual experience. The data in this chapter presents a different picture of the boys, many of whom appeared tentative about sexual encounters. Indeed some may wish to prolong their childhood which includes the close friend- ship of other boys, and all that that encompasses, such as having fun and avoidance of strong commitments or responsibilities. Many of these boys did not experience responsibilities about their schooling at all. Fun and enjoyment was high on their list of priorities.

However, whether or not they had girlfriends while at school, their masculine identity is closely tied in with sexuality, and mas- culinity and levels of scholastic attainment are closely interwoven. As such this aspect of boys' lives and its relation to education does require further exploration, particularly if, as seems to be the case, present day youth culture denigrates scholastic attainment. Changes in level of pupils' attainment can only be partially altered if this particular ideology is replaced by a more positive one on scholarly attainment.

PART THREE

THE CURRICULUM

CHAPTER SEVEN

Knowledge and control

Introduction

What people learn at school is not simply determined by their individual motivations, psychological make-up, or inherent ability. As already noted, individual pupils are subjected to a range of controls which interact with various social formations, including the peer group culture. These controls provide the structural basis in which the learning situation takes place.

The content of education is the curriculum which conventional wisdom holds as comprised of separate and discreet areas of knowledge made available to pupils. This is clearly not all there is to it. The curriculum comprises differentiated knowledge and hidden agendas, known as the hidden curriculum, which relates to ideologies on work, gender differences, class differences and so on. The curriculum may be the site of struggle within the teaching profession, and there is no consensus about what should be taught in schools, although there are moves to create a national core curriculum which has had a mixed reception. There is little doubt that the working of the curriculum is not straightforward. In the final analysis, it is a highly effective form of control over pupils.

This chapter will examine the curriculum as it was conceptualized at Berkeley. To do this and to place it in some context, a brief discussion on some of the discourses on the curriculum will precede it. What is taught and how change may be effected in the curriculum can be a source of friction and an example of this will be given, as it has implications for effecting overall changes in the curriculum, particularly relating to gender differences. Finally, as one of the aims of the school was to operate an integrated programme, with a common curriculum that would not differentiate between boys and girls, how this was to be achieved, what the views of the key teachers were and how parents reacted, will also be discussed.

Some comments on discourses on the curriculum[1]

The curriculum is the essential core of both the form and content of knowledge transmitted by schools. Amongst other things, the conceptualization of knowledge has been in terms of its control by the dominant group in society, with knowledge seen as 'cultural capital' (Bourdieu and Passeron, 1977). This notion became widely adopted and was interpreted, as Apple (1981) says, as the transformation of culture into a commodity by the ruling groups enabling them to maintain and control this 'cultural capital'.

The value of this concept lay in its application to the processes of the maintenance of hegemonic power by members of the ruling group, which in the course of ensuring their control over the access to knowledge, also ensured their entry into powerful and controlling occupations. This implies, quite correctly, that the curriculum is differentiated and that access to that part of the curriculum which is directly linked to high-powered jobs is not automatically available to all pupils at all times. This point may be simply illustrated by a comparison between two extremes – public school pupils of, say, Eton, with those of a comprehensive school in a metropolitan city area such as Toxteth in Liverpool. A boy from the latter is simply not going to have learned or acquired the knowledge that his contemporary from a top public school will have gained at the time of leaving school. Thus there is a differentiation that occurs on class lines. But what none of the many commentators recognized was that the differentiation also included gender.

The example of class differentiation is true at the most general level. But these extremes are more complex than the clear-cut example above suggests. In comprehensive schools, the same stock of knowledge is not readily available to all pupils equally. The various techniques employed in the course of making 'normalizing judgments' involving streaming and the demarcation of pupils on the grounds of their 'ability', and which largely correspond with class membership, are accompanied by the presentation of different forms of knowledge. There is no way that a fifth form girl in a non-GCE class would have been studying the same history that her sister in a top stream would be doing (Keddie, 1971). The syllabuses differed markedly. (Nor is there any basis for believing that the new examination system will eradicate these differences: different levels will still continue to exist and operate.) This lack of homogeneity in terms of the content of knowledge is both inter- and intra-school.

In the 1970s, the basis for accounting for the effectivity of schooling in maintaining stratified society was attributed to the role of specific ideologies (Althusser, 1971), particularly those relating to the work ethic, and their internalization. As discussed in the general Introduction, Bowles and Gintis (1976) popularized this[2] and, as Whitty says:

> These authors suggested that there was a 'correspondence' between the social relations of school and the social relation of work [which] makes a contribution to the reproduction of an appropriate skilled and disciplined workforce for capitalism (p. 22, 1981).

This account was superseded by that of cultural reproduction (as also discussed in the general Introduction) with Willis' work spearheading this type of analysis (Apple, 1982). In spite of the importance of the role of the curriculum the focus was on 'the level of social relations, on how the people involved interact'.

This analytical development has contributed to the shortage of concrete studies on the curriculum at the general level (Whitty, 1981). However, there has been a considerable input of feminist work on gender differences highlighting, in particular, those areas which could be seen as part of the 'cultural capital', especially subjects such as mathematics and the pure sciences (Whyld, 1983, Walden and Walkerdine, 1982, Kelly, 1981). But the analytical framework has begun from the premise that girls as a whole are disadvantaged compared with boys as a whole. Assumptions have been made that all boys have equal access to all the educational goodies, or 'cultural capital', which has been systematically denied to girls, largely because of male power or patriarchy.

Such a form of analysis is unproductive because it fails to take account of the complexities and variations within the curriculum. The understanding of differentiation on the basis of gender requires to be contextualized so that the full complexities of the system may be appreciated.

The curriculum does effectively make available those aspects of knowledge which are thought suitable for the particular group of pupils. Consequently there is a form of control which may effect class and gender differences. The curriculum includes more than one set of ideologies and these work together with the other determinants which operate in the schools, including those discussed in the preceding chapters.

The curriculum at Berkeley: The ideology behind it

Berkeley occupied a highly privileged position in the borough. It was to become its first and only purpose-built comprehensive school and consequently enjoyed, in its developmental phase, the fullest support, both financial and otherwise, from the educational officers, the local councillors and, in particular, the Chairperson of the Education Committee who also, conveniently, was Chairperson of the Board of Governors.

Given that the school was starting from scratch, one could have anticipated that there would be a great emphasis on curriculum development, experimentation and the confrontation of current debates surrounding curriculum issues. However, what proved to be the major thrust and which reflected the views of both the Chairperson of the Board of Governors and the Head was the concept of Community School, albeit rather loosely defined by both these people. They both spoke in general terms, advocating that the school serve the local community, and to this end the long-term plans included the school doubling up as a community educational centre in the evenings, with a separate set of staff to present an evening programme. Initially the main focus was on involving parents in the school through an active Parent/Teachers Association, extra-mural activities involving parents, and so on. Innovative ideas about the curriculum were not high on the Head's list of priorities and his mark was to be on the integrated programme which affected home economics (HE), physical education (PE) and Humanities.

He allocated the role of curriculum development to his deputy, Mr Burns, although he, like Mr Burns, did have definite views about the form the curriculum should take. For both these men the class position of their pupils was of paramount importance and one which they both thought would influence the form and content of the curriculum, although each held a distinctive position.

Mr Trim spoke in general terms about working-class parents and their effect on the pupils. He identified two problems which were linked: 'They either think that they can't afford to keep their kids at school, or that the children must go out and earn some money'. To this extent he was reflecting a commonsense view that all working-class parents were either financially unable to support their children's education or largely disinterested in their children's education; but whatever position, they wanted their children to enter the labour force and contribute to the household budget. In either event he saw the parents as playing a key role in their children's education, although from a negative perspective. Given that his school was composed almost entirely of working-class children, he was concerned to combat what he saw as these two evils.

He anticipated that teachers could play an active role and positively affect parents' attitudes by establishing and maintaining personal contact with parents both through home visits and through parents visiting the school. This contact would enable parents to recognize and accept benefits that education could bestow on their children. For this reason Mr Trim emphasized his 'link scheme' which he said could avoid 'either a total withdrawal (by the parents) from any contact with the school or an aggression directed to the sort of thing like, "What are you doing about my kid, why are you unfair?" type of situation'. The link scheme would end working-class parents' lack of confidence in the school.

This reflects Mr Trim's ambiguous and somewhat contradictory view of working-class parents. On the one hand he had claimed that they were not concerned with their children's education as such and were keen to get them into the labour force, for one reason or another, yet on the other hand he said that they mistrusted school because they thought their children were being discriminated against. Irrespective of his own confusion, Mr Trim clearly perceived his pupils as having different educational needs from those of middle-class children whose parents cooperated fully with the school and supported their children's education. The working-class pupils were 'culturally deprived' and he anticipated that his school would fill this gap, as he explained when he discussed part of the integrated programme.

Apart from the fact that he established the principle that teachng in the first three years was to be conducted in mixed-ability groups, there was to be a fully integrated programme which Mr Trim proudly emphasized would not separate boys and girls in any subject, at least in the first three years. All teaching was to be fully integrated with boys and girls pursuing the same curriculum. Although it may no longer be seen as innovative, this was a new departure as far as Mr Trim, Mr Burns and, particularly, Mr David, the craft teacher, were concerned. They publicly supported these developments enthusiastically, although privately they expressed their doubts, as the subsequent data will reveal.

Mr Trim referred to the integrated programme as comprising a 'balanced diet' which all boys and girls would receive at school. It meant that:

> All children should do woodwork or craft, including sculpture and carving and so on. Artwork would include pottery, home economics would include home management and personal relationships, health education and, finally, needlework.

But he found the term needlework unsatisfactory because of its close association with feminine activities and, as such, the terminology had to be altered to make the subject more acceptable to children (presumably boys!) and parents alike. In a discussion with me he said:

> We are trying to redesign needlework as material design to get away from the concept that needlework is a thing which old ladies do or girls do, or mums do, mostly mums, and that moving towards the up-to-date idea is that needlework is a very exciting proposition in materials. In fact, we leave the word needlework . . . material design and when one thinks of, for instance, embroidery, boys or girls could produce in embroidery the sorts of pictures, collages that they could produce. I think, myself, ultimately, that we will have a new cultural direction.

Clearly Mr Trim was getting carried away by his own enthusiasm. He saw the school as a potential creator of good taste, an agency for counterbalancing the so called poverty of the culture of the environment:

> I think that this is my main point, a new cultural direction of ability, the effect of these abilities, because ultimately one hopes that they see possibilities in a thing like material design,

wood sculpture, wood carving, and this will lend itself or bring some sort of dividends in the making of their homes.

Mr Trim's statement on the potential and wide scope of home economics throws light on the extent of his ideas on the meaning of integration. He felt obliged to change the name of needlework because of its feminine connotations which he thought would exclude boys from taking such lessons. But this was not sufficient. He had also to change the content of the course because it would not be adequate to teach boys as well as girls the usual form of needlework; needlework had to be altered to become a 'creative' activity, thereby simultaneously enriching the lives of the pupils and hence the local community!

In this way the school would have a concrete effect on what he clearly saw as an impoverished, culturally deprived community. The school would improve the quality of their lives and bring about a 'new cultural direction':

> We are offering the kids that opportunity to experiment in areas, aesthetics, if you like, which they would not [experience otherwise]. Now they can take it or leave it . . . we are adding to their cultural enrichment.

Mr Trim's conception of culture illustrates the point made by Raymond Williams (1961) which drew attention to the commonsense way in which high and low cultures were defined, with the former obviously referring to the socially acceptable and desirable set of values, while the latter referred to a working-class set of values. Exactly what constituted Mr Trim's aesthetic standards was not clear, but the message was unambiguous. The school could affect children's aesthetic values and introduce them to the more desirable values of the middle-class high culture.

Mr Trim's concept of integration also included girls doing wood-work. On a separate occasion in one of our many meetings there was a discussion on parents' apprehension about their daughters. Mr Trim said:

> One parent did complain and say, 'We would rather our daughter did academic subjects than get on with woodwork', so I said to her, 'Well, let's see how it goes'. I wasn't disposed at the time to go into great moral discussion as to why we are

integrating boys and girls, but I am very happy about how it is going. There is no subject where boys and girls go separately, and if I want justification for it, I would say it's jolly good for a girl to be able to develop a facility in the use of tools in a workshop. It is very good for a boy to be able to develop the ideas behind *some* home economics or home management . . . all girls when they get homes *will want to put up shelves*, perhaps. *All boys will have a home in which they perhaps want to do a bit of cooking.* This would aid in overcoming the barrier between what constitutes whose job was whose or 'that's cissy' or 'that's manly' (my emphasis).

This revealed very clearly the extent of Mr Trim's notion of what constituted an integration of curriculum between boys and girls. In effect it didn't deviate from traditional gender roles, in that woodwork for girls was in relation to household activities, and nothing more than this; and home economics for boys was no more than teaching them to do a bit of cooking, helping out in the home. He held no views about technological literacy or alternative employment for women. While integrated classes did not threaten traditional gender differences, there was nothing to fear.

The only other areas in which integration would occur would be in PE. Mr Trim foresaw no difficulties in this regard but, as will be discussed in the next chapter, his attempt to integrate PE was short-lived.

Integration, however, meant running classes without separating boys from girls. This referred only to those lessons which in the past were seen strictly in terms of one or other's group. Mr Trim was satisfied that his programme of integration represented the means to ensure equality between girls and boys. He did not recognize the existence of other factors which contributed to this differentiation.

Mr Burns was more specific about the differences which he considered demarcated middle- from working-class pupils. He believed that the former, in fully accepting the school culture, did not truant, did not constitute disciplinary problems, pursued school goals keenly and, in the end, would successfully sit GCE examinations. Working-class pupils differed completely. They simply did not pursue these educational goals, a belief which he attributed to the influence of parents whom he said had 'been only too pleased to get out of school, had felt school was irrelevant to their adult lives and whose children were likely to have similar attitudes'.

His perception would have direct consequences on the whole curriculum development in the school. Entering pupils *en masse* for the higher-level public examinations was not on the agenda and he would find some other means for involving pupils in school-work. Although he did not consciously recognize the control which the examination system exerts over pupils, he was aware that he had to devise means of keeping the pupils' interest alive. To this end he wanted to solicit the active support of parents, he wanted to eliminate all forms of negative effects of 'normalizing judgments', and he planned to introduce a new course, 'Design for Living'.

Involving parents in their children's education would take two forms. The first was informing parents of exactly what was on offer at the school, and the second involved practical measures designed to aid parents' supervision of their children's homework. To achieve the former, an evening meeting for all parents (which Mr Burns would address) was to be held annually. In regard to the assistance of parents, Mr Burns ran a class on new mathematics for parents.

Although this particular idea was received enthusiastically by the parents, in reality the number who availed themselves of this opportunity were small and tended to be parents of children who, in any event, were 'high-fliers' and who were likely to encourage their children. The first two years there was no assessment by either Mr Burns or Mr Trim on the effectiveness of their attempts to involve parents, nor how this affected parents' treatment of their children. Rather, both these men seemed to treat these measures as ends in themselves.

Mr Burns' concern with labelling reflected teachers' overwhelming rejection of selective examinations such as the 11+ examination which had dire consequences for those who had failed to pass such an examination. To avoid labelling, Mr Burns opted for teaching mixed-ability classes until such time as pupils had to 'choose' the subjects after the third year of schooling.

In order to free children from the effects of such examinations, Mr Burns opted for the introduction of Mode III examinations in many subjects, although not excluding the taking of public examin-ations by pupils deemed capable of so doing. Mode III assessments 'were set and marked internally by the individual school and moderated by one of the appropriate Regional (Educational) Boards', thereby enabling individual schools to develop, present and examine their own specific syllabuses. Although moderated externally by a professional peer group, these examinations have not been viewed favourably, particularly by prospective employers who are familiar with the other examination systems and the particular grades. Consequently, pupils with Mode III levels of qualifications could be disadvantaged in the open labour market.

So, although the introduction of Mode III examinations in itself had much to commend it, there were, nevertheless, negative and unintended consequences for pupils. But this was a problem which Mr Burns did not address. Rather, the use of a Mode III assessment appeared to him as an alternative means of engaging pupils unlikely to sit public examinations. It was assumed that public examinations covered syllabuses which are of little interest or relevance to working-class pupils as a whole, while Mode III syllabuses would be tailor-made for the particular pupils, cater for their own interests, and have the consequence of having pupils attend and participate in classwork. So it was anticipated that truancy would decline, pupils would be committed to their studies and control over them would not constitute a major problem.

Associated with Mr Burns' decision to encourage staff's utilization of Mode III form of assessment was his own contribution to the curriculum development. He planned the introduction of a course called 'Design for Living' which he said would 'familiarize pupils with essential information'. In effect, what this meant was to make them fully conversant with 'the working of the social welfare department, local studies, and current affairs'. Local studies, when the course was introduced, became the means of introducing pupils to the different consumer outlets in their area. How much 'current affairs' was taught is unknown, but clearly Mr Burns believed that his pupils' future would be somewhat restricted: they would live and work locally, few if any would continue with higher education, and they were likely to make use of the social welfare department at some time in their lives. Clearly, and probably realistically, he did not see the bulk of his pupils as comprising an upwardly mobile group, but rather fixed in their social class, likely to have to call upon social services.

In order to develop the necessary 'self-discipline' which in turn involved the ability to study on one's own to develop the 'correct attitude', and to complete allotted tasks, all of which he regarded as prerequisites for pursuing Mode III examinations, Mr Burns proposed to introduce the tutorial system. Although this sounded highly commendable, in practice it amounted to no more than a single period on a Monday morning which was devoted to the form tutor completing the numerous bureaucratic tasks required of him or her. During this period children would be charged with reading and working on their own, although they mostly utilized this period for continuous chatting, catching up on the weekend's exploits of their classmates. And yet the phrase 'tutorial system' became incorporated into the everyday language of the school.

Mr Burns did not appear as enthusiastic about the integrated programme as Mr Trim. He did, though, speak about it at a parents' evening in which he outlined the school's future policy. He spoke of a 'common curriculum' which both boys and girls would follow. He used the phrase 'common curriculum' in two distinct ways. It referred to providing children with what he termed a 'real education', that is, 'a bit of everything', as well as providing all children with an identical curriculum. (For a full discussion of such distinctions see Lawton, 1975 and Whitty, 1981.)

As an example of all boys and girls following a common curriculum, he said that boys would be expected to do some home economics and girls, handicrafts. He presented this as innovative and advantageous to all pupils although he, like Mr Trim and others, privately expressed unease and concern with such a scheme.

Mr Burns asserted that boys would not be excluded from pursuing commerce 'because they may take up commerce training later on. Instead of doing it later on, why don't they do it at the beginning? . . . . It includes so many things.' He never spelt out exactly what it included, nor did any parent question him about this. But this provided him with a cue to talk about girls' employment:

> My idea is that if a girl is trying to be a secretary and wanted
> to make a really good career out of it and not simply become
> a typist in a large office bashing away at a typewriter all day,
> a personal secretary or something like that, then perhaps one
> would suggest that they took a language as their other choice
> because that would be quite a useful thing for them to have.

He expressed the commonsense view that secretarial work was preferable to either factory or shop work and, perhaps even more importantly, his views about the scope of his female pupils' future employment. Private secretarial work represented the pinnacle of success, and was the best one could hope for amongst Berkeley's female pupils, there simply was no question of further or higher education as an alternative goal!

On the question of boys doing needlework and cookery, he realized that there could be some opposition, and had this to say:

> There is the question of boys doing needlework and cookery. I think that it is probably more difficult for a boy to accept doing needlework and cookery than it is for a girl to do woodwork. It is going to happen, but I think that it will take a little time before everybody accepts the fact that doing needlework is not cissy. Cookery is perhaps not as bad but needlework is more feminine than cookery.

This reflects quite unequivocally the status of female-labelled activities. Boys' self-esteem could be lowered if they engaged in such activities, and their masculinity would be questioned!

He gave no indication then of his opposition to this. At a planning meeting with Mr Trim, Mr Burns subsequently said that needlework was a 'dead loss' for boys, a view which Mr Trim did not question or take up. Perhaps he too shared Mr Burns' views about boys doing needlework, but publicly he had to support its availability for boys, otherwise his claim for an integrated curriculum could not be made.

The parents' evening was the only occasion at which Mr Burns spoke directly about gender differences in relation to curriculum provision. Mr Burns did not locate his discussion on curriculum development in terms of the debates which had dominated academic literature, nor in regard to gender differences. He was faced with problems relating to resources, both human and physical. The immediate resolution of the provision of particular courses was determined by the availability and expertise of the teachers who had been appointed and this is what occupied his mind, the practical issues. He, like many teachers once out of college, resolved problems pragmatically. The balanced curriculum with 'a bit about everything to start off' was to be compartmentalized into four sections: Humanities, Mathematics and Science, Communications, and Design. These were sub-divided as follows: Design: home economics and craft; Communications: French, physical education and music; Humanities: English, history and geography. This grouping was designed for purely practical reasons based on existing staff appointments, what they specialized in, as well as the grade at which they had been appointed. If his classification coincided with four out of five of Lawton's (1975) prescribed five core areas – mathematics, physical and biological sciences, humanities and social studies, expressive arts and moral education – then it was more by chance and custom than by careful consideration of the problem. In addition he had to resolve questions of timetabling, a duty which appears to take up a good deal of time of many deputy headteachers.

The integrated programme was something he had to accept but, on the basis of his remarks, he did not think it important. Far from it. He was not in favour of boys doing needlework and he did not offer any opinion on girls doing woodwork. Gender differentiation brought about by the curriculum was not an issue as far as he was concerned.

And what were the parents' views about the integrated programme? Mr David expressed amazement at how many parents had come up to him on open evening:

> They weren't annoyed, but they were surprised that their daughters were doing woodwork and they didn't think much of it. I pointed out to the parents that woodwork is not the same these days as it used to be when I was at school, you know. Most of the woodwork is artistic. You have to go that way because if you decided to make something in the classroom they could go out and buy it cheaper in plastic. I do a lot of sculpture and things like that. . . . I think it is purely the old traditional sort of workshop kind of study. I think they will be surprised.

So woodwork for girls was legitimate as long as it was linked to 'artistic' activities and not as part of a formal basis for learning fundamental techniques and skills such as joinery, etc. This was something that would come later and be taught to senior boys.

In a group discussion I held one evening with some of the parents, I asked how they felt about their daughters doing woodwork or handicraft, and boys doing home economics. Contrary to the impression given by the above, the immediate response, with both men and women trying to enter the discussion, was approval and general acceptance, but with certain provisos: 'I think that it is a jolly good idea. When they grow up they will probably live on their own anyway'; 'It's quite a nice idea, occasionally' (from a father), 'as you say, like, women doing most things like welding, woodwork, everything, you know, like, probably twenty years back it would have been wrong, but now you accept it, you know; but there are some jobs, some things that women don't do, there are some things'. He did not elaborate on this point. And whilst this particular father recognized that the scope of women's work had altered, he was certainly not convinced that girls doing woodwork would enable them to enter areas previously dominated by men. But his views were met with laughter and he said defensively that 'women only left the job for us. Bascially woman is equal of man'. But this did not get much support, apart from one woman who said:

> I am terribly against these schools that take girls and lead them to the typing pools and hope that they will get a nice little office job. I don't know, perhaps many girls would like it. It is a jolly good thing to know. Let them learn all things, let them learn to type, let them learn shorthand yes, but also let them do the other things.

For the rest they were content to see girls do woodwork as long as it was restricted to the privacy of their homes. It was not seen in terms of aiding them to obtain qualifications or skills in technology. Indeed, their views permitted them to accept a boy doing needlework as long as it was seen as a hobby. 'There is no reason why a boy who wants to be an engineer shouldn't do needlework, not as a job, but as an interest, a hobby.' Provided the boy was doing a man's job it would be legitimate for him to pursue a hobby that could be defined as feminine. This led one father to discuss the implications of boys doing needlework and cookery. 'It is probably more difficult for a boy to accept doing needlework and cookery than it is for a girl to do woodwork.' Interestingly a girl's femininity was not threatened by her doing woodwork. The reason for this could lie simply in the fact that nobody took girls' attending classes seriously, nor did it amount to anything more than acquiring a particular skill which could be of use in the privacy of the home. As such, it was in keeping with their major role and therefore their femininity was not at stake. The father who raised the question of boys doing needlework speculated that the time would come when boys would do needlework but that 'it will take time before everybody accepts the fact that doing needlework is not cissy. Cookery is perhaps not as bad, but needlework is more feminine than cookery'.

Some of the parents had had sons who had done needlework at junior school but, whilst they had accepted this at that time, they were cautious about the potential problems. As one parent put it, 'We are very careful not to give him any impression that he was doing anything girlish. But I think if anybody had said to him, "Oh, you are a girl. . . " '. The sentence was not completed but the implication was quite clear. Such activities would have immediately been banished had their son's masculinity been doubted.

The only serious objection to girls doing needlework seemed to have come from the parent who had expressed her concern to the Head and was more interested in her daughter's pursuit of 'academic' subjects. Apart from that, this form of 'integration' on the whole seemed quite acceptable to the parents. It is interesting, though, to note how the introduction of this topic led the parents on to discuss the implications for their sons doing traditionally female subjects. For them there was a strong element of doubt about their sons doing home economics, particularly if it included needlework.

These comments on the curriculum by Mr Trim and Mr Burns do not alert one to the possible conflicts and tensions which can arise between members of staff on the content of the material they wish to teach. These conflicts may spill over into other struggles between the staff. A brief description of what occurred with the Humanities team provides an interesting example of the type of struggle that may take place within a school and how the changes they wished to introduce were prevented.

The Humanities programme represented a serious attempt to integrate various subjects. The term 'Humanities' referred to the interdisciplinary course devised to include English, history, geography and moral education. Mr Trim originally emphasized the importance of this development and said it could represent a milestone in educational terms, a view which Mr Burns publicly shared. Mr Trim emphasized that Humanities would break down the discipline boundaries. Implementation and realization of these ideas were left to Mr Warne, an enthusiastic teacher who headed the Humanities team, all of whom were young, mostly inexperienced, and two of whom were probationary teachers in their first jobs and first year of teaching. Mr Warne, whose subject was English, argued quite correctly that it was impossible to separate history and geography from English: 'The problem is that English underpins everything else and really it is a core subject on the Arts and Humanities side. It is the means of communication, like maths is in physics.' From the outset he was dedicated to integrating these subjects and this principle was adopted by the other teachers appointed that year.

The course team did not minimize the problems that needed resolution if they were to realize their goals. Mr Warne always emphasized the need for all the staff involved to engage in detailed planning so that everyone knew what everyone else was doing at any one time.

It is not surprising that issues relating to gender differences were not high on their list of priorities, given the staff's dedication to pursue this policy, to create a new work programme and to fulfil the many calls made on their time outside the classroom. They seemed to take it for granted that no discrimination would take place and that the girls would not be disadvantaged in any way. This was, after all, the early 1970s, in which consciousness about the women's movement had reached an all-time high.

For the first eighteen months or so there was a Herculean effort on the part of the teachers to have a fully integrated Humanities course. The original group of teachers met regularly in the evenings at one or other of their homes with the specific aim of discussing the contents of the course, how to integrate the different disciplines, how to prepare the necessary material and how to combine all this with the problems surrounding English as a written language. Their efforts reflected the enthusiasm they felt, not only for their own project but also for the aim of creating a new and stimulating environment for their pupils. There was no talk amongst them of devising specific strategies for what Mr Trim clearly saw as an underprivileged group. The principle adopted by the Humanities team was to teach their pupils in the best way they could devise. The team did not take into account class membership of the pupils and this element did not dictate the content of form of the material to be taught. Rather, they were concerned with the more abstract nature of their material and the accompanying practical problems that their venture induced.

However much Mr Trim paid lip service to an interdisciplinary approach, his enthusiasm for this scheme soon waned and reflected his disenchantment with the Humanities group as a whole. This became apparent in the planning sessions he held with Mr Burns and at which I was present.

After the scheme had been operating for three months he voiced his doubts, claiming that the scheme was 'sacrificing depth for study'. He became more and more uneasy about the work of this group. Although he represented their deficiencies in terms of the content of their work, his disenchantment stemmed from the emergence of this group as an oppositional force within the school.

As a direct result of their constant meetings and working together as a team, this group of teachers emerged as one with a distinct character, presenting a unified voice on many policy issues at staff meetings. For example, they were anxious to democratize decisions and wanted to participate fully in the running of the school. They consistently questioned Mr Trim's decisions publicly at staff meetings. This was, originally, in conformity with the ideals Mr Trim himself had propagated, namely that the staff would all be directly involved in decision-making and, in the first few months of the school's history, he had actively encouraged staff to do so. However, as soon as his own authority was questioned, he drew a line and soon surrounded himself with teachers who did not question his decisions and whose support he could rely on wholeheartedly. The polarization which followed split the staff into two distinct camps, with the Humanities team, together with two other staff members, representing an opposing force. All subsequent staff appointments over the next eighteen months – and there was to be a massive increase in the number of staff – would be made very carefully, ensuring a consolidation of Mr Trim's position of authority.

The first new appointment was a geography specialist. The teacher concerned had an impeccable academic background (Oxbridge degree), a great deal of experience and in the interview made it quite clear that she wanted control over her subject area, thereby threatening the continuation of an integrated programme.

In point of fact, although there were a number of conflicts initially, Mrs Graham did cooperate with the team and did not disrupt their programme. Although her appointment did not have the desired effect, Mr Trim adopted other strategies and effectively undermined their morale through a variety of techniques. One was to isolate the group by having private 'morning tea' with other staff members before school; then he denied any of them promotion at the end of the year in spite of tremendous effort and time put in during the course of the year. By the end of the school's second year, all but one member of the original Humanities staff had resigned from the school.

It was impossible to assess the success of the Humanities team's efforts over such a short period of time. There were difficulties from the outset. They had come together at the beginning of the term, and had had to cope with problems that a new school was bound to experience, with all the makeshift arrangements that had to be made. Two of the team were probationary teachers and the other two had not had a great deal of experience anyway. Mr Warne, the head of the scheme, was currently completing a part-time degree and had this to contend with, as well as the coordinating tasks. The team had to devise a complex programme, while at the same time devoting a great deal of energy to extra-curricular activities to which they were all committed. In addition, and this is probably the major problem, to integrate subjects required extensive and highly structured plans which the group could not meet, especially as many of their meetings were devoted to the solution of technical problems, such as the reproduction of materials and worksheets, rather than with details of what should constitute the content and how the integration would or could be effected.

In order, therefore, to effect a major and permanent change in the curriculum, it is necessary to have the support of those who have positions of authority. The interdisciplinary effort in the Humanities programme failed because of the internal opposition the team experienced. This is likely to apply to any new programme which either directly or indirectly threatens the status quo.

Another source of discontent amongst the staff can arise through problems associated with allocation of time for particular lessons and external interference in the content of the lessons. Both these examples were experienced by Mr Leon, the science teacher.

Like many comprehensive schools, Berkeley had a general intro-ductory science course, the nature of the course having been deter-mined by the school's scientific adviser. Mr Leon, the first science teacher appointed, expressed his discontent at this. Apart from his overall criticism of the nature of scientific teaching, he complained that he had been thrust into teaching a particular syllabus in accordance with the authority's scientific adviser. He personally would have preferred teaching scientific principles through the study of the history of science and the development of scientific methods, rather than through the employment of abstract principles and the introduction of a set of empirical skills which this particular syllabus called for. In addition, he objected to the manner in which the timetable allocation was made for science classes. He had only three periods a week for science, one of which was a double period and the other a single period. The latter he considered a waste, as the time spent in setting out and clearing away equipment ate into the period and left little time for either teaching or practical work. Here is an example of difficulties relating to an important part of the curriculum, none of which have any bearing on gender differences. Mr Leon's concern was with how best to make pupils aware of scientific principles.

Conclusion

The introduction to this chapter referred to analyses which maintained that control over the new generation was exercised through their differential access to knowledge in the education system. Others, such as Willis (1977), focused on the dominant role of peer group culture, thereby minimizing the role of education and the process of the transmission of knowledge. These discourses failed to take account, significantly if at all, of gender differences. When analyses have specifically referred to gender differences then factors of class and culture tend to be ignored.

This chapter has set out to take account of these factors empirically through examining the discourses of some of those who determine the conditions and, consequently, the selection of those aspects of the curriculum generally available. The empirical evidence demonstrates just how complex the educational system is.

Although Mr Trim's primary goal was creating and maintaining control over the pupils through various disciplinary procedures, his concern in regard to what knowledge would be available to the pupils was dictated by what he regarded as the specific needs of the working-class pupils who constituted the bulk of the school's intake. He clearly thought the school would bring 'culture' into their lives. Mr Burns' ideas were more clearly defined than this. He considered that the pupils in this school would not take public examinations because of their working-class origins.

It was the class composition of the pupils which ultimately determined the level at which subjects would be taught. Given that

Berkeley, like all comprehensives, is charged with providing a general education for its pupils, all pupils are required, in practice, to take a range of subjects including 'academic' subjects all the way through. But it is the level at which all subjects, particularly the academic ones, are taught which is of paramount importance because they determine the future life chances of most of the pupils. Their access to occupations and further and higher education are directly linked to the level of certification attained. This level was spelled out by Mr Burns through his emphasis on the Mode III examination system. Whilst the Mode III system opened up the possibility of devising interesting and meaningful syllabuses, nevertheless there was a limitation on their effectiveness in providing pupils with acceptable levels of certification. To this extent then, both men played crucial roles in setting the scope and limits of the school curriculum. They were responsible for a set of conditions in which the pupils as a whole would be disadvantaged in that they were neither given full encouragement or access to standards and courses which would provide the pathway to positions of power and authority within the society.

Teachers have always been fully aware of the contradictions implicit in this system and have been torn between providing their pupils with an interesting and progressive education, or teaching in order to advance pupils' chances of successfully competing in the public examinations. This tension was not a problem at Berkeley in the early years as the 'normalizing judgments' would not take place for several years and the pupils' choices would not have to be dealt with until the end of the third year. The immediate concern was with problems associated with teaching mixed-ability groups, and effecting integration in the Humanities programme, amongst other things.

Yet both Mr Trim and Mr Burns wished to appear 'progressive' and alert to educational requirements through the innovative measures they were proposing. The first of these, which Mr Trim emphasized, was the breaking down of discipline boundaries through the introduction of Humanities. But his aims were soon overridden by his need to counter the influence of the group which constituted this team because of their opposition to many of his decisions and plans. This scheme dissolved by the end of the second year and the school reverted to the normal subject boundaries. The second was the integration that would occur across the board. No differentiation would be made between boys and girls. In effect this would occur in three areas: HE, craft and PE.

The question that now arises is how successful an integration programme could be in countering sexist practices in the school. Mr Trim was proud of the principle of integration and claimed that this would ensure that girls and boys had access to all subjects. But in spite of his claims, the comments made by Mr Trim and the other senior staff indicated that their commitment to such practices was cosmetic and did not go very far. Although Mr Trim, Mr Burns and Mr David all supported this scheme publicly, it is clear from their comments that none of these men took the principle of integration seriously. They expressed scepticism and none anticipated extending the teaching beyond the first three years of secondary school because, they argued, there were limited resources.

Integration was to occur in HE, craft, and PE. The provisions in the first two areas was to be made in such a way that existing forms of gender specific division of labour and ideologies relating to these would not be questioned, as for example, the use girls could make of skills learned in woodwork classes as women in their own homes. The extent of Mr Trim's conception – and this applied to the other male staff as well – of breaking down gender differences did not extend beyond home-oriented activities. Whether it was boys doing home economics or girls doing craft work, the value of such 'innovatory' teaching was defined in relation to practical use for both boys and girls in their homes as adults. The curriculum provisions were in accordance with existing and acceptable forms of division of labour, particularly in the home. There was no attempt to confront questions which might arise from a reformulation of these divisions. Nor were questions on the division of labour at work questioned.

The availability of integrated teaching programmes in themselves cannot overcome the differentials operating between boys and girls in the schooling system. Whilst such teaching schemes expose both groups to aspects of knowledge they would not otherwise experience, such exposure cannot ensure a breakdown of gender differences. The breakdown has to occur at all levels, ideological and practical, both at home and at work.

To sum up the question relating to the transmission of knowledge, Berkeley, and the way in which the school was organized, confirmed the theoretical discussions which point to a differentiation in the education which working-class children may receive in contrast with that of middle-class pupils. These differences were legitimized by a number of ideologies expressed by the staff who held positions of authority and responsibility. Their concern to tackle gender differences was nothing more than cosmetic and the way in which the curriculum was conceived would not counteract existing social conditions.

CHAPTER EIGHT

The curriculum at Berkeley

Introduction

At the most general level, the curriculum is a major mechanism in the establishment and maintenance of one of the specific forms of control over the school population, including the teachers, as discussed in the last chapter. The control is more obvious when class factors are considered than is the case with gender differences.

Given the range in content as well as in standards attained in all school subjects, it is extremely difficult to generalize about the way in which school subjects have a differential and decisive effect on girls and boys. And yet girls do emerge from school with different expectations and different subject groupings.

To identify systematically those aspects of the curriculum which contribute to maintaining traditional gender differences is a complex task. To do so, subject areas which are unequivocally gender specific, such as home economics and craft, need to be examined. These are the only two subjects in the curriculum (both in the non-academic section) which are directly and openly related to the major divisions. Ideologically and in practical terms they are characteristic of female and male roles in society. A third subject area in the non-academic sphere is physical education, in which gender differences are most apparent.

In the academic area these differences are not as obvious. The content, for example, of subject areas such as mathematics and science do not overtly distinguish between boys and girls because of their abstract nature. But it is the 'hidden curriculum' which contributes in no small measure to the perpetuation of gender differences. The 'hidden curriculum' may be conveyed through teacher expectations to the pupils, or in the presentation of the content of lessons. As Lobban (1978) says:

> The official curriculum details the skills the pupils are supposed to be learning, and the avowed aims of the school and the education system of which it is a part. A number of authors have shown that the pupil learns a variety of other things in addition to mastering or failing at academic skills. . . . The term 'hidden curriculum' is used to describe this learning (p. 52).

Whatever form the 'hidden curriculum' takes, the content may be presented to the pupils in such a way as to demarcate gender differences. In addition to this broad, blanket definition, it may be useful to draw distinctions between actual content, the often unwitting signification by teachers of what constitutes gender appropriate behaviour, and the actions and statements of the teachers which include their expectations regarding pupils' gender specific performance and attainment. All three elements will be commented upon in this section.

The separation of non-academic from academic subjects is a distinction that most closely approximates the convenient mental/ manual division in the labour force. The former is a somewhat crude and over-simplified division but the relevance of this will be examined in detail in the following chapter, given the importance attached to particular qualifications, particularly mathematics and sciences where gender differences are discussed.

This chapter will examine the curriculum as a whole as it was presented at Berkeley, concentrating on HE, craft, and PE in the 'non-academic section', and Mathematics, Science and Humanities in the 'academic' section. It will describe some of the teachers' ideologies about their particular specialist areas, where these link directly with gender differentiation and give examples of some of the ways in which the 'hidden curriculum' operates.

It is important to recognize that owing to the diverse nature of the curriculum, there is a limit to the amount of time spent overall on any one subject, as the following table indicates. It details the amount of time per period allocated to each subject. This distribution should be recalled when the influence or importance of any one subject is considered. Mathematics, for example, has only three periods in any one week! Music was the only subject with a single period. The Humanities block with seven periods was supposed to cover English, history and geography, each of which was allocated two periods a week.

Table 1: First Year Timetable

Subject	Double period	Single period	Total per week
Tutorial		1	1
English/Humanities	3	1	7
French		2	2
Science	1	2	4
Art	1		2
Games	1	1	3
Maths	1	1	3
Music		1	1
Handicraft	1		2
Physical education	1		2
Home economics	1		2

At Berkeley, as already mentioned, teaching in the first three years was to be conducted in mixed-ability groups, a principle established from the outset. Furthermore, and this was a point which Mr Trim emphasized proudly, there was to be no separation between boys and girls in any subject, at least in the first three years!

Home economics (2 periods per week)

Home economics, the current term for classes covering cookery, home management, child care, sex education and so on, has a long history associated specifically with domestic training and needlework. The latter was introduced in many elementary schools by 1840 before cookery, although the level of teaching, as with other subjects, was far from satisfactory. By 1870 a 'mild form of domestic training for girls' was introduced, and as J. Kamm (1965) pointed out, 'in addition to the usual sewing and knitting, cookery lessons – at first only theoretical – were started after 1870, together with lessons in hygiene and elementary housewifery and by 1888 more time was spent on domestic subjects'. This applied, of course, to the elementary schools.

Home economics, as it is now known, therefore has a long history with particular emphasis on the imparting of 'useful knowledge' to working-class girls in particular who, as the policy makers consistently pointed out, needed to learn the rudiments of hygiene and preparation of food in order to contribute to the health of the working population. British sensibilities had been rudely shocked at the turn of the century when it became apparent that the ordinary soldier serving in the Anglo–Boer War was a sickly, puny individual, unable to discharge military duties.

Over the years, changes have obviously occurred, but home economics still remains an almost exclusively girls' subject. By 1984, of 5,041 candidates at 'A' level in 'Domestic Subjects', 36 were boys, of whom 26 or 72 per cent passed; this contrasts with 5,005 girl entrants, of whom 65 per cent or 3,264 passed.

Mrs White, the first appointment in home economics, had just completed her training as a mature student. At college she had been taught that home economics represented a 'skill in cookery, nutrition, meal planning and so on' and she hoped to concentrate on cooking and associated aspects of nutrition. She said that at college they had focused on teaching methods and how to 'get it across to the pupils'. She denied that home economics was primarily concerned with girls as future housewives. She claimed that the current feeling in the early 1970s was that fast foods and convenience foods would become more readily available, with the result that 'we are all going to be eating pills, boys and girls alike', so that cookery would become a leisure pursuit, 'something like flower arrangement now'. She failed to see that 'flower arrangement' courses were the stereotypical courses available for housebound women seeking some creative hobby!

Her ideas became translated somewhat differently when she described the aim of the actual teaching programme she had devised. The main aim would basically be 'to enable both boys and girls to cope with any situation which arises when they leave school, whether they are living on their own, married or whatever'. They would learn 'practical things', but she would include the theoretical aspects 'covering the greater role that nutrition plays in modern life'. She summed it all up when she repeated that the course would 'equip them to cope with life when they leave school . . . so that they can go home and cook themselves a reasonable sort of meal', an ideology which the children shared (see Chapter 9). She did not overlook the fact that many of the girls she taught would leave school and marry and she was concerned that they would be able to 'cope with feeding a toddler' and having 'to cope with an old grannie'. To this extent she was realistic about the future role of many of her girl pupils who would undoubtedly marry and set up homes of their own. Nor did she anticipate that the boys would play a significant role in either child care or looking after ageing relatives.

A similar view was held by Mrs Craig, a woman in her mid-forties with many years' teaching experience who was appointed in the second year as head of this section. Home economics was 'dead easy', she said, and was designed to 'make kids cope with a home and family situation'. Neither woman spoke about boys studying this at senior level. It simply did not arise. Home economics, although available for boys at the lower end of the school, would remain almost exclusively female at the senior end.

A part of the HE department was needlework. Mrs Francis, the woman appointed with special responsibilities for needlework, clearly shared some of Mr Trim's views about the potential creativity of her subject. She said that if boys were to be included in the needlework classes then it would be necessary not to teach the basic seams anymore, which comprised orthodox needlework syllabus, but introduce them to 'the more creative side of needlework' which included macramé, drawn thread work, and embroidery. She thought the girls would benefit from the extension of the course and one can only presume that she was assured that girls, by virtue of being female, would have 'mastered' these basic techniques. This view of needlework being more than 'just making dresses' was expressed by Mr David, who shared Mr Trim's notion of needlework being creative and artistic. 'I mean, there is a lot of art to needlework', he asserted. But he was less sure than Mr Trim about the value of introducing this new needlework to boys.

This immediately raises questions about what form the needlework classes would have taken if boys were to have been excluded. It suggests that it is acceptable to present girls with orthodox needlework syllabuses, but presumably such dull, boring work would have not proved suitable for boys. To this extent, Mrs Francis' attitude does support some of the claims by many feminist writers that the more interesting work is seen to be the province of boys whilst girls may be given the less demanding, less interesting, more conventional type of syllabus.

The prevailing message is that boys doing cookery is tolerated, provided that their masculinity is not threatened. Specialization in HE at senior level for boys was an option they did not entertain. Needlework for boys might barely be tolerated, provided it was in the realm of creative work which could be seen in commercial terms, i.e. fashion designer and not just as a hobby.

All three teachers referred to the exception. This was the participation by senior 'difficult boys' who attended cookery classes, already referred to in Chapter 5. As is well known, the older the pupils, the more difficult are problems of classroom control. Mrs White had found in teaching practice that fourth year cookery classes were inundated with boys keen on 'getting into the kitchen and being let loose on gas cookers'. Mrs Criag said all the truants would turn up for cooking:

> They like doing practical things so they don't miss the lesson. . . . They have something to show for it at the end of the lesson. And of course it is therapeutic, this playing with flour and water. They like it, whatever age they are, and it is amazing that truancy is quite alright from our point of view.

Truancy did not constitute a problem in her classroom. Nor did she experience a problem with the boys having to take the aprons home for washing. Using what amounts to strong sexist expression, she said, 'Even with a bitch of a cookery teacher, they will come rolling in and you have to cut down the class size and somebody is going to get hurt.' The third teacher, Mrs Francis, held similar views, an account of which was given in Chapter 5.

The fact that cookery is successful with older, difficult boys is surprising, especially given that cookery is so closely identified with femininity. As was suggested in Chapter 5, sexuality and some of its associations partially accounted for this. Provided boys' masculinity has been well established, they are unlikely to suffer identity crises or pejorative labelling such as being termed a cissy or a 'poofter' for doing such feminine subjects as cooking. Further their attendance at HE classes is done on a group basis and it would seem that they experience immediate gratification on the completion of a particular task; at the end of the day they have produced a concrete object (non-alienated labour).

Craft (2 periods per week)

In an interesting article on the introduction of craft work to girls, Grant (1983) singled it out as 'the most strongly sex-stereotyped area of the secondary school curriculum' (p. 216). He argued that girls should be taught craft because of a number of advantages that would accrue. In the course of acquiring these skills they would enhance their employment prospects in an increasingly techno-logically-oriented society, although how this would occur was something he failed to address.[1] It could have a positive effect on their cognitive processes. Knowledge about consumer goods would become accessible and they would cease to be technologically illiterate. He felt that basic interest in such subject areas could be developed in girls, through stimulation.

As pointed out earlier, Mr Trim viewed the availability of craft courses for girls in the first three years of school as a major step forward in breaking down gender barriers: the mere act of making such a subject available appeared an end in itself. He qualified his comments on the availability of this. Woodwork for girls as a straightforward acquisition of skills would be of use to them as adult women in their own homes. Consequently he saw no need to extend the training beyond the first three years, at the most, of school; the senior years would be devoted to the boys.

The subject was to be taught by Mr David who, at the age of forty-five, was the oldest member of staff. He had left school at fourteen and had been apprenticed as a carpenter/joiner. He had obtained a City and Guilds Certificate, a vocational qualification, through part-time study and worked in the building trade until the age of thirty-one when he had taken up teaching in a small boys' school. He said he had felt self-conscious about his lack of formal academic training, particularly given the increasing number of teachers with university degrees, and so recently had had a year's secondment to study. This, he said, had been very important in that it had established for him a link between art and woodwork. The projects he proposed would be of an artistic nature and so enable him to include girls in his class. Clearly he could not teach girls woodwork in the same way as he had previously taught the boys. Women are seen by him as the arbiters of good taste. He had told his class that his wife always selected the pattern of wallpapers and the coloured paint for their own home. He clearly defined girls and women entirely in regard to their home-making roles, and the provision of woodwork for girls was to accommodate this vision.

Observations in Mr David's class provided clear cut examples in which the 'hidden curriculum' operates and this will be discussed below.

Physical education (PE) and games (5 periods per week)

PE is assured a place in all secondary school curricula in spite of its low status in the school hierarchy. PE as such has a long history with its provisions and forms varying in the nineteenth century according to class and gender. Hargreaves (1977) suggested that its development was linked to the dominance of the Protestant Ethic[2] with its pejorative attitude towards 'enjoyable and wasteful pastimes' which the middle classes condemned as one of the reasons for the ruin of the working classes while they upheld the virtues of 'competitiveness, victory, aggression, aestheticism, and training and dedication' (quoting Charles Crichter). Such qualities were thought to be realizable in games such as rugby and cricket which were the main activities in boys' public schools. Organized games in girls' public schools came much later. To begin with, there was a concentration on specific calisthenic exercises for them. 'The vigorous exercise which boys get from cricket, etc., must be supplied in the case of girls by walking and calisthenic exercises, skipping, etc, etc,' said Miss Beale in her evidence to the Schools Inquiry Commission in 1868 (quoted by Kamm, 1965). The introduction of Swedish gymnastics was welcomed by Miss Beale. For both working-class girls and boys in elementary schools, however, PE took the form largely of military-type drill (Browne et al., 1983). So PE has both a class and gender differentiated history.

Ideas expressed on PE are constantly being reworked and reconsidered. Yates (1977), in an article dealing with the ideology of PE, identified three distinct abstract aspects: leisure, movement and skill, which are removed from class and gender differences. He said in spite of a great deal of attention paid to all three aspects no major curriculum innovations had been developed, but there has been change in emphasis in school from physical training to physical education as such. Movement studies, for example, represented a welcome change from an emphasis on sports and games to what he saw as a creative element in PE. Such comments, however, recognize neither class nor gender differences.

Concentrating on gender differences, a useful distinction may be drawn between PE and Sports, both of which are the concern of the PE department. Sporting activities are noticeably gender specific, and their cultural identity is such that the question of integration in sports in secondary schools is almost unthinkable at the present.

Mr Trim's avowed policy of running a fully integrated school did not extend to the sporting activities of PE. However, his policy was to insist that boys and girls would do PE together. By the end of the first year this was no longer the case and fully segregated classes had been adopted. Various reasons were given for this reversal. The Head's main argument was that some parents had reported that the boys had laughed at the girls in their knickers and he could not permit this to happen, so he banned mixed classes. There was no question of confronting the boys and discussing their reaction, indicating his lack of serious intent to ensure that integrated classes could exist, or considering why the girls should have experienced embarrassment.

Mr Burns, on the other hand, offered a completely different reason for the reversal of the decision to hold integrated PE classes. He said that they had experienced problems with the woman PE teacher and here he was referring to problems of girls' attendance at games. It is interesting to note, in passing, that a woman had been appointed in the first year of the school's life, but in the second year the second appointment was a man who was also made head of PE.

Mr Burns had added that Miss Brand, the PE teacher, had asked for a man to be appointed, and had also opted for holding separate classes. When asked about this, Miss Brand said that she had wanted to introduce modern dance but could not do so in mixed classes. She said that modern dance was a means of expressing oneself and she was keen for the girls to experience this. She herself had discovered the value of dance while at college. Boys, she felt, would not react favourably to dance 'as they would regard it as cissy and not very nice, which in turn would affect the girls' enjoyment of it'. When interviewed, the new head of PE said that he had never entertained the notion that PE should be integrated. Girls simply did not concern him, although he claimed that integration operated between boys and girls in athletics, rounders and tennis. But he said this at the height of summer when track events were being offered to both boys and girls, as well as those games more directly associated with the summer months. And he anticipated that there would be even more mixed games by the fifth and sixth years. He hastened to add that he did not find girls less able than the boys, for 'the girls were every bit as strong as the boys, and boys and girls can achieve the same standard in this work', referring specifically to athletics and rounders, both summertime activities.

These varied views of the teachers suggest that there is no single cause for the reversal of Mr Trim's decision. PE is composed of both physical exercise and games, and both these activities are linked to sets of beliefs about the differences between men and women. For one thing, as Browne et al. (1983) point out, there is the notion that women and girls are modest and that men are stronger. This is a convenient way of masking issues surrounding sexuality. Girls who perform PE in scanty clothes may be viewed in sexual terms. This has to be avoided in schools which suppress questions relating to sexuality as far as possible. Girls who mature physically faster and more visibly than boys have to be shielded from the boys' gaze. Integration therefore is not a feasible option under the present circumstances.

Turning to sporting activities, there are massive differences in the status of girls' and boys' sports, as discussed in Chapter 2 in reference to playground activities. Football dominates boys' lives from an early age, and not to play football or not to have an interest in the game can marginalize a boy immediately. Furthermore:

> Pupils see the status of sport in society reflected in the school department. The head of department is male, since men's sport is more important than women's sport. . . . Announcing football results in assembly also gives competitive sports, mostly male, undue importance. So girls learn that PE is more important for boys than it is for them. (Browne et al., 1983, p. 273).

Nor were games at all popular with the majority of the girls or amongst the women teachers who were obliged to do some games' duties.

Where gender differences are most striking is in the labelling process that accompanies non-participation in sports. As pointed out elsewhere, the failure of boys to do PE or play football can damage their reputations, as occurred with Graham. Also, they could not express interest or enjoy certain activities like the 'creative dancing' so admired by Miss Brand without being labelled 'cissy'. Girls, on the other hand, had little danger of being labelled because, quite simply, they were excluded from doing anything which could be labelled masculine. Their reputations were not at stake and resisting participation in PE or Games conformed with being feminine.

The level of girls' participation in team games or sports appears to be of an individualistic nature, rather than on the basis of team work. This is in keeping with the ideology that emphasizes individualism and the development of the self. Amongst adolescents this ideology is particularly strong and is inextricably connected to their developing sense of sexuality. In accordance then with this duality – that is, the development of the self and the concentration on sexuality – it comes as no surprise to hear that in only one particular area girls' participation is high, and that is in athletics. Mr Barry, the head of PE, said that the reason for this was not that girls enjoyed it but rather they did so because they had an audience of boys. And he found the reverse occurred, that is, the boys did it better because of the presence of girls. Two elements – one of competition and the other of impressing members of the opposite sex – were included. Girls certainly do not have an audience of boys when they play hockey or netball; these are team games with a small female audience.

Associated with this presentation of themselves as sexual objects is their accompanying sense of femininity. Now, the 'natural' progress of PE is often seen in terms of developing the physique, or muscle power. This is a desirable quality amongst boys but hardly that amongst girls. The stereotypical desirable female form is not one of developed muscles, so the well-developed muscular woman PE teacher is seldom taken as a role model by the girls. However, the well-developed male teacher often epitomizes the ideal masculine type and is a model for most of the boys. He may even, through his physical being, exert a certain amount of control over the pupils (see Chapter 5).

The above discussion has concentrated on those subject areas in which differentiation on gender lines is built into their content. There is a direct link with divisions of labour in society and their legitimating ideologies where HE and craft are concerned. PE is linked to gender specific cultural formations. Together these three areas comprised 29 per cent of pupils' formal lessons (taking the total number of lessons as twenty-seven, excluding the one tutorial period).

In regard to the content of the other parts of the curriculum, there are those of an abstract nature, such as mathematics and science, in which there are basic principles which may be unrelated to gender differences. It is the ways in which these subjects are taught and their representations that contain distinctions relevant to gender differentiation. Similarly with music and art. Here the distinction may apply in reference to the preponderance of male musicians and artists. Together these subject areas comprised ten periods in a week, or 37 per cent of the school's timetable. Over a third of pupils' time was spent, therefore, in subject areas of which the content was not gender specific.

Mathematics and science
(3 and 4 periods per week respectively)

Mathematics and science are two subject areas which have generated a great deal of research and comment for the obvious reasons that knowledge and understanding of these areas open up the possibility of work in technology and its multifarious ramifications. It also has a direct bearing on everyday life.

As is well known there are far fewer girls who qualify in these subjects than do boys. For many years now this has been recognized and every now and again when shortages of skilled personnel in technology is discussed, suggestions are made that the untapped resources from girls could alleviate the problem. Over the last few years, with growing recognition of differences in relation to gender performance at school, papers such as the *Times Educational Supplement* have highlighted the differences. The problem remains one of accounting for why these differences occur.

It is generally recognized that girls' under achievement is largely due to social forces (Kelly, 1981) and not because of any inherent differences in their genetic makeup. Mixed classes have been identified as a major factor in this. Arnot (1984) said that the: 'Tendency overall was, therefore, that boys and girls were more polarised into the science/arts split in mixed schools than in single-sex schools' (p. 51). Shaw (1984) commented on experiments in mathematics classes which showed that girls benefited and made marked progress in single-sex mathematics sets. Similarly Hawes, a senior lecturer in physics at Avery Hill College of Education, said: 'I believe that as far as possible in mixed schools it should be a matter of policy that the third, fourth and fifth year girls are separated from the boys to be taught their physics and chemistry' (*Times Educational Supplement*, 3 July 1981). Smith (1984) has argued that it is necessary to qualify all supporting evidence in regard to such claims. Others have focused on the content of the subject matter. Harding (1980) blamed the nature of science teaching and its content. A group of teachers from two large comprehensive schools have emphasized the need to make mathematics more relevant, interesting and comprehensible for girls (Stantonbury Campus Sexism in Education Group, Bridgewater Hall School, 1984). This same group pointed out that textbooks represent science as a male occupation and most scientists as male. To counter this, apart from a change in actual representations in text books, the curriculum content has also to be examined and altered. The most extensive study which involved action research, was Girls into Science and Technology (GIST) reported on by Kelly et al. (1984). The success of the project in ten schools was limited. They found that there was a decline in stereotyping in the 'actions' schools, with only slightly more positive views towards science by the girls, in spite of all the efforts. They were disappointed to find a reluctance on the part of the teachers to acknowledge any changes in themselves arising out of the project (Whyte et al., 1985).

In the final analysis neither mathematics nor science are of any considerable interest to a substantial number of girls and boys. At a conference held at Homerton College in June 1987, Alison Kelly called for a humanizing of science rather than its presentation as a series of isolated facts. She referred to the work of the Association of Science Education, a large and significant group concerned with curriculum changes. Since 1976 it has produced a variety of working papers calling for a move towards science for all; and away from the developments by Nuffield Science which Kelly claims were specifically aimed at getting clever boys to do science, particularly at select schools.

But at Berkeley the questions of low level attainment in scientific and mathematical knowledge were not addressed at this early stage. All pupils were taught mathematics (like all other subjects) in mixed-ability classes.

Teaching mixed-ability groups has direct consequences for the slower pupils. They simply fall behind more and more in what seems to be geometric proportions as time passes. Given that mathematics is built on a series of fundamental principles, failure to comprehend the one level has direct consequences for subsequent understanding. The lack of repetitive exercises which reinforce and solidify the basic principles is an element among the slower learners who never appear to grasp completely the first step before following on to the next. What occurs both in the classroom and at home is that the quicker and 'cleverer' pupils do more mathematical work than the slower pupils. They complete the work in class and are able to repeat such exercises at home in the course of doing their homework. The slower pupils never can catch up. Even though mathematics is taught all the way through school, as a compulsory subject, the level at which it is taught in the senior years is little less than arithmetic.

What emerged in the mathematics class in the first two years was the marked contrast between those who could follow the simple mathematics and those who could not. The divide did not appear to be gender-related at all. There were very few who did do well in mathematics and the top positions were filled equally by two boys and two girls. The subsequent failure of these two girls to pursue mathematics or the physical sciences was attributed to their increasing interest in their social life and related sexual concerns. This coincided with an overall decline in their interest in school work *per se*.

The failure of the *vast* majority of pupils to study mathematics may have a simple and straightforward explanation at senior level and that is that at the early stages of secondary schooling they fall behind and are never able to catch up, whatever the cause of this may be.

Mr Burns did not appear to discriminate in favour of either boys or girls. He referred to the pupils as 'people' and maintained a strict discipline in the classroom. There was no evidence of boys receiving differential treatment in class. Mr Burns did recognize that parents could play an active role in encouraging pupils, as discussed in Chapter 7, and the number of parents willing to learn more about mathematics was limited.

During the course of Mr Leon's science classes there was, like the mathematics classes, no overt examples of differentiation between boys and girls. Mr Leon's overriding concern was with teaching his subject. He set up experiments for the whole class to do. What the field notes reveal is that there were a number of both boys and girls who successfully avoided doing any work at all during the course of these lessons. This was partly consistent with their overall behaviour in all lessons. The example of two girls stand out in particular. Neither Cheryl nor Monica completed any one task. As discussed in Chapter 2 they were adept in task avoidance, a pattern which was repeated in all the classes they attended. They either sat at their places doing nothing, or walked around. This walking around was something that several boys did as well to avoid doing the experiments. In the course of pretending to be interested in what others were doing, they successfully did nothing themselves. In science, as in all other subjects, it was the 'high achievers' who performed well and here, as in the mathematics class, two of the girls were the outstanding pupils, together with two of the boys, though in the end both girls dropped out of science and only one of the boys, Adam, continued with this subject.

Mr Jason, the science teacher appointed in the second year, had definite ideas about the form the syllabus should take. He said that in the first year there should be a broad introduction to general science, carrying out simple experiments. The second year should concentrate on academic attainments which he defined as learning how to evaluate experiments. The third year would introduce the pupils to physics, chemistry and biology, laying the foundations for future specialization.

He anticipated that by the end of the third year, pupils would be aware of the relationship between science subjects and job opportunities. In other words, he conceptualized scientific knowledge in vocational and practical terms. He said it was his practice to organize talks on different careers by people for pupils and their parents. He felt that the 'choice' of school subjects would be made more effectively if the pupils and their parents knew what prospects were available, although he said that pupils did have set ideas of what they wanted to do in the future and their choices were often affected by their likes and dislikes of their teachers.

He felt strongly that science should be closely related to everyday life. It would be 'useless talking about light rays and bacteria because these aspects of science were outside of the pupils' everyday life'. In other words, he set a definite limitation on the level of scientific knowledge that he regarded as suitable for his pupils. And it was in the course of elaborating on this point that the distinction he made between boys and girls became apparent, even though he had claimed that he fully supported an integrated curriculum which did not differentiate between boys and girls. In his view, the sciences 'are needed for girls and boys in their jobs – so many jobs that are now done require a knowledge of physics or chemistry and there can be no difference between the girls and boys'.

In spite of this he said that there was a difference between boys and girls in relation to the ways they reacted to science:

Girls in general would tend to look at the subject in relation to their enjoyment. They tend to be a bit girlish about snakes

215

and spiders and things like that. Boys, on the other hand, relate
to apparatus. Girls have a much more mature approach to
science. They will look at the experiment, their notes are
neater and more concise. In fact, the *more interesting* questions
all come from the girls; the boys are usually more interested
in the flashes and the bangs.

In accordance with his views, Mr Jason proposed tailoring a
scientific course which would cater to girls' interests, which he
said varied from those of boys and necessitated, as he said, various
practical measures. By way of illustrating his technique he cited
the following example. Oil was used in the production of face
cream, foods, make-up, perfumes, soap and commodities, such as
paint. To comprehend its use he proposed to get the girls to make
their own mascara, lipstick, and talcum powder. For boys, deodor-
ants and after-shave would be the items they could make. So the
course would be equal but different.

In this way Mr Jason introduced a contentious issue of how lessons
may be made relevant to pupils' lives. When a claim is made about
the relevance of the curriculum to girls' lives, there is the very real
danger of seeking a correspondence between girls' narcissistic
interests in themselves, their physical appearance and the content
of the course. In this instance Mr Jason was assuming that, if he
related science to make-up, scientific principles would become
acceptable and understood by the girls. What he failed to realize
was that he was introducing his pupils to empirical knowledge and
experimentation – how they themselves could create make-up utilizing a set of practices – without necessarily learning the
underlying principles or theories on which this knowledge was
based. That which constituted relevance to pupils' lives was that
which would appeal to them immediately and not that which was
necessarily dictated by the nature of the subject under study. Similarly it has been argued that, in order to make pupils more
mathematically skilled, one should introduce them to practical
problems of immediate concern such as, for girls, how to bake, or
dressmake. Again, the basic principles of the subject area may be
subsumed by the practical solutions. How successful such
strategies are needs very careful evaluation. On the surface there is
every possibility of divesting the disciplines of theoretical and
abstract content and replacing it with empirical, observable data.

Mr Jason's statements contain a number of confusions, contradictions and hidden meanings. In the first instance he claims that girls, unlike boys, only pursue subjects they 'enjoy'. Given that the school offers practically no selection in the first three years, and that whole sections of the curriculum are compulsory, is he arguing that girls reject all subjects they do not enjoy? Conversely, do boys pursue those subjects which they do *not* enjoy? Patently such a claim simply does not stand up to analysis. Talking to pupils reveals that there are huge sections of the curriculum which neither girls nor boys enjoy. Next, consider girls being 'girlish about snakes and spiders and things like that'. What constitutes girlishness? Presumably he is referring to a revulsion in handling reptiles and particular insects. Even if this were the case (and, again, there are many men who cannot handle either snakes or spiders), how crucial is the handling of such creatures to scientific knowledge? Does a nuclear physicist have to handle snakes and spiders? These traits of girls are then contrasted with those of boys whom he claims 'respond to apparatus'. Again, some boys do, but equally so do some girls, as the evidence in the classroom indicated. Yet, having made all these claims, Mr Jason confusingly asserts that girls are not only more mature than boys in terms of their handling scientific experiments but they even ask the 'more interesting questions'. How can Mr Jason account for all these contradictions? He does not attempt to do so as he is bound by his own ideological fix which clearly sees science, in general, as a boys' subject in spite of educational requirements which call for all pupils to have a general introduction to science, and girls' obvious ability to learn scientific data. He had definite expectations about girls' performance in relation to science and no doubt he would have transmitted these ideas in the course of his everyday practice within the classroom situation and this would have had an impact on the class. This is very different from the more general views which Mr Leon held about the subject. For Mr Leon, the pupils appeared as non-gendered subjects, into whom he wanted to induct scientific truths. In Mr Jason's case it was the gendered subjects who imposed a restraint on the subject matter.

Humanities (7 periods per week)

The remaining areas of the curriculum – English/Humanities and French – together had nine periods or 33 per cent of the timetable. Of these, French, with its linguistic distinction between masculine and feminine nouns may be seen to contribute to a recognition of gender differences through its construction. But when one examines English/Humanities there are obvious examples of gender differentiation in the content and in the 'hidden curriculum' of these subject areas.

Beginning with the actual *content* of the Humanities course, it was particularly in those classes in which history was taught that examples were apparent. History, as is well known, is one of those subjects which consistently has portrayed men as the active creators of our cultural heritage and women as passive, nurturing onlookers. Mrs Ivory was particularly prone to representing men and women in this fashion. Take her lesson on the Minoan Empire. What was discussed was its founding, the development of legends, and how legends reflected part of history. In the course of tackling the worksheets, a discussion ensued on the form of dress of the Minoan soldiers followed by a question by one of the boys about whether women went to war. Mrs Ivory emphatically replied 'no', her tone of voice indicating the absurdity of the question. But she paused and then corrected herself while recalling the Amazons. Had Mrs Ivory been attuned to feminist issues she might well have seized this opportunity for highlighting the particular role of women in relation to war. But this did not occur and she moved on to discuss the life of Spartan boys (all in the same lesson). She presented Spartan boys as children to be pitied, children who were taken away from their parents at the age of seven and put into barracks to toughen them up where they lived until the age of thirty. Although allowed to marry at the age of twenty, the young men were not allowed home to their wives for a further ten years. In the course of learning to fight, they were also taught general lessons and poetry.

This type of lesson, giving vignettes from historical epochs, was repeated many times. One lesson focused on the Vikings and the use of the great hall in which segregation between men and women occurred, with the women having their own hall but still being responsible for caring for their men, as in the pictorial depiction of a woman serving a meal to two men, and another bathing a man in a large wooden tub.

Both these examples illustrate several points. That which constitutes historical 'fact' and is portrayed as such within the classroom is often reduced to simple descriptions and divorced from historical content. This point may be best illustrated by taking the way in which the life of Spartan boys was depicted. Here all boys were defined in terms of being snatched away from the bosom of their families and systematically taught the rudiments of war-like behaviour before resuming 'family life' at the age of thirty. Family life was depicted as it exists in the present day western world. Boys were denied, by implication, a normal childhood and family life.

There was no recognition on the part of Mrs Ivory of the historical specificity of different forms of family life. Her simplistic portrayal ignored the complex social structure of that period in which the position of women was very different to that of women in advanced industrial societies; family relationships were not of a nuclear family kind; homosexuality between men was the order of the day; and the society was highly stratified, with slavery providing specific labour requirements, to mention but a few structural elements.

Therefore, to portray boys outside of this social formation, as though the normal forms of behaviour approximated that of contemporary family life, results in a distortion of the institutions of that community. The example of the Vikings' way of life was similarly interpreted, utilizing the present day nuclear family as the basis for comprehending what life was like amongst the Vikings.

Related to this is another aspect associated with this failure to depict situations in the context of the specific historical social formations. This is the unintended consequences of reinforcing the ideological statements about what constitutes women's and men's 'normal' roles throughout history, women as the wives and mothers, and men as the warriors and the adventurers.

That such statements occur again and again in the course of such lessons needs full recognition. They constitute an important feature of on-going aspects of both the actual and the 'hidden curriculum'.

The above discussion illustrates the ways in which the ideological views of the teacher – here reference has been made specifically to gender differences – are inserted into the formal curriculum. The effect of this is to reinforce stereotypical views about gender appropriate forms of behaviour. As will be appreciated the range is wide, from family life, to specific feminine/masculine interests. The pupils, as the recipients of this wisdom, are subjected to such influences covertly. These are examples of the 'hidden curriculum' as they may appear in all the subject areas.

Scripted forms of the 'hidden curriculum'

There is another aspect of the 'hidden curriculum' and this is more directly related to the processes of the scripted forms of behaviour referred to in Chapter 5. Examples will be given of the ways in which teachers impose on the class their views of what constitutes gender appropriate forms of behaviour.

Take Mr Sands' class. Mr Sands had recounted the mystery surrounding the disappearance of all hands from the boat, the *Marie Celeste*, which was found floating without any trace of its crew nor any indication of what had caused their total disappearance. He set the class the task of writing an account of the mystery. Whilst the children were busy completing the task, Mr Sands chatted with me (a common occurrence when I was observing in his classroom). In answer to my question of what type of reply he anticipated getting, he said there would be a difference between the boys and girls: 'There's a difference between the boys and girls in the context of the subject. The girls will write a more airy-fairy story whereas the boys will provide a practical solution to the problem'.

Although the boys were supposed to give down-to-earth, concrete, adventurous types of accounts and girls, presumably, to resort to supernatural, fairy-tale explanations, their written responses did not conform at all with this expectation. The reality was very different. There were a number of short answers which could not be classified in either way. They were written, in the main, with little command of the language, with minimal content, bad spelling and ungrammatically. Of those who did submit a reasonable piece of work, there was no way in which Mr Sands' expectations were borne out. Some girls wrote straightforward, 'down-to-earth' accounts as did some boys; and there were examples of supernatural accounts from both boys and girls. But this substantial evidence did not cause Mr Sands to change his mind, nor his expectations that girls on the whole would write totally differently from boys. (Mr Sands did not comment on what constituted work of an alarmingly low level of attainment.)

There are several points that emerge from these incidents. The first is that such examples were not daily occurrences in the classroom and cannot be said to be typical of each Humanities lesson. Quite the contrary, but each time they occurred they did represent a subtle and covert manner in which gender roles were both defined and reinforced in conformity with pupils' own gender identities and their own experiences. The pupils themselves had fully mapped-out cultural expectations and such incidents were confirming their blue prints for behaviour.

To conclude the discussion on the operation of the 'hidden curriculum', examples of what took place in Mr David's woodwork class highlight the tensions between adopting a policy of integration and ensuring that the spirit of the notion was effected in practice. In Mr David's class the former existed but the latter was never achieved. The 'hidden curriculum' was a persistent reinforcement of particular aspects of feminine identity, gender visions and maintaining stereotypical notions of both boys' and girls' behaviour.

In the course of interviewing Mr David and observing his classroom practice, breaking down gender barriers was very limited. For example, he said that muscular differences between boys and girls were significant. So if furniture had to be moved, the boys would be called upon 'to get your jacket off and get to work' whilst the girls would be allotted paperwork tasks. In spite of this, girls would also participate in moving things around, although Mr David ignored them. His position was unequivocal; 'Some things need more strength, a bit of muscle power, and that is where the girls need more help than the boys', he argued. Quite clearly his views did not coincide with reality because at this stage of the pupils' development their physical strength was somewhat unequal, with the girls tending, if anything, to be more physically developed than many of the boys and, indeed, actually stronger than many of the boys whose growth spurt had not yet started. But in ideological terms Mr David had no doubts.

The fact that Mr David considered girls weaker than boys also provided him with the rationale for positively discriminating in favour of the boys. This occurred all the time. If there was a shortage of particular equipment, boys would be given preference over girls. Chisels, on one occasion, were handed out to the boys, but the girls were told to use something else which would be less dangerous!

If the boys were slow to respond to questions and the girls, in their eagerness to answer, held their hands up in the air, he would chastise the boys for their failure to reply. 'I shouldn't be getting answers from the girls', he would remonstrate.

If the girls helped the boys, this again would result in Mr David ridiculing the boys concerned and ignoring the girls' efforts, as happened when Robin broke a piece of dowelling, referred to in an earlier chapter. Mary, who noticed this, immediately intervened and offered to fix it for him, an offer which Robin rejected and resisted. But she was insistent and a scuffle ensued while she tried to wrest the dowelling from Robin who threw it down in a fit of pique. Mary was much bigger than him and much stronger. She ignored his anger, picked it up and repaired it. None of this went unnoticed by Mr David who rebuked Robin in strong terms. 'Shame on you for letting the girls do it for you.' Obviously unmanly and unmasculine for a boy to be assisted by a girl! Mary did not let this go by unchallenged. She responded defensively by saying how much she liked woodwork and how she often helped her older brother. She obviously felt it necessary to justify her actions and yet it is interesting to note that she did not appear to be affected by these overt, systematic discriminatory practices by Mr David. She continued to work hard in woodwork classes and enjoy them.

Mr David had positive things to say about girls in private, even though his classroom technique was to avoid public recognition of their abilities or keenness. He claimed they were more patient than boys and had:

> a better sense of design. Boys are interested in the subject until it comes to the final bit . . . the cleaning up of the work. They find that a bit boring, they are not prepared to clean up to the quality I want. Girls are very good in that respect. They are quite prepared to knuckle under and finish that work off, as it should be. They work neater, most of them – this is only a generalization of course – but they work very often in the early stage when accuracy is called for and the marking out of anything. They are generally better, I find, than the boys. Boys are so keen to get on with the actual manual part, you know, the using of the tools, that they skimp the marking out and the accurate measuring. Over-keenness I suppose, really.

He attributed the girls' better sense of design not only to their greater level of patience but 'they are more interested in things in the home', yet another example of his defining girls in relation to home-oriented activities.

Whilst in the past it could well have been argued that many boys, especially working-class boys, would have benefited from craft classes in that it would have been a preparation for their future apprenticeships, this is no longer the case. With the diminution of manufacturing and the ensuing deskilling process, it is more and more difficult to argue that boys benefit in terms of their future employment from the acquisition of such knowledge and skills. Apprenticeships are few and far between. However, craft courses have direct relevance to men's domestic roles, working on their own motor cars, or 'do-it-yourself' in their homes, for example. The ideological input of craft work for reinforcing male identity exists.

Conclusion

It now remains to draw some general conclusions from the detailed discussion on the working of the curriculum at Berkeley. Overall, it is difficult to evaluate this operation in terms of its pedagogical value. As an observer, I experienced extreme boredom sitting in class, day after day. Many of the teachers spent an inordinate amount of time remonstrating with all the pupils about the need to work quietly and well, and to settle down. Others seemed to have minimal difficulty in achieving this sense of order. But, whatever the case, many of the lessons seemed to lack depth of material and, indeed, the amount of constructive input by the pupils also appeared remarkably scant. There were occasions when that which passed for knowledge was questionable. Mr Sands, for example, spoke in passing about witch doctors. He portrayed them as ignorant, uncivilized and untutored people practising magical rites. However, this section is concerned with evaluating the methods in which knowledge is transmitted, the ideologies embedded in the knowledge, the contradictions and, finally, how girls, as a group, fare in comparison with boys. Each of these points will be considered within the context of the everyday life of the school.

In regard to woodwork, which constituted the first two years' syllabus, Mr David presented the subject as a recreation/hobby/home-oriented activity. He seemed to have, consciously or subconsciously, recognized the limitation of craftsmanship in a society in which skills were becoming more and more obsolete because of increasing technological developments. He even warned boys of the future limitations in becoming skilled workers, and so concentrated on the uses of woodwork for the pupils in their own homes.

Nor was there any marked difference with home economics

with particular reference to cooking and nutrition, which was also cast within the context of home-oriented activities, except these were seen as the main province of women, and only of use to men when absolutely required by force of circumstance to either cook or keep home: in such cases it would be of a temporary nature prior to the boys' future marriage, or when their future wives would be indisposed.

As for PE, the integration was short lived and soon reverted to separate classes for girls and boys with little reaction to this. The reasons given for this varied but, clearly, integrated PE appeared neither successful nor desirable. Arguments such as girls like to dance and boys would refuse to do so, or the unacceptable phenomenon of boys laughing at girls in their underwear were separately advanced to legitimate this change which partly reflects the marginal position that PE and games occupy within the school hierarchy. Nor did anyone speak of the problems in relation to emerging sexuality amongst the boys and girls, a point which was conveniently glossed over.

Nevertheless, in spite of all these caveats, some boys, as they progressed up the school, did pursue classes which were traditionally a feminine preserve. But there were no girls who pursued craft work in the senior years. Does this reflect a marked change and a move towards the breaking down of gender specific pursuits in spite of the deeply-felt reservations the staff expressed? The evidence is not all that encouraging. Those boys who did pursue such feminine-labelled classes, textiles or home economics, in their senior years were treated pejoratively by some of their peers. But this has to be recognized as linked to the apparent serious intent of such pupils, particularly when the examples of boys in other schools doing similar subjects is considered. In other schools where boys whose masculinity was unquestioned because of their deviant acts, it appeared legitimate for them to do more or less what they liked, particularly in classes where no formal examination procedure is likely to take place and the class resembles a leisure-time pursuit. However, the opposite does not appear to be the case for girls. There was never any mention of difficult girls, or girls who truanted, turning up to do woodwork classes. They probably would neither wish to attend such classes nor be permitted to do so.

Given these factors, the practice associated with the integration of subjects for boys and girls appears restricted by a set of ideologies which relate specifically to gender identities in terms of home-centred activities. In other words, it is quite legitimate to integrate all courses, provided this does not represent any threat to the status quo of the gender-based division of labour, both in the home and place of work.

In the course of proposing and conducting an integrated programme, several ideologies have been expressed: equal opportunities for girls and boys alike and education to equip pupils for adult life. It is this latter one which incorporates the ideology relating to the home and family formations. At no stage was there any consideration or questioning of the form of labour in the home.

In conducting the classes in home economics and craft, the teachers revealed their close identification with this latter ideology; both activities were home-centred, particularly woodwork for girls. Nor, for that matter, did the pupils differ. They, like the teachers, identified the subjects with the appropriate home-oriented activities, as the following chapter will demonstrate.

The situation is less direct and gender specific when the content of the other subjects is considered. Bearing in mind that these subjects comprise roughly three quarters of the timetable allowance there is much covered in the course of each lesson which has no bearing on the division of labour between the two groups and which is not directly related to male or female identity. Large sections of the academic subjects comprise abstract knowledge. It is too early to pass off the contents as male dominated as some writers have done in the course of trying to account for the failure of girls to select or successfully study particular subjects (Spender and Sarah, 1980). It is difficult to conjecture how the principles of working in fractions, or what constitutes the theorems, may be defined in such terms. There is a wide range of knowledge – factual and abstract – which appears to be neutral.

Where differences emerge they are, in most cases, part of the 'hidden curriculum', reflecting the teachers' own perceptions, belief systems and practices in regard to gender divisions of labour. The effect of these practices is likewise hidden. It reinforces the already existing blueprint that pupils have about gender differences.

Finally, the working of the curriculum is a complex set of processes in which a number of different elements meet and overlap. These processes are ones in which the teachers and the pupils are active subjects meeting against the restraining backdrop of the disciplined classroom. In the course of the schoolday, ideologies intermingle with facts and all interact on the already constituted gendered subjects – boys and girls – who receive this input not as passive receptors but as active agents who already have existing blueprints about what constitutes expected forms of gender-appropriate behaviour.

The complexities of the curriculum in the course of both defining, creating and reinforcing existing gender divides is indeed varied. Such empirical evidence needs to be further explored if we are to succeed in the educational enterprise, both in terms of educating pupils and in terms of breaking down rigid gender barriers.

CHAPTER NINE

The curriculum
and work

The ideological component of the curriculum and its impact on
gender differences has been examined. What remains to be considered is the link between the curriculum and the preparation
pupils receive for future work. The recent changes in technological
education with the introduction of TVEI (Technological and Vocational Education Initiative) bear witness to the attempts at state level
to establish a more direct, practical link between schooling and
work.

Exactly how important and in what way schooling prepares
pupils for work in the labour force is difficult to establish, and has
been the basis for a great deal of study. There is a strongly held
view that girls, in general, have inferior education to boys, and that
most girls, by virtue of their gender, are automatically disadvantaged in comparison with most boys; that their schooling does not
give them the basis for competing on an equal footing with boys
for jobs.

It is obviously difficult, if not impossible, to assess adequately
the effectiveness of the curriculum the pupils have followed at
Berkeley in terms of the work they would do in the future. But
their own assessments can be given. In order to place their views
in context this chapter will begin with a very brief review of some
of the current thinking and developments on the relations between
school and work followed by a more detailed critical examination
of the notion that all girls are disadvantaged in comparison with all
boys. This will provide the basis for examining the mental/manual
dichotomy in the curriculum and its effect on future job
opportunities.

In a review essay on the relation between schooling and employment Brown (1984) pointed out that:

> Since the mid-1970s at the latest the balance appears to have swung back towards a predominantly instrumental view of education as preparation for work, and considerable emphasis has consequently been placed on the questions of how and how far schools prepare their pupils for employment (1984, p. 97).

This has been coupled with the ever present concern about youth unemployment which has mirrored the growing numbers of unemployed in the country. The outcome has been the development, largely through the work of the Manpower Services Commission (MSC), of a new vocationalism which has taken as axiomatic the failure of the schools to provide appropriate skills and attitudes amongst the school leavers.

To overcome what has been seen as this general deficit of educational provision is the notion that work experience must be introduced to pupils *before* they leave school. This may be achieved through a change in the whole curriculum, through experience in work situations in 'work experience courses', and through 'work creation schemes' involving local employers, local authorities and the schools in various projects.

The major initiatives have been through two programmes: Lower Attainers Project (LAP) and Technological and Vocational Education Initiative (TVEI), with the latter obtaining far greater resources and media coverage. The projects have excited a great deal of comment and a certain amount of hostile reception (Bates et al., 1984), not least because the schemes are seen to be conflicting and contradictory, neglecting educational goals at the expense of trying to enforce a training programme. Brown (1984) sums it up as follows:

> The message is clear. There has been a refusal to accept that youth unemployment is primarily a problem of *deficiencies in the demand for labour*, combined with a faulty or inadequate understanding of the youth labour market (p.100, my emphasis).

The assessment of the schemes are currently being made

(Cockburn, 1987, Finn, 1987) and the findings are now appearing. In regard to the efficacy of these programmes confronting differentiation and effecting change through opening up new opportunities of employment for girls the results, not surprisingly, are disappointing. Millman (1985) pointed out that sex stereotyping had not been altered and girls remained largely in three areas – retail, hair dressing and community care. When girls did cross the divide into traditional male areas of work they were marginalized. She regards this as unlikely to alter because 'the majority of male dominated project teams and steering groups lack the expertise necessary to achieve' a change (p. 66).

This conclusion is not surprising given the tendency to see girls as victims of a lack of qualifications rather than as having to fit into an existing labour market which determines in the main the conditions of the working population. Thus: 'For most girls, schooling leads to a position where they have neither the skills nor the attitude of mind to compete equally with boys for jobs, money and the power that goes with them' (Platt and Whyld, 1983, p. 7). This statement automatically assumes that irrespective of the new vocationalism boys leave school with skills and appropriate attitudes which enable them to compete for jobs with money and power. Such an assumption needs to be questioned and the following will do so by examining what constitutes skills, what qualifications pupils obtain at the end of their schooling and how this differs on a gender basis and, lastly, how 'attitudes' towards their future may be assessed. In the final analysis some assessment of the school curriculum can be made.

Skill is one of those generic terms which can include several different meanings. It is important, as Beechey (1982) argues, 'to clarify what is meant by skill if one is interested in the reasons why particular categories of labour . . . have generally been excluded from skilled occupations'. Much of the work women perform, for example, is not classified as skilled labour. Beechey identifies three main components. The first relates to 'complex competencies' which may involve objective criteria involving both the 'conception and execution' of actual labour, the second includes 'control over the labour process' and the third refers to 'conventional definitions of occupational status'.

What constitutes objective criteria of 'complex competencies' is problematic because of the ever changing nature of production processes. In the past there were certain clearly definable skills which required a long period of apprenticeship. Today the production process has stripped many jobs of their skill components, but, as in the case of typography, organized labour has preserved the classification of particular jobs as skilled even though the nature of the work has been greatly transformed.

Consider whether school leavers possess skills or 'complex competencies'. Beginning with the boys, do all boys leave school with marketable skills as the Platt and Whyld statement would have one believe? The answer is in the negative. Those boys who have gained qualifications in vocational courses may have some skills but are they sufficient to enter the labour market without further training? Apart from anything else, as already commented upon, apprenticeships have practically vanished, the production process has been consistently deskilled, so it is unlikely that those skills which boys acquire in the vocational courses are directly marketable. Furthermore the change towards a technologically oriented society is shifting the focus of what constitutes skill, and what constitutes desirable skills. So to suggest that such boys have qualifications which will enable them to compete for jobs which are likely to generate money and power is not the case. Nor do the boys who have pursued an academic course at school possess 'complex competencies'. What they may have attained is the means to further qualifications and training. And then there are boys with no qualifications whatsoever.

The girls with vocational skills have them in areas which are directly related to traditional female occupations – sewing, cooking and so on. They suffer from the same disadvantages that the boys have but with the additional factor that these are not socially recognized skills. Girls with academic qualifications have possibilities (as do the boys similarly qualified) of pursuing further or higher education and thus enjoy an advantage over the boys who have only vocational qualifications. And as for the girls without any or only minimal qualifications, their work opportunities have to be compared with boys of the same level. Furthermore, for such girls their position is not without contradictions. While they occupy the lowest paid and lowest status jobs at the same time the increase in part-time jobs both in manufacturing and the service industry means that they may be able to get employment whilst boys of the same low level of qualification may find it impossible to get a job.

The second component of skill according to Beechey relates directly to the workplace and so is not relevant to school leavers.

The third element of skill which refers to 'conventional definitions of occupational status' is the one which has direct bearing on school leavers, and in particular girls. Take the example of a woman who cooks in the privacy of her home. However skilfully she may do this she is not defined as a skilled worker but as a housewife fulfilling her marital duties. She does not get paid for her labour, her tasks are socially defined as housewifely and hence unskilled. In contrast a man who cooks is likely to do so as an occupation for which he is paid. He is defined as a skilled worker. The conventional social definitions of what comprises skill have been founded in past struggles and in social definitions of what skill is.

On the basis of the above the first section of the general statement by Platt and Whyld that 'schooling leads to a position where [girls] have neither the skills . . .' needs rethinking.

If there is no point in comparing girls with boys in terms of skill at school-leaving then what is the criterion which can be used for comparison? The basis may be in terms of qualifications. On the grounds that qualifications 'serve mainly to establish competitive differences between applicants and to attest the presence of certain general dispositions' (CCCS, 1981) a comparison between boys' and girls' qualifications will be made.

According to available statistics from the DES it is possible to compare four different levels of attainment for all school leavers and this will be done for the period from 1971–2 to 1985 (see Table 2). The first category refers to pupils who get one or more A level passes (and note that up to the early 1980s prior to the enormous cutbacks in University places, entry into University required a minimum of two A level passes, whereas now the requirements are mostly a minimum of three A level passes and often of a high grade); the second category is one or more Higher Grade CSE or O level; the third category is one or more grades in CSE or O, but not at the higher grade; the last category refers to pupils who leave school without having passed any examination at all. What constitutes the 'higher grade' needs clarification. According to the DES 'Statistics of School Leavers CSE and GCE England 1981':

Prior to 1975 O level candidates were awarded a pass or deemed not to have passed. From 1975 onward O level candidates were awarded a grade A to E or ungraded. Grades A to C can be regarded as equivalent to the former pass level. For brevity, O level passes grades A–C and CSE grade 1 are re-

Table 2: Levels of Attainment of School Leavers 1972–84

		1971-72	1972-73*	1973-74	1974-75	1975-76	1976-77	1977-78	1978-79	1979-80	1980-81	1981-82	1982-83	1983-84
With 1 or more A level passes	Boys	17.34	26.27	16.44	16.25	17.00	16.72	16.46	16.26	16.15	17.02	13.91	13.97	14.19
	Girls	15.06	23.76	14.53	14.53	14.74	14.49	14.51	14.46	14.98	15.88	14.26	14.73	14.49
With 1 or more higher grade O level or CSE results	Boys	26.27	42.91	30.80	31.41	31.31	33.00	32.52	33.62	33.38	32.93	34.28	34.93	34.86
	Girls	29.22	48.82	35.95	36.80	37.50	38.99	39.43	40.04	39.69	39.64	40.19	41.21	41.30
Without higher grade O level or CSE results but 1 or more other grades	Boys	14.00	22.89	31.25	32.69	34.28	34.49	35.78	36.08	36.87	37.07	39.10	39.19	39.31
	Girls	11.96	20.83	30.27	31.13	32.33	32.65	32.82	33.90	34.59	34.65	35.90	35.79	39.38
No GCE or CSE Qualifications	Boys	42.36	7.93	21.50	19.65	17.39	15.77	15.22	14.02	13.57	12.97	12.69	11.89	11.62
	Girls	43.74	6.57	19.23	17.51	15.49	13.85	13.22	11.58	10.71	9.71	9.62	8.24	7.32

* 1972-73 has lower number of school leavers because of raising minimum school leaving age from 15 to 16.

Source: DES Statistics of School Leavers CSE and GCE England 1981
Statistics of Education School Leavers CSE and GCE 1984

ferred to as 'higher' grades, and the remaining graded results as 'other grades'. (p. 2)

Although candidates may appear to have GCE O or CSE qualifications after 1975, in effect those below what constitutes a higher grade do not have what was the equivalent of a pass prior to 1975. Therefore, although the figures of those who appear in the column of passes without 'higher grades' is high, the *level* of their grades is not sufficient to enable them to continue with A levels and hence ultimately higher education. This distinction is important given the numbers of pupils who fall into this category.

On examination of the figures, a number of interesting details emerge. In the first instance in 1971–72, prior to the raising of the school leaving age from fifteen to sixteen, 42 per cent of all boy school leavers and 43 per cent of all girl school leavers had *no qualifications* whatsoever. Absence of qualifications applied equally to boys as it did to girls. With the raising of the school leaving age this figure appears to drop dramatically, but what in effect has happened is that far more boys and girls may attempt either O or more probably CSE examinations, but do not succeed in getting higher grades, or the equivalent of what, in the past, constituted a pass. At a cursory glance it appears that they have CSE or O grades, but they have not reached any comparative level of qualification. So although there is a steady and ever rising increase in the number of both boys and girls without higher grades but with one or more O or CSE grade, these figures combined with those without any qualifications still give cause for concern. So notwithstanding the extension of educational facilities, there is a significant number of pupils who leave school without any meaningful qualifications, if the basis of qualification is after ten years or more of compulsory education taken as passing examinations which enable pupils to continue with higher education. It should be noted that the absence of qualification is not gender-specific, as the statement at the beginning of this section would lead one to expect. Failures apply equally to boys as to girls; boys as well as girls leave school without any qualifications which would enable them to compete for jobs.

There is, however, a positive side. There has been a steady, indeed quite dramatic fall in the numbers leaving school without any qualification, as well as an increase in the numbers passing examinations at all levels up to the A level. In 1973–74 20 per cent of all school leavers had no qualifications but this figure had dropped to 10 per cent by 1984, a fact often overlooked by critics of the comprehensive system. Those with CSE or O level passes below the higher grades have also increased from 34 per cent to 37 per cent in the same period. The next stage up, that is those with higher grade CSE and O level passes, also increased but at a slower rate, from 33 per cent to 34 per cent between these years.

If one examines these trends in terms of gender, they are somewhat different to the view expressed in the statement by Platt and Whyld. The improvement has been particularly marked for girls up to A level. At each stage the girls as a group have shown an improvement, the most dramatic being in the category of O and CSE passes at the higher grades. In 1971-72 only 29 per cent of all girl school leavers fell into this category and by 1983-84 this had increased to 41 per cent. The improvement occurs at the lower levels as well. In 1975 15 per cent of all girl school leavers got no qualifications at all. This figure had dropped to 7 per cent by 1984, a change which cannot be ignored. The reasons for this increase in girls' performance needs to be explained and cannot be dismissed, as did Shaw when commenting on pass rates and the narrowing of discrepancies. She said:

> To expect that trends will simply continue uninterrupted is as politically and socially naive as it is to fail to see that if girls now achieve about the same number of 'O' level passes as boys it is also the case that 'O' levels 'are becoming increasingly irrelevant to pupils' future careers. It is short-sighted to be content with improved pass rates at CSE and GCE level in the light of knowledge that girls still end up in the worst paid, least secure and least interesting jobs available (1980 pp. 69-70).

There are two different issues. The one is qualification and the other is the structure of the labour market itself. Qualifications open up *access* to further studying and to certain occupations but do not guarantee employment. The nature of the available work is determined largely by the enterprise itself and is not dependent on the qualifications of the workforce. Thus the nature of the work women do is not determined by their qualifications but by factors predominantly related to the economy (Beechey, 1978, Wolpe,

1978) which, as Phillips (1983) says, is not neutral when it comes to differentiating between men and women.

However, the question of the formation and differentiation of the labour market does not constitute the main concern here. Rather it is the relationship between schooling, qualifications and skills, and gender differences that are at issue. To pursue this further a distinction needs to be drawn between academic and non-academic schooling and the associated mental/manual dichotomy in the labour market.

Beginning with pupils with an academic record at school, much of the work on gender differences has concentrated on the academic side of the curriculum, and, in particular, has singled out the mathematics/science areas as the ones in which women are massively disadvantaged and under-represented, as discussed in the previous chapter. The interesting and wide-ranging literature highlights girls' failure to study mathematical and pure science subjects at A level which blocks their entry into fields of advanced and applied technology.

When the numbers of boys and girls passing science subjects are compared, the figures do indicate big differences, as seen in the following figures:

Table 3: Passes at GCE Advanced Level Summer Examinations

	Thousands	
	Boys	Girls
Mathematics	49.261	20.059
Physics	31.066	8.216
Chemistry	22.725	12.987
Biology, Botany or Zoology	12.949	18.952

Source: DES Statistics of Education School Leavers CSE and GCE 1984.

However, comparison of these numbers with the total number of school leavers in each group presents a different perspective. In 1983–84 there were 351,400 boy school leavers. Of this number only 49,261 passed mathematics at A level or *13.78 per cent of all boy school leavers*. There were 351,200 girl school leavers. Of this number 20,059 passed mathematics or 5.7 per cent. While there are almost three times as many boy school leavers than girls passing A level mathematics, the figures of those who *do not pass* should

235

be considered. In all only 14.19 per cent of school leaving boys, and 14.49 per cent of school leaving girls had one or more A level passes in that year, so that when talking of these subjects the reference group must be taken on the basis of these figures and not the total boy or girl school leaving population. When talking of girls who are disadvantaged in regard to not studying these subjects at A level, then comparison must be made with the top section of boys, and not with all boys. The number of boys and girls who do not have a scientific or mathematical background at the higher level is extremely high amongst the total school leaving population. Taking mathematics, only 86 per cent of boys and 95 per cent of girls have no advanced mathematics at all. Obviously the figure is far worse where girls are concerned but overall the school leaving population is not advanced mathematically. A dearth of knowledge in these fields is a *general phenomenon* and not one specific to girls.

There are other differences which are also often commented upon in regard to disadvantages of girls in comparison with boys. These refer to the propensity for girls to study biology, arts and humanities in greater numbers than boys. But once again these discussions have meaning only when reference is being made to school leavers destined for higher education and fail to take into account those school leavers who do not pursue any further education on leaving school and who have no meaningful qualifications at the end of their schooling.

What should also be noted is that over the years there has been a steady increase in the number of women attending universities and institutions of higher education. Yet in comparing the attainment of boys and girls passing one or more A level, as already seen, the numbers have remained constant over the years except for boys since 1981. From 17 per cent of all boy school leavers getting these results there was a dip to 13.91 per cent in 1981 and the figure has remained fairly constant over the succeeding three years. This change should be linked to the overall performance of all boys. As yet there does not appear to be an account of this.

Broad generalizations about the disadvantages girls experience in comparison with boys should, therefore, be avoided. The figures that have been given amply demonstrate that undifferentiated comparisons cannot be made; comparisons may be drawn only between like groups.

Regarding the non-academic subjects; they include the most

obvious vocational and technical subjects which may open up work possibilities to both girls and boys but in those areas which are defined as the traditional work places of either group. Reference was made in Chapter 8 to the distinction between mental and manual work and the parallel that this has with the divisions in the curriculum. The question that will now be addressed is the attitude of pupils towards work. Again this is a very broad field so comments will be restricted to a consideration of some points raised by Willis (1977).

He argued that 'mental work is associated with unjustifiable authority'; it is seen as being all the same and is invested with 'masculinity'. Although he says that the division between mental and manual labour is an artificial one, and of an ideological nature, 'it is a construction upon the real which is dislocated from its originating structure, transformed and reapplied' (p. 157). When it comes to applying this distinction to the lads in his study, Willis says they define labour as 'emphatically manual rather than mental'. And so he is able to account for their rejection of formal schooling.

Indeed it is never clear what exactly Willis' lads studied at school and whether they attended any classes, and if so, which ones. But they labelled pejoratively those boys who were seen to be clever and do their schoolwork. In fact it was that classification of the boys as *clever* which was invested with femininity. It was not the *subjects* the 'ear-'oles' studied, but the *level* at which they studied. After all, all pupils are supposed to have studied a number of 'academic' subjects from the beginning of their schooling and it would be interesting to determine at what stage this rejection of certain subjects occurred, which subjects they were, and whether such subjects are labelled 'feminine'. Willis lays blame on the school for being responsible for the lads' resistance to mental work making the assumption that this applies to all academic subjects:

> It is the school which has built up a certain resistance to mental work and an inclination towards manual work. At least manual labour is outside the domain of school and carries with it - though not intrinsically - the aura of the real adult world. Mental work demands too much, and encroaches - just as school does - too far upon those areas which are increasingly adopted as their own, as private and independent. The 'lads' have learned only too well the specific social form of mental labour as an unfair 'equivalent' on an exchange

237

about control of those parts of themselves which they want to be free. In a strange unspecified way, mental labour henceforth always carried with it the threat of demand for obedience and conformism. Resistance to mental work becomes resistance to authority as learnt in school (p. 103).

However, there is an alternative way of examining this divide: the lads associate a *level* of study with mental work, a level which is outside their experience. They have no direct or intimate knowledge of adult work other than manual work; they have no knowledge that academic subjects provide a step into another world, because that other world is simply an unknown; they have no knowledge of what is required for further and higher education. Because the level at which these subjects are studied constitute part of an unknown they are divested of any importance. The legitimating force in their rejection, is to invoke pejorative terms about those who appear to achieve the level they are unable to achieve. So they label such boys as feminine. The school subjects may become identified in this way but this occurs at a time after they have been excluded from studying such subjects. It is at this stage that the boys' achievements are labelled as 'cissy' or feminine.

The tendency actively to reject the notion of achievement in academic subjects by boys cannot only be understood in terms of their identification with the shop floor culture. The causes extend beyond this and must include the cultural heritage which denigrates intellectual pursuits.

But this type of behaviour is not restricted to the older more spectacular boys who have filled the pages of work on youth culture. This process is an ongoing one which probably started in junior school when patterns of learning were established and pupils were able to recognize differences between those who could do the schoolwork and those who consistently failed.

Nor is this process of rejection of school culture only found amongst boys. Girls do so as well and their reasons are as complex as amongst the boys, reflecting their cultural heritage. Their rejection of the pursuit of academic subjects cannot be accounted for in terms of their identification with shop floor culture. On the contrary evidence from this study indicates that girls reject the harsh work such as factory work. Those girls whose mothers have worked in factories opt for work which is very different. Nor can their rejection be accounted for on the basis of domination by boys as the earlier data has indicated. In the end ordinary girls and boys reject school culture.

It is now appropriate to examine the empirical evidence. In their first three years all pupils would follow the same curriculum and be taught in mixed ability groups. This would continue until their 'choices' would be made following the 'normalizing judgments'. The concern of the teachers was with the present and that is controlling the class. The messages they were transmitting were ones on behaviour – being quiet, good, sitting still, listening, settling down to work. The ideologies extolling the virtues of learning and the excitement of intellectual pursuits were not on the agenda at Berkeley; the emphasis was on a vague and unspecified level of attainment to prevent unemployment – 'if you don't do your schoolwork you won't get a job'.

The cohort at Berkeley was a group that clearly did not fit into the top section of the school-going population. Their ideas on schoolwork were defined because of its compulsory nature. There was nothing else one could do. As you had to be at school you might as well enjoy yourself: you could meet your friends, have a laugh; schoolwork interfered with this, the real business of their lives. Thomas seemed to sum up the attitudes and messages received while at school and reconciled these with what actually happened in the end. He recalled as follows:

> I think the thing we always used to talk about between ourselves is considering we were all sort of lazy at school, virtually all of us as it were. We'd always been told if you don't work at school you won't get a job, you will be out of work. But we all seem to be working.

They were to study to get a job, not high status jobs, or jobs with career prospects, but any form of employment.

There was no tradition in their homes of pursuing education beyond the minimum school leaving age. When I interviewed the parents, so many of them said that they did nothing at school and they hoped their children would not repeat their mistakes. But their children seemed to be replicating their parents' behaviour. Many of the parents thought the children should work hard, but it was not goal directed. Further and higher education was something they knew little, if anything, about and it represented a world beyond their knowledge or experience. Nor was the school out to do much to alter this image and enlarge the horizon of the pupils. There were, of course, exceptions as with a West Indian mother who did night nursing in order to cope with child-rearing and to bring in an income. She set aside whatever money she could to pay for extra tuition for her children. Although her son's school performance was mediocre in the first two years, he succeeded fairly soon after leaving school, owning his own business and car within a relatively short space of time.

As could be expected the majority would not attempt O or A level examinations. English and some form of mathematics (arithmetic?) were to be compulsory, irrespective of their options in the fourth year.

We have already seen how the boys associated academic achievement with non-masculine behaviour and how at least one girl associated her cleverness with her failure to attract the boy she had a crush on. But this does not give a clear indication of what their specific views were about the different parts of the curriculum. Did they associate particular subjects with specific beliefs? Did they have definite views about the value of academic subjects? How did they differentiate between those subjects that were vocationally oriented and the more academic subjects?

When first interviewed, between the ages of eleven and twelve, in response to what subject or subjects they considered the most important in their schooling their inevitable response, both girls and boys, was English and mathematics. 'English – that's very important because you have got to know English to get a good job. Maths is important because you have got to have maths, in case you get a lot of adding up'. '. . . if you can't do maths when you go for a job they could easily catch you out of a couple of pounds'. 'Maths is important because I think that everyone should know a bit about maths: for example, if you are going shopping or something and somebody adds up the total and it is wrong and have charged you too much, it is useful if you are to know adding and that, so that you can add it up yourself'. Comments about the use of English and mathematics were restricted entirely to the most basic level. Neither the boys nor the girls conceptualized the use of such subjects as a means to further education. It was simply a question of aiding one in talking correctly and seeing that either your pay packet or your shopping was totalled correctly. Mary was the only one in the class at that stage to reflect on the possible advantage of studying science because it could lead 'to going to a university perhaps', but that was not something she contemplated. She also thought home economics very useful for girls who would become housewives. Robin listed Humanities as very useful because he said 'you have got to know what is going on like, got to know about Africa and all the other places'.

At that stage the pupils had little idea about the relationship of what they were studying nor the general application of their schoolwork for the future. They had very restricted views on the role of education and the parts the various sections played.

The same questions were asked of them when they were fifteen. They expressed very similar views. English and mathematics were still regarded as the most important subjects and for similar reasons. There was a beginning of an identification of particular subjects with possible future jobs. Shirley said:

> The most important subjects are English and Office Practice because when I leave school it is the most likely thing I will need. I was going to be a secretary when I left school or something in that line, you know, but really what I needed was English and Office Practice mainly and I think that those two are the most important. But, now I want to change my mind, and I think Textiles is more important because I want to be a fashion designer or something in that line.

She wanted to change but expressed a realistic view of her chances. In the end she became a hairdresser and married at nineteen.

Julie thought English and maths had to be important because they were compulsory. 'I suppose because we have to take them, we have no choice about them – I suppose we think they must be important.' Nor were there changes amongst the boys.

This reaction of the pupils reflected the narrow vision they held about the role of particular subjects. Their plans for the future will be discussed in the following chapter. They were conforming to the expectations expressed by Mr Burns. Apart from Adam and Graham, they were not aiming high: they wanted to talk 'properly' and be numerate. They did not conceptualize that schooling did much else for them. In the main, both boys and girls were mirroring the views their parents held. Their class position had locked them into a mould from which there was little likelihood of breaking out. Not for them the anticipation of a university career, or a professional or managerial occupation.

Furthermore, in listing the important subjects the pupils were reflecting the divide between mental/manual view of school subjects. Apart from one girl who had specified home economics as important for girls, none of the pupils selected vocational courses as influential. In this regard there is a convergence between the girls and the boys in their conceptualizing the value of schooling.

Did they have views about differences in their schooling and different advantages one group may have over the other. Questions dealing with this were only asked in regard to their views on the attempt to integrate home economics and craft. As noted in Chapter 6 the pupils were more concerned with gender identity in regard to these subjects. At the earlier levels of schooling the possibility of these subjects having direct reference to work when they were adults was not recognized.

Now to consider the 'vocational' courses, that is craft and HE. Given that there was to be no separation in the early years, the question that arises is to whether this had any impact on either group, particularly in relation to skills that could be used in work.

Between the ages of eleven and twelve, the question of girls doing woodwork did not evoke a great deal of response from either the boys or girls. When asked, the boys made few if any comments about the girls. 'It's O.K.' summed up the attitude. Nor did the girls appear surprised about entering such classes. Like the boys they said it was 'alright' and shared the view that it was something which could be useful to them in the home. Most assumed that they would get married and anticipated that woodwork could prove useful 'because girls might want to do things to a house and I think it is an enjoyable subject'. One girl recognized the dependence that women have on men to do certain things in the home and said, 'It's a good idea because girls have got to learn to do these things if they don't get married and be independent for themselves'. Only two thought it irrelevant because 'we don't really do it when we grow up'. On the whole they found woodwork a legitimate subject as it was cast in terms of traditional female roles. Woodwork was related to necessary chores or pleasurable activities around the home. It could not clash with women's rightful roles. There was no question of learning this because it could lead to skilled labour in the workforce.

By fifteen, woodwork had become an option for boys and in the interviews conducted at that time nobody expressed regret at this. Both girls and boys saw it as having provided the girls with some useful skills they could employ around the home. Robin voiced his grievance at unfair advantages the girls had had in being allowed to do metalwork in the third year. 'But when we were in third year they do metalwork but we never had a chance to do that, so we complained. But they seem to get on with it alright.' Integration in craft ended after the second year!

Interestingly, girls' pursuit of such a masculine activity did not result in their becoming tainted or labelled in pejorative terms. Their femininity was not at stake even if it was 'her best subject' as Robin said of a younger girl he knew. Girls doing woodwork were not seen as 'lessy' or butch.

What of boys who did HE? At an early age HE was identified as cookery. Boys in cookery classes were seen by boys in purely pragmatic terms. They were learning a skill that could prove useful to them as adults either as bachelors or, once married, if there was a crisis in the home and their wives were incapacitated for some reason or other: 'I like cookery. I'm very good at it really. I think it will teach me a lot in years to come. If I never marry and I'm a bachelor then I need to cook – I don't want to eat burnt sausages.' But once they were older this was no longer the case even though some would have liked to continue with cookery. Elliot, for one, was regretful that he could not do this even though some people 'might not think it is for boys'. He had been told by Mr Burns that he could not fit it in and so chose engineering science. Robin, on the other hand, thought it 'was alright for boys to do it' although he himself had not chosen it as one of his options 'because anyway what I need to do, like snacks and so on, I know how to do already'. He felt that in the past when he had been in home economics classes the value he got from attending depended on the things you wanted to make:

> because you have always got a cookery book to help you, but there are certain things if you didn't have a cookery book around, or didn't want to take it from the book it would be good for you to kind of do it off-hand from memory, instead of just start flicking through pages and be able to remember.

He was required to help a great deal at home. He was the eldest in the family, with two younger sisters and a mother who worked full time. He vacuumed the house when he got home from school, gave his sisters their afternoon tea and had food ready for his mother when she returned from work.

Robin commented on the two boys who were doing cookery and how good their standard of work was:

> There are only two boys in our class that take that, and what they make is pretty good, pretty good for boys. You would ex-pect girls to make the things better than boys, but what they make is pretty well made.

He obviously did not regard this as an illegitimate course to study, probably because cookery could always be linked to adult work as a chef.

On the whole, the boys were fairly easy-going about their past attendance in what was identified as a typical female activity: doing home economics in the lower school constituted no problem, but the older they got the less acceptable it became. On the whole boys were likely to be labelled gays or 'poofs' if they did cookery or needlework, particularly by the girls.

What did the girls think about the boys encroaching on their territory? In the first round of interviews they shared the same view as the boys about the usefulness of boys learning to cook and do things in the home. They, like the boys, viewed this in pragmatic terms relating to the home. Shirley thought, as they all tended to when younger, that certain skills could be of use to a boy if:

> he doesn't want to live with his parents for a long time so it is teaching him to get a flat and decorate it and cook on his own. Or if he didn't get married until late they could cope on their own, cook their own meal. They wouldn't have to keep going down the fish and chip shop. Making the homes more cheer-ful and how to decorate them.

During the second round of interviews, at a time when they were well into adolescence, the girls questioned the identity of boys who did subjects such as cooking or textiles. At fourteen, Doreen thought that it was 'alright' and that the boys would not be called 'poofs' because 'there is writing involved as well and . . er . . . I don't really know because I am in an all girls' group at cookery so I don't really know about that'. Provided there was some other activity which was not specifically identifiable as feminine – such as writing – this legitimized boys' attendance. She was less tolerant about boys doing textiles. She said there were two boys in her textile class and 'people thought they were poofs, I suppose, I don't know – they kept saying that'. She thought their attendance was 'really funny'. As the boys got older the girls thought they would be subjected to a certain amount of teasing. In other words, as long as they were still childish and before they reached puberty boys could legitimately engage in feminine pursuits. But once their masculine identity was at issue the situation changed. Shirley put this view point quite bluntly. 'The two boys that do textiles and home economics out of school are a bit cissy.' They were damned in her eyes.

These reactions illustrate a change that had taken place over the period of three years, during which all boys had no option but to do home economics. This coupled with their youth did not involve their masculinity being questioned. But once it became optional, those boys who voluntarily *chose* a feminine subject ran the risk of being labelled a 'poof' by girls and boys alike. Exception to this has been referred to in the discussion in Chapter 8 when those older boys who were defined as 'problems' joined cookery classes, but this was done *en masse*, and they had already established their masculine identity in the school through their active acts of resistance.

In the first few years of their secondary schooling the pupils overall did not indicate any personal direction in their studies. They had to do the subjects in accordance with the timetable; there was no choice in the matter. What they studied seemed to be separate from their real lives and they gave no indication of connecting their schooling with adulthood. It was remote. The pupils enjoyed school but it was on account of their friends, the social aspect of school and the companionship. Learning was somehow divorced from all this.

The mental/manual division was not something that these pupils made. The relevance of the vocational courses was largely related to their own personal lives. Not even the boys spoke of craft courses as aiding them in terms of getting them jobs in the future, but then this is hardly surprising given Mr David's attitude about the unlikelihood of skilled craftsmen still being able to make a living. The pupils' concern was with *level* of attainment, as will be discussed in the final chapter.

Epilogue

This study which set out to examine school processes that re-inforce gender differences became far bigger than I had intended. This was so because the processes that initially had appeared so clear and identifiable evaporated against a complex patchwork of social structures that intersected at different levels. These processes defy neat compartmentalization and monocausal accounts.

This book has argued the need for contextualizing the processes which differentiated between boys and girls through examination of the related structures which create the conditions in which the differentiation may occur. Many of these structures operate for both girls and boys and it is necessary to identify these before the specificities relating to the differentiation process may be examined.

The starting point of the book was the disciplinary system which physically constrains and controls all pupils, and without which the school cannot operate. In ideological terms no distinction is drawn between boys and girls. The ideology on the need for disci-pline is represented in statements referring to the moral order which is overtly observable in the behaviour of the pupils. It is at this point that gender differences intersect because of the socially constructed differential expectations about the way girls and boys behave.

There is a universal assumption that men and women, boys and girls behave differently, and this is represented in a range of stereotypical views. Not surprisingly, teachers' discourses reflect this belief and their treatment and handling of girls and boys in the classroom is the outcome of this. All this masks the fact that girls resist control just as the boys do, but the form of their resistance is different and less physical. Girls therefore are not passive agents in the classroom situation – quite the contrary.

This leads to a refutation of some current feminist literature which has constructed its own set of stereotypes about boys' behaviour. The literature holds that the effect of boys' behaviour is the cause of girls' overall failure to do well at school. As pointed out above, the evidence in the book refutes this. Girls are not victims. Furthermore, both boys and girls recognize certain stereotypical forms of behaviour relating to each group but at the same time they are aware of contradictory forms of behaviour.

Whilst there is a set of disciplinary constraints on all pupils, emerging sexuality amongst the adolescents provides another set of constraints on their academic careers. Much of recent feminist literature has focused on the repressive effect of boys' sexuality and power over girls. This monocausal account ignores a range of elements including the way in which school deals with sexuality, the interrelationship between the two groups and the effect of girls' sexuality on their lives.

The section on sexuality began with an examination of the school's means of confronting sexuality amongst its pupils. In the main it is subsumed under the rubric of moral order. In the course of informing and teaching pupils the correct moral order, sexuality of women is defined in terms of monogamy, marital and maternal relations thus reinforcing one of the major ideologies about women's life. The emotional and erotic elements of sexuality are obscured or ignored. Where sexual intercourse is acknowledged it is in terms of contraception, deviancy and health hazards.

But sexuality is ever present in the school and is seen in everyday classroom interaction. Teachers, both women and men, exploit their own sexuality in the course of maintaining control in the classroom. Where sexual issues are obvious the tendency in the main is to ignore their manifestations because they are seen as a 'natural' part of children's development, which if commented upon or acted upon may have a damaging effect on children's perceptions about sex. Underneath all this is a view which endorses existing beliefs about the differences between male and female sexuality.

Sex and sexually related questions appear to preoccupy the pupils and this at a time when their schoolwork could be very time consuming. As already pointed out, some of the literature has emphasized the oppressive form boys' behaviour may take at this stage. But age related to physical maturation is an important factor. There are marked differences in terms of their behaviour, ideas, and concerns according to age: a twelve-year-old girl is very different from a fifteen-year-old. The argument that is developed is that, as with classroom behaviour, girls are active agents and not passive victims. They are active in their interpersonal relations. Their interest in boys tends to be directed to older boys; boys of the same age are often immature and physically less developed than girls. For girls who have up to this point done well academically, they are diverted from studying by the effect of their developing sexuality. For the others schoolwork has never been a top priority and their increasing interest in boys is another diversion in their lives.

The third set of constraints which operate within the school situation exists in the curriculum which comprises differentiated knowledge and hidden agendas. It is at this point that class factors most obviously intersect. The class position of both boys and girls will determine to a great extent the content of the curriculum they will be offered.

There are two main areas in which gender differentiation occurs primarily in the vocational courses, home economics and the second is in the 'hidden curriculum'. In regard to the first, this occurs primarily in the vocational courses, home economic and craft, which are identified and associated with traditional female or male occupations. The second is identifiable in all aspects of the curriculum and may take different forms as discussed earlier.

To overcome overt differentiation in the curriculum, the school planned an integrated programme which, in effect, meant full attendance by all pupils in HE and craft. The programme failed overall, particularly for the girls, because of lack of serious intent to effect fundamental changes. The programmes for the girls ended, in effect, after the third year. Nor was the 'hidden curriculum' challenged. It was never intended that the provision of these teaching schemes would challenge existing ideologies about gender-specific divisions of labour in the home or at work.

Gender differentiation is less obvious in the academic courses in which the content may be abstract or of a factual nature not related to gender issues. The differences which do occur are part of the 'hidden curriculum' which reflect teachers' conventional views and practices, and cultural practices at a more general level.

The courses studied and the qualifications obtained at the end of the day provide a pathway to future jobs and attendant life styles.

These qualifications represent the end product of schooling. The divide between academic/non-academic subjects roughly corresponds to the mental/manual division which characterizes the labour force. Some of the present day literature depicts girls as being disadvantaged in comparison with boys at this stage of their lives because they do not have comparable academic qualifications. This assumption is questioned.

Evidence is presented which argues that, overall, a significant proportion of all boys and girls are ill equipped to compete on the open labour market for high status, and well paid jobs. The pupils have low levels of aspiration, and this correlates with their standard of work. It is by no means only the girls who are unqualified or inadequately qualified.

This links with the contentions about girls' motivations which are supposed to be the outcome of the differentiated processes they are subjected to in the course of their schooling and will be examined briefly before presenting the pupils' views.

This chapter sets out to present simply what the pupils themselves said about their aspirations for the future. It takes account of their home backgrounds by way of illustrating that generally there were uniform class and social conditions for these pupils. The data on the backgrounds is derived both from home visits and what the pupils themselves said.

Work and their aspirations

Chisholm and Holland (1986) acknowledge that 'a crucial aspect of women's disadvantage lies in their labour market position' (p. 355). Their research was into girls' occupational choice and was action based. Their aim was, through units in schools, to make interventions into the curriculum to influence girls' aspirations. Underlying this project, is the belief that through raising consciousness amongst teachers and pupils changes may be effected, although how is not spelt out.

This was the problem that Furlong (1986) confronted in his longitudinal study. He reappraised the relationship between schools and girls' occupational aspirations. He argued, correctly, against what he described as the dominant view in sociology of education which is that 'the experiences of young women with the education system are largely responsible for maintaining the existing sexual division of labour' (p. 367). He rejects this and instead apportions responsibility to their family experiences. He says that girls have restricted aspirations by the time they leave school, and their horizons are dominated by their feminine role which is strictly familial. He develops the argument when he says that 'the image women hold about themselves . . . prevents the majority applying for, or even considering, many jobs'. Following on from Sharpe (1976) he says that these views emanate from their mothers.

In the course of examining what goes on in schools he found that some of his data contradicts well established ideas. For example he found that teachers in his sample thought their female pupils were more competent academically than the boys, and were also more likely to enter professions than boys.

His conclusion is that girls' position in the labour market is a direct outcome of their aspirations for which their families are directly responsible. In the course of this he is critical of my analysis. He says:

> Wolpe (1978) suggests that a radical restructuring of female aspirations is not possible without prior changes in the structural base. Changes in the ideas of women, she suggests, are insufficient to change their overall position within the labour market. I would suggest that Wolpe's position suffers from structural overdeterminism (p. 375).

In support of his argument he gives the famous quotation from Marx that 'life is not determined by consciousness, but consciousness by life'.

> So increasing labour market participation by women will structure the work expectations of the next generation through family experiences (p. 375).

This is a somewhat romantic notion of the power of consciousness. The history of the struggle by the working class for better working conditions (including a family wage) has not been achieved through consciousness and aspirations forged in the family hearth. It has been achieved through struggle, conflict and confrontation. Women may, and indeed have, participated increasingly in the labour market; their numbers have shown a remarkable increase over the past decade, but still their aspirations have not matched their increasing participation. To match aspirations requires opportunities and at this stage their opportunities are restricted to what work is available. These are unlikely to change simply through increased aspirations and motivations, although these combined with active struggle both with employers and male workers is a necessary ingredient. Furlong has not addressed the question of how demands for labour are generated, and met.

What were the pupils' views about their future? Their responses to what they were taught gives a clue to their overall views on the goals of education and what they anticipated they would obtain from their schooling. Their vision of their future, what they hoped to do when they finished school, indicated they wanted something better than their parents but their goals were limited and restricted. This applies equally to girls and boys and for the latter presents a somewhat different picture to Willis' 'lads' who seemed to have no ideas other than following in their fathers' footsteps onto the shopfloor. The pupils were questioned about their future both at the ages of twelve and again at fifteen and what actually happened to some of them emerged from the interviews when they were young adults.

When first interviewed as twelve year olds, unemployment was beginning to occur nationally and there was evidence of some fathers joining the dole queue. The fathers' occupations were wide ranging: there were two chronically sick fathers, one did some home-work aided by his wife when she was free from domestic duties which were onerous (five children still living at home); there was a casual labourer who, according to his son, was 'on labour' (getting unemployment benefits); there were several self-employed men in the building/decorating business, factory workers, a bus driver, a manager of the local branch of an undertaking firm, another who had moved into personnel management and was studying part-time in order to improve his promotion chances. There were several clerical workers. Some had always lived in the area, some were immigrants predominantly from the West Indies and Cyprus.

Initially about a third of the mothers worked, but three years later more mothers were working. Their work varied as much as the fathers'. There were factory workers: on telephone assembly, clothing, packing; there were nurses, clerical workers, cleaners, a 'dinner lady'. Some of the mothers had to negotiate the work they did in order to cope with family responsibilities. Mrs West, for example, an immigrant from the Caribbean, worked in a nursery school so that she could have school holidays with her family, but in addition she worked on Saturday nights as a nurse so that, said her son, 'we can have clothes, that we can eat and that we are able to stay in the house and she wants us to have a good education. She likes to see her family happy'. Katherine said her mother worked because there 'was not very much work to do in the house, because it is mostly tidy and so I think she goes there for company'. Family obligations dictated what some of them could do.

The employment of the mothers meant a shifting of family responsibilities in some cases onto the children and this applied to some boys as well. Robin, as set out in the last chapter, helped out and said 'Well seeing that mum has to go to work and I have to stay with the girls, I've got to find something to do during that time because I can't go out and leave them'. So he hoovered the floors. Elliot prepared his mother's evening meal. Leslie felt burdened by his responsibilities and wished that his mother did not work so that 'she could pay more attention to the home, for my sisters as much as anything' although when he described his out of school activities he spent a great deal of time out on a bicycle, or watching TV or meeting his friends. Alice had the main burden of looking after her younger brother and sister, tidying and cooking. Her brother did nothing to help, just sat and watched TV and refused to help her 'because he says it is a woman's job'. Alice's mother, who was separated from her father, had two jobs. Alice said she hoped it would not happen to her. Her mother rushed home from one job, grabbed something to eat and went out to clean offices for another two hours. Alice hoped for herself that she would not 'rush all the time from one job to another and not have time to look after my children'.

Irrespective of whether the mothers worked or not, the girls were expected to help at home. Tricia gave a graphic description of what she did when she was twelve:

Well usually we go into the kitchen and the first words I hear – 'Are you going to the shop, or will you go to the supermarket'. I get the shopping and come back. Then the little kids have their tea before us older ones . . . After we have had tea my mum usually retires to the front room. We have all to make sure that the rooms are tidy. The bedrooms have to be tidied every day and we make sure that we have everything ready for school the next day, like all our books and everything and then after we have done that we can go down and watch the telly.

The extent of the help the girls reported they gave at home varied. They seemed to take this for granted and only one girl expressed her dislike, claiming that it interfered with her homework, 'I am up all night doing me homework' (no doubt something of an exaggeration – her schoolwork did not bear out this claim). She said she could not combine the two.

Some of the boys had specific tasks – Simon had to polish the brass pipes, and helped his mother with 'tea things and that' – others claimed they did things their mothers wanted them to do. But as one boy said, his mother preferred him being out of the house otherwise 'he got under her feet'. Football, messing about and street games occupied him.

As the girls got older they reported that they avoided domestic chores as they interfered with their social life. Their activities became more self-centred, spending time with their friends, even those who had done well in class admitting to spending less time on their homework. They would listen to records, visit each other at their homes, go out or spend time with their girlfriends talking about clothes, or fixing their clothes. Shirley said how she was allowed out at night after she had finished the washing up after seven, but she had to be in by 9.30. She said she was 'crafty' in the way in which she avoided doing household chores, and that she really wanted to be out most nights. Life was there to be enjoyed. The boys similarly reported on out of school activities and seemed to have fewer responsibilities.

The second set of interviews took place in summer and their activities were characteristically summertime. Adam was the one who spoke about the extra schoolwork that he did – he stayed on to use technical drawing equipment to save himself having to buy it. He played the clarinet in a youth orchestra, he played squash, and worked in a radio station at a hospital on Sundays. His schoolwork took up a great deal of time. Graham's work had begun to go downhill. He was no longer considered one of the two top boys in the class. He played the piano at home and listened to early jazz records. The others did not spend time at home on homework or helping out, except for Robin whose chores continued even though he was older.

The boys were involved in group activities with their mates.

They now wandered the streets, looking at shops, meeting friends, riding bicycles and going to each other's homes. One or two claimed they did homework when they got back from school, but mostly their accounts were of outdoor activities. 'Sometimes we get blamed for anything we don't do, such as smashing windows or shouting. We never shout. Now and again I might have a go. . . .' said Fisher.

The picture that emerges as these pupils get older is an involvement in gender group activities. Girls met with girls, boys met with boys. Schoolwork appeared low on their list of priorities. The notion of working hard was one they recognized. They knew that people got on better with qualifications, but they did not apply these notions to themselves, apart from Adam and to a lesser extent Graham.

Their fathers' lives appeared quite remote. The boys did not appear to identify with their fathers. Only two of the pupils spoke highly of their fathers. Katherine recognized that her father had improved his position, including going to night classes. She said:

> He has always been very ambitious and he has always wanted to try and do something better all the time. I admire him for this really. Obviously he did not have a very good education but he was still willing to do some out of school and that is what I really admire.

Adam expressed similar feelings about his father who had progressed from being an undertaker's chauffeur to local manager. He did not come home 'from building sites covered in dust'.

For the rest there was no strong feeling of closeness or admiration. Time and again the boys said they wanted more out of life than their fathers had. Where the fathers were working in factories the sons spoke of doing different work. Not for them the shop floor. Unlike Willis' 'lads', shopfloor work was not something they automatically saw themselves doing. Michael's father was a shift worker in a factory and he said:

> When he comes in in the evening he is tired. He doesn't want to talk he just wants quiet. He sits in the chair and falls off to sleep. If his dinner is ready he sits down and then watches the telly and goes off to sleep in the chair.

Michael wanted some 'life before I get married. Live my life until about twenty-five, then I would think of marriage'.

Similarly, the girls did not want to repeat their mothers' lives. Those whose mothers worked in factories were adamant about not doing similar work. They said their mothers came home tired, and many referred to their mothers' domestic responsibilities. Katherine was the only one to speak about her mother's lack of education and how this had affected the type of work she did. Katherine was emphatic that she wanted to achieve more than her mother. She did not want to be like her mother:

> I want a little bit more than my mother has achieved really because she had to go to work when she was 14 and so her education wasn't that good and I would like to get a standard that I could get a better job really. Really she has been brought up to be a housewife which I wouldn't like to start very early in my life. I would like to make a success of something and then go to be a housewife. She worked in a dressmaking place, putting all the pieces together. I would like something that you use from your brains rather than work like a zombie all the time.

There was ambivalence about the role of women's work in the home. Most of the mothers did all the housework even if they worked, and their daughters recognized that this put an extra burden on them but took it for granted. They did not question this. Even though they wanted better lives than their mothers this was not conceptualized in terms of changes in the division of labour in the home. Half of them thought that men had better lives than women, and often this was related to women's domestic chores. But they did not suggest ways of changing this. As will be seen below marriage was something they all anticipated.

So what work did the pupils envisage doing at the end of school? What emerged from the initial interviews was the limited range of their employment aspirations from both boys and girls alike. The girls at the age of twelve all assumed they would work though they had given little or no thought, in the main, to what they would do. Social work, work with animals, secretarial work, and hairdressing were on the list and some said simply they had no idea, although the two at the top of the class, Katherine and Carol, each had more definite ideas to begin with.

Katherine hoped to be able to do architecture but thought this too ambitious and difficult. She dismissed this and was prepared to settle for something less. 'So I thought I would like to do a job that I could get something out of and I could say that I did that and as I thought well I could be an architect.' She recognized the difficulties this would incur and said that she would have 'to think about what you're going to do and taking into consideration what other people's views are on living and things like that'.

By the age of fifteen Katherine's attainment had lessened. She had begun to lose interest in school and was more into enjoying herself. Although she said that she was worried about the mock O levels and found physics particularly difficult, her comments throughout the interview highlighted the contradictions between schoolwork and enjoyment. She found that boys occupied her thinking but felt that it should not interfere with her life. She still had ambitions at the age of fifteen, she wanted to be a draughts-person. Universities or colleges were unknown to her. Money had become a more important criterion in terms of her assessment of her future in contrast with her parents. Where previously she had talked of doing work that differed from the kind her mother had done on leaving school, now she talked in terms of being 'a bit better off because things get a bit tight sometimes, and it's a bit difficult'.

Career guidance would only occur in their senior years, and this was limited, according to Katherine who recalled:

> I had one careers talk, and that was in the fifth year after I had chosen my subjects, so that wasn't any much help. But virtually all they could say, the person, I don't know if it was a man or a woman, said 'Do you know what you want to do?' and I said 'No'. 'What subjects are you doing', and I told him. They said 'keep looking around'. I think at the time I wanted to work on a magazine. She said 'you need English for that' and I thought I will see how I get on. They never gave me any definite help. I can't even remember them saying anything positive about suggesting things.

She got five O levels, did one year of A levels and then left school. She worked during a vacation for the Central Electricity Generating Board and got a permanent job. She said she was not happy at school. She had thought of becoming an art teacher but had been told there 'was an enormous amount of teachers out of work and it was a very difficult area to get into'. She appeared to be on a career ladder and felt that because of her experience she had definite advantages over graduates who came into the organization without any practical knowledge.

Carol, the other high flier, at the age of twelve wanted something to do with art and if she could not get a job as an art teacher 'then there's always something else I can do'. Her mother at the time was child minding in a private home, and was quite ignorant about higher education. Carol said 'I would like to go to universities and study typing or something like that'.

By the age of fifteen she wanted to work in textiles and display and fashion work. She had thought about becoming a veterinary surgeon 'but after a while it wore off'; she had changed her mind because 'I have always liked dress designing'. All she wanted was to be successful in her job and be happy and have a good family.

She said she had loved school. As a result of a chance meeting she got a modelling job during the vacation and with the advice of Mrs Francis decided to leave school. She became a freelance model and had travelled fairly extensively when I last interviewed her. But she found the work unsettling because there could be long periods when she was unemployed and so planned to open a boutique.

This is what the two top girls hoped for and what actually happened to them. The others, apart from Lara, had had vague ideas about what they wanted to do. Work and a career was not something they anticipated.

Jane, for example, was bright but did little work at school. At the age of fifteen she had no idea whether she would be in CSE or GCE classes, nor was it important to her because she had no plans for her future at all. She would do whatever work came along and she planned to marry and have a family. She did eventually work in the West End in a shop. She continued living at home although she had a relationship with Robin and her parents did not approve, partly because he was of Afro-Caribbean origin, partly because he had fathered a child, did not work and had committed petty crimes.

Shirley wanted to be a dress designer when she was fifteen. She became a hairdresser and was married by the age of nineteen. She had mapped out exactly what she wanted and was on the way to achieving it.

Doreen, who had been defined as quiet and not very bright,

admitted as an adult that she could not read. This point, commented on elsewhere, obviously affected her notion of what she would do. She thought she would become a hairdresser because this would enable her to work and look after children because of flexible hours. Indeed her thoughts centred on marriage and she did this as soon as she left school and had a two-year-old daughter by the time she was nineteen.

Lara was very conscious of how easily women could be dependent on men. At the age of twenty she said that she had experienced being dependent on her boyfriend and she 'didn't like the thought of becoming what my mum was really'. Her mother was then thirty-five but as Lara said:

> She can't do a thing without my dad. She had two children before she was nineteen, totally lacks confidence in getting a job . . . even if she wants a new dress she has to ask my dad for the money. And I wouldn't like to have to go around asking for things . . . my mum used to talk to me and say 'don't be like me' and I don't really want to be like her in that way.

By the age of nineteen Lara was running a betting shop and earning a high salary. The work the others did was clerical or as shop assistants.

The range in measured ability was wide, as could be expected, but the level of attainment and aspiration for the majority of the girls was low. As school girls they did not talk in terms of alternatives. Nor do age factors seem to have played a role in their emerging aspirations. They were ignorant of job opportunities and never thought of themselves in high status jobs. Their attitude towards future work was limited and this was affected by their goal of being mothers. They wanted to be married and have a family. While they had no specific aspirations, on the whole, they did not appear to suffer from low esteem, particularly in contrast with the boys. They reflected their social and cultural backgrounds. They did not want to do dirty work, or work in factories and, after school worked as clerks, shop assistants, and hairdressers.

The boys' aspirations about their future jobs were also low and unclearly formulated at the age of twelve, although, as mentioned above, they wanted a better life than their fathers had. Where the fathers worked in factories the sons spoke of white collar jobs.

Epilogue

There was a feeling of restlessness. Fisher said that he wanted to get out of England: 'I don't like being in one place. I don't like England all that much. It's too kind of over-populated. I've had me heart on going to America, and I am going to go.' Fisher wanted to become an airplane designer which would assist him in his travels abroad. Elliot did not want to work in a factory as his father did. 'It seems to me so boring. I like to work in the West End. I like it places like that. I would like to work in a big store. I would like to be like a manager, so I could be adventurous'.

The two boys who started out as top of the class differed somewhat from the others. Adam, at the age of twelve, had set his sights on working in a bank. Graham at the age of twelve had obviously given it a great deal of consideration. He said that he could come to no decision. He wanted to be an architect but realized that this involved a good deal of hard work. He was interested in set designing 'for TV but you've got to start from the bottom and work your way to the top'. He had also thought about dealing in antiques but recognized that this required capital.

By the age of fifteen some change had occurred amongst all the boys but not that marked given that the boys were now at the end of their fourth year and at the point at which their subject choice had set them on the pathway into the occupational system. Given the difference in the occupational structure and the emphasis that our culture places on the work men do, ideally these adolescents should have some idea about their future work or further study. There were still several who had no idea what they wanted to do although, like Elliot, they had some notion of further study. He wanted to pass 'the important exams' but did not know which they were or whether he could rewrite the ones in which he got low marks. Although he was fifteen he knew nothing about further and higher education or how he could get access into one or other of these systems. Fisher now wanted to be a policeman in a blue Rover 'roaming about and once I kind of had that, about thirty or forty, I would just like to stop what I'm doing and start travelling'. His urge for travel had not abated, but he now added that he 'would make sure I have got some money behind me, and if I'm married I would have to have them along with me'. His knowledge of training and requirements was very limited. He said he would have to have 'CSE grade 1, or O levels or A levels to get into the police force. And once you are in there for six months you do what you want but you have to start reading books and start catching up on

259

the traffic. Things like that you have to do'. Graham was consistent. He still wanted to do something with designing and now felt that architecture, which he said required physics, took too long and was too technical for him.

Adam, by the age of fifteen, had set out a specific pathway. He was the clearest and also the most ambitious of all the pupils. He was the only one to specify that he wanted to study at a university. He had a great deal to say about his future plans which he had all mapped out. First university to study physics, then a Ph.D. followed by some research somewhere. 'I'll hit at the right time with the job application.' He saw himself as a member of the school's élite and consequently had no doubt about his ability.

Of all the boys, Adam was the only one whose school qualifications were sufficient to set him on the right path. Although he had considered himself one of the top boys in the school, he received a rude shock about his overall results in comparison with boys from other schools. His results were not good enough to gain him a place at Imperial College; he went to one of the Northern universities.

Details of Michael's progress will illustrate what happens to boys with minimal qualifications. He got a City and Guilds qualification in the sixth form (a curriculum innovation in the school and forerunner of TVEI). He tried to get into the Civil Service but there were no openings for someone with his qualifications:

> I was home one morning and me mum's looking through the paper and she must have been looking for jobs but I wasn't really looking. There was a job advertised for a qualified cartographer so mum kept on at me to see if they would take on trainees, and I did phone up and they took on trainees and so I went along there.

He got the job which he enjoyed at first. After a year someone at work suggested that he do a part time evening course at a college. He tried it, but found it reminded him too much of school. He felt he was at a dead end:

> I look at it as a dead end job in a way, because I am not learning anything apart from how to draw. I learnt that pretty quickly and I just can't see it, if I stay there, I am not going to get anywhere. What I am thinking of doing now is taking a

job as a postman because I will be in a dead end job but I will be earning twice as much as I am getting now. So you might as well do a dead end job that's worthwhile.

Michael enjoyed school but regarded the lessons as interfering with his enjoyment: 'I enjoyed the social side of it more with me mates and that. The lessons really were in between the breaks like. After school it was great.' School had not provided him with qualifications or skills with which he could compete on the labour market. His prospects were not good.

Thomas, on the other hand, also did a City and Guilds course and qualified. He felt that his results had helped him get the draughtsman job he was doing. He had not wanted to be a motor mechanic because he did not want to 'lay under cars in pouring rain and all that sort of thing'. He had always wanted to be a draughtsman, so was pleased with the job. However, he found that what he learnt at school was regarded as a handicap:

When I first started I thought it's just going to be like the drawing we did at school, but the first thing they said to me was, right forget everything you learnt at school because it is no good to you at all. And that sort of puts you right off. And you sort of just pick it up and you do it how they do it.

Thomas felt that he did have prospects for promotion without any further training or qualifications as the next step up was as assistant manager which was open to him. He felt that if he did get higher up the ladder he might do further studying on a part time basis.

For these two boys the City and Guilds qualifications had proved useful indirectly. Although their training was not directly relevant – or indeed even a handicap – it had proved that they could qualify in something and it would seem that it was this that had secured them their jobs. Neither of these boys had worked hard at school, on the contrary. After a history of doing as little as possible in school they did achieve something in their last year. Possibly their imminent entry into the labour market spurred them on. They, like so many others, could have left school with nothing to show for the years they had spent there.

Their future and marriage

The first section of this chapter has illustrated the gap that exists between the belief, and the reality, that education provides pupils with the necessary skills and aptitudes for the labour market. The pupils have ill formulated views of available work and how to set about getting jobs. Problems associated with work was not something with which they were concerned. Up to the age of fifteen all but one seemed relatively unperturbed about their prospects. Both girls and boys seemed to accept their limited horizons without question; although they all wished for lives different from their parents, they did not know how to achieve this. In spite of the limitations in terms of their aspirations, the boys were aware that further study could enhance their job prospects. Although their aims, on the whole, were low, some, at least, contemplated the possibility of further education, something which none of the girls did. It was as though that was something quite external to their experiences, although day release colleges had brought further education into the homes of working-class people.

There was a general expectation that the girls would become wives and mothers and all but two of them took family life for granted. The girls were familiar with the work their mothers did and they recognized that they would have to combine work with family responsibilities. They were probably aware of the limitation of job prospects for women, particularly given their socio-economic backgrounds. What is not generally commented upon is that the boys can also see family life as their ultimate goal, accepting the notion that it is the responsibility of men to support their families.

Family life can burst upon them quite quickly on leaving school. For others it can be postponed. Whatever the case may be the pupils' projection of the future at the age of thirty was married life with children. The following gives some of their views about marriage.

At the age of twelve, Doreen was defiant about not getting married because her husband would not allow her to do the things she enjoyed doing:

> My dad reckons I am going to get married and I'm not going to get married. I think if I get married I want to be able to do things as I am now, paint and decorate. Maybe my husband will let me do it but I reckon he would do most, so I wouldn't get married.[1]

By the age of fifteen she had undergone a massive change. She planned to leave school as soon as she could, wanted to be a hairdresser because she could return to it when her children were older. She now wanted to be married by the age of twenty-one 'to have the key of the door, just to be happy with my husband and with life'. Having children would give her the status, dignity and authority previously denied her. Children 'were someone you could look after yourself and they would have to depend on you no matter how stupid you were'. She had always been conscious of being defined as stupid both at school and by her mother. She said she was not 'brainy enough to work in an office although that doesn't bother me'. She saw children as a way to prove herself capable. She did not anticipate working when they were young and because she thought it would be lonely being in the house on her own with children 'with no one to talk to' she planned to take up dressmaking 'because that's what me mum does when we are indoors'.

Within a year of having said this Doreen eloped with her boyfriend to Gretna Green to get married but the place was closed. They split up for a while because her boyfriend's parents objected to her on religious grounds. When she discovered she was pregnant they married.

At the age of twelve Shirley wanted a big house in the country, with a big garden and a swimming pool. She wanted 'two to four nice children'. She would make sure the children were not spoilt. Her husband would be 'kind, gentle, a non-smoker, and not drink a lot'. At the age of fifteen her aspirations had not changed. Marriage was something she wanted, although she fantasized about being a fashion designer:

> When you find somebody that you want to marry there is no reason why you shouldn't although I think if it wasn't for my parents I would rather live with my boy friend as opposed to getting married . . . and I really don't know what the situation would be like if I want a family or something like that. I think it is nice for children to have actually married parents. It's all so different. I change my mind every five minutes.

When she was nineteen she thought that men should shoulder financial responsibility:

I still think it's nice for the men to go out and earn all the money and you can be at home and bring the children up. I don't think that men have got it in them to bring up children at all. I know some girls say I would like to go out and earn all the money and he can stay and look after the children but they don't have the same instinct like its mother. You can't put a man in place of a woman. They are totally different. A man hasn't got the soft tone in his voice for one. So I don't think they could play.

Her future marriage occupied her spare time and she regretted she no longer continued with dancing:

Yes, I was always keen dancing in the evening. That was what took up a lot of my time, dancing and ballet but I gave that up quite some years ago, which I also regret because I would have loved to continue with that, but I think that was what kept a nice figure. I had a hobby to do in the evenings. I find now that I haven't really got a hobby, no matter how much I tried to get interested in something. I can't really get that interested in things. I am hunting around for a hobby . . . I got a form on some of the evening classes but I said I would do that after I got married and once everything is straight. At the moment we are so sort of busy with the wedding, honeymoon and the furniture so really, saving. I can't afford to like . . . we save.

Shirley's world revolved around her domesticity and she was married by nineteen. Neither she nor Doreen had got any qualifications. Doreen had accepted the definition of herself as stupid and initially had wanted a life outside a conventional feminine one. Shirley had never envisaged anything different. She would not want to compete on the open labour market with men. She did not want an interesting job or a career.

The following accounts of the two girls who had been top of the class for the first three years and who had wanted some sort of career are somewhat different initially, but in the end domesticity does feature prominently for one of them.

Carol had never questioned getting married and having children. At the age of twelve she had worked out how she could combine both marital and family duties by getting a job as an art teacher in a school which would give her free time during school holidays. Family life was never far away from her ultimate goal.

She had been a fairly successful model since leaving school but the nature of the work was sporadic. She planned to save sufficient money in order to have her own shop which would mean:

> I would be able to work from home anyway, because I still think, I wouldn't like to work while I had young children. I think I should be at home. If I had seen you a couple of months ago and I was still with my boyfriend, although we weren't thinking about getting married, because we both thought that we were too young, we were actually thinking about getting a flat and so, it would have been easier to think about marriage. But now it seems too far away, marriage, and I have just got no idea when I am going to get married or anything.

She shared Katherine's sentiments about her contemporaries who were now young mothers:

> I know that ever such a lot of girls, not necessarily in my class, but from my year, have got babies, at least one. Lara had her first when she was fourteen. I think she has got two more now. . . . I don't know if that's what they want, but to me, it seems a bit of a waste somehow. I think they are so young, babies when they were sixteen or seventeen.

In spite of her work aspirations at twelve, Katherine anticipated that she would be married, would have children and bring them up much as her parents had brought her up. By fifteen she was beginning to enjoy herself and said that she did not think she could plan ahead about marriage, although only after some prompting did she say it would be nice. By the age of twenty she said about marriage:

> I don't really want to do that yet. Well for one thing I haven't met anybody who I would like to settle down with. I don't know really. I suppose I am too young . . . I don't think that marriage is important. I am not against settling down if somebody came along tomorrow and I really felt that I could get on with him. I would be prepared to. . . . The way I am at the moment I don't feel settled myself enough to go with somebody else.

Although she said she did not wish to have a solitary old age, she did not feel it was necessary to marry at the time. At fifteen she was no longer so sure about having children, 'We saw a film at school about giving birth and it looked very painful and nasty and I don't think I would like that.' She was never very enthusiastic about children, and at the age of twenty said:

> I can't really imagine myself with children. I mean I like other people's children, but I like to give them back at the end of the day. I don't think I would be very patient because I tend to over indulge children, and I wouldn't like the consequences of bringing up a load of spoilt brats. I don't think I would be a very good mother. . . . A lot of the girls in my class are married now with children. I don't think they can have seen that much of life. Alright, there is so much you can see. Going out with your friends and having a laugh and having to worry about paying the bills and making sure that you are back in time to feed the kids. Things like that. I don't think that I am ready for things like that yet.

She spoke about the girls who had married as not having had much interest in anything when she knew them.

Katherine was echoing the same desire for freedom from responsibilities that some of the young men spoke about. She saw marriage as a financial burden, and having children as a major responsibility which would impair her enjoyment, but did not speak about this in terms of her independence.

As a schoolboy Thomas did not see marriage as a top priority; his projections for the future were a good job, money and a nice car. He accepted the probability of being married, as though it was inevitable. By the time he was twenty he regarded 'marriage as responsibility, lack of freedom and commitment'. He recognized that many girls got married young but said:

> I mean they must have wanted to. I think you have got to be a bit daft to get married when you are so young because you lose your freedom, which I think is very important. Marriage is like getting tied down, you know. That puts the screws on it. Your social life is finished. I mean if I had just one week to decide that I was going to pack my job in and go abroad sort

of thing, I can do that. But if you've got commitments then you've got to stay at work to earn money.

Thomas held very traditional views on women's role within marriage. He would be responsible for the support of his wife although he reluctantly agreed that if there were no children it might be permissible for his wife to work. His role model was his mother who he said had always been at home and he had 'got used to that and I think that's what would be right as well'.

Michael's fantasy was to become a professional footballer or boxer. He envisaged marriage by the age of thirty and he too had traditional views about the role of women in the home. At twelve he said she would have to be, 'someone who would be in when I got in and someone who doesn't keep working all through the night, like washing up and clearing up.' By the age of fifteen he wanted his wife to be a good cook and to look after the children. At the age of nineteen he was living with a girlfriend in his parents' council apartment. He felt that 'girls don't seem to do anything really' and that girls are really interested in marriage. His girlfriend kept: 'pestering [me] about getting married . . . but I put it off polite and that . . . I get on with her really well. She is more like a mate. It's always the same. *You feel trapped and that*' (my emphasis). He felt that he had got into a situation from which there was no escape. He was ambivalent about his girlfriend and did not know how to handle the situation. He did not want to marry her although she was very keen to do so. He did not like upsetting her which happened if he went out on his own or with his mates, and he also admitted to thinking about girls a lot. 'It's wicked when you have got a girlfriend. But I think about other girls.'

His sister was married at sixteen because she was pregnant. He thought her boyfriend was to blame:

I can see him thinking that I have been really stupid getting my sister pregnant and having to marry her. And when that day comes and he has to ask himself that question, he is going to blame, not her, but that's the way it goes. He will take it out on somebody else . . . it bothers me.

But he also thought that girls 'looked forward to getting married and having children whereas the majority of boys look forward to having a car'. He was convinced that girls wanted marriage and material goods:

> They get all these grand illusions they are going to get married and settled down. You have your house with your nice settee. They don't realise the bloke isn't 100 per cent into it or maybe the girl isn't into it. He don't want to spend all his wages on a table. I mean that is what I think buying a house and all that. No I would think twice. I would maybe go out at night and maybe have a wife at home. I know I wouldn't be dedicated 100 per cent not unless I wanted to. I mean if I wanted to you that's how it works. . . . I think partly she was pleased that she had a baby. She didn't have to go to work and she could stay at home and look after the baby. That's what I think. It may not be true . . . she was pleased when it was all over and she had actually had the baby. *It was an excuse not to go to work and things like that* (my emphasis).

Conclusion

Reference was made in Chapter 9 to a statement which claimed that schooling does not lead most girls to have the 'attitude of mind to compete equally with boys for jobs. . .'. The data contradicts this and suggests that neither the girls nor the boys had highly developed work ethics. But girls did anticipate working and regarded this as a permanent feature of their lives. Their home experience had taught them that mothers did work, so for many of them the problem was what they would do when their children were young. To this extent their aspirations regarding work reflected their family backgrounds.

Overall the projections of both the girls and the boys for their future reflected a restricted view in regard to work. Only one aimed to go to university. For the others further and higher education was clearly beyond their family's experience and something that they had little or no information about. Their schooling did not seem to introduce them to this option. While both the girls and the boys wanted to improve their life styles in comparison with their parents, they lacked the knowledge of how to go about it. They had a restricted view of the labour market itself, and details about further and higher education appeared quite outside their experience. Both the girls and the boys knew what jobs they did not want to do, but they were less clear about what they did want. While some knew vaguely that qualifications were necessary, and that certain types of jobs required qualifications, such as architecture, they had little concrete information about the nature of the qualifications or how much studying was required. It was only in the sixth form that some of the boys did obtain some qualifications that seemed to be useful, such as the City and Guilds which had only recently been introduced. For the rest it seemed that what happened to them was a result of chance factors once they had left school. All this seems to contradict Furlong's (1986) contention about girls' aspirations being forged in their homes. The situation is more complex than that.

Would it have made a difference to both boys and girls had the school been oriented towards widening their horizons about work and job opportunities, and training schemes been made part of their curriculum from the outset? After all the deputy head had set the sights of the school curriculum within the narrowest possible range and this could well have had a hidden impact on the pupils together with the limitations they brought with them from their own cultural backgrounds.

Taking into account more specific elements within the curriculum, this also raises serious doubts about the nature of such courses such as Design for Living. What exactly is the purpose of such a course? To what extent are the pupils made aware of the direct and concrete effect of qualifications and at what age? Career guidance is something which is carried out outside of the normal range of the curriculum and although individual teachers may be charged with some responsibility in communicating information to the pupils, the Local Education Authorities provide external guidance and all such guidance, in any event, stands in jeopardy if recent proposals in education are carried out.

The question is to what extent should such data become an integral part of their education and furthermore how concrete should pupils' experience of vocational aspects of work be. These are obviously questions on which TVEI are focusing and, as seen in Chapter 9, the success of the scheme has yet to be established, although there are clear indications that these are limited and girls are even less likely to benefit from these innovations.

However, what is clear is that the aspirations of the pupils in regard to work – both girls and boys alike – are cast in terms of individual goals, reflecting the competitive individualism of our society. They all want better lives than their parents had, and this is to be attained through individual effort. There is no sense of working together as a group, within a community, or for the improvement of society in general.

It is in regard to projections about marriage that the differences between the girls and boys are more marked. The extracts from the many comments made about their future marital state reflect the different perceptions of traditional gender divisions. In the main the girls accepted marriage as their primary goal although there were a few exceptions as with Katherine who wanted to postpone such responsibilities. The boys recognized that they would marry, except for Graham who said from the outset that he would always be a bachelor. The comments by Thomas and Michael reflect the growing awareness among the young men of the burden they *thought* would be theirs with marriage. Unlike a section of middle-class men in America who have shied away from marriage on the grounds that they can have many of the benefits of married life without the responsibilities (Ehrenreich, 1983), these young people did not question marriage. Thomas wanted to be the sole supporter of his family; Michael simply saw marriage as a cutback on his freedom and the need to meet the demands of the consumer requests of a wife. Both he and Thomas were wary of taking on such responsibilities although they both recognized the inevitability of marriage. Most of them would marry, although many would land up divorced, separated (as Mavis was at the age of nineteen) or as single parents, according to present day trends.

What is interesting is the relationship between schooling and the family. Domestic labour is taken for granted and is never spoken of as 'work' because it is not part of production for consumption on the market. For this reason it is not included in the terms of reference when training for adulthood is being discussed. Priority is given to vocational training. Yet the family is where the majority of girls will spend a great deal of time and effort throughout the course of their lives. Furthermore, given the increased rate of unemployment and the decline in the hours of the working week, men are also likely to spend more time in the family.

This suggests the need to examine more carefully the relationship between family and work. Many married women, or women who are single parents, work and inevitably the burden of homecare falls on them. The changing nature of employment in this country can alter, dramatically, the relationship of men to their families, more so if they spend more time at home. Already there are marked changes. Men push babies in prams and in pushchairs; they shop at the supermarkets; they go to launderettes. There seems to be some shift in attitude towards what a man may do in the home without being laughed at. It is eminently sensible to envisage training men to participate more fully in the life of their families and in housework. This, together with possible job share schemes, and maternity leave which could enable men or women to remain at home with children while they are still very young are possibilities which schooling could consider. An equitable division of labour should take place both in the home and in the workplace.

To effect changes for girls' education requires, amongst other things, drastic changes in the education system: it needs systematically to be reviewed and restructured. It is possible to heighten teachers' and parents' awareness through various programmes, and is a worthwhile enterprise in itself. But this cannot by itself bring about a change which will affect future generations of girls. There are many problems still to be resolved within the educational system and perhaps the time has come to rethink many of the principles that stand as sacred cows.

Notes

Introduction

1 For a reappraisal of the contribution of Bowles and Gintis, see Cole (1988).
2 There was a concentration on cultural formations as exhibited in politics (Corrigan and Frith, 1976), style (Hebdige, 1979) and deviancy (Pearson, 1975) of male youth culture and it was male oriented.
3 There is an extended critique of the application of the experiential in Wolpe (1988).
4 In passing it should be noted that such analyses have also occurred in work on racism and has become a dominant feature of much of Black feminist writing. According to the emphasis on the experiential it is only women (or blacks, or black women) who can know and understand oppressive behaviour of men (or white racists).

CHAPTER ONE *Within these walls*

1 This analysis is explored in greater depth in Wolpe (1985).
2 Wolf, Goldstein and Silver in an article in the *Guardian*, 3 June 1986 pointed out that the reliance on teachers' ability to assess raised serious problems for the success of the GCSE scheme. Not only the time involved but also the techniques required constituted problems. They said 'What must be worrying is the notion that the new system will provide completely specific and unambiguous information about what an individual "can do" '.
3 Truancy has always comprised a problem in schools and this form of resistance has always been present. Humphries (op. cit.) concluded that the 'systematic and coercive efforts made by the state to control and eliminate [truancy] from the late 19th century onwards' is not located in altruism but rather in a form of class control. On the basis of the discussion on discipline, it would seem that overall control,

irrespective of the class nature of the pupil population, is what is at stake.

4 These figures are derived from an article by De Waal, a Head of Year in a large South London Comprehensive School (*Observer*, 30 May 1982). He referred to these truants as '20,000 potential petty criminals'. Humphries (1981), drawing on oral history, recorded some very poignant accounts by women and men of their school avoidance. These included examples of brutal treatment as pupils. They were not 'potential petty criminals' at all but children sometimes negotiating the conflicting demands being made on them by members of their families.

5 In an article in *TES* (6 January 1984) Gerald Haigh discussed a privately published book *Memories of a School Inspector* by A. J. Swinburne who retired in 1912. Haigh quoted Swinburne on corporal punishment: 'A London mistress, whom I discovered administering unjudicious punishment, flew into a temper on my remonstrating mildly with her.' She was boxing a girl's ears. Swinburne wished to establish with the teacher that it was her 'slack surveillance at fault . . . Vigilance is an indispensable factor of good teaching, yet how often a child is punished because the teacher's surveillance is slack.'

6 The whole issue of corporal punishment has been hotly debated for many years. In 1982 The European Court of Human Rights ruled that 'children have a right to be educated in schools where they will not be beaten' following an application by Scottish parents. In June the *Guardian* reported that 'head teachers accepted that the abolition of corporal punishment was inevitable but warned the Government that a considerable increase in resources would be necessary to keep order in school' (4 June 1982). After several local education authorities decided to ban corporal punishment, the Assistant Masters and Mistresses Association set up a working party to consider the possible outcome of such action. They, like others, concluded that this would result in a need for financial input if disruption owing to the banning of corporal punishment was not to increase (*Guardian*, 16 June 1982). Quite contrary evidence is available to this gloomy prognosis and indeed at the end of the same year there was a report in the *TES* by M. Dueham on the record of the Punishment Book of an inner-city mixed comprehensive school:

> It turned its back on the cane in 1970 after its current headmaster had been in place for three years. He is still there. 'I began to feel that caning was wrong. It wasn't a blinding flash of light but a gradual realization. So I said to my staff, "Let's try and do without it for a while".' Nothing was said – officially. But two months later the canes were thrown out for good. The

pupils quietly adjusted and two years later when a supply teacher whacked a boy the rest of the class were indignantly able to tell him that theirs was not that kind of school (3 December 1982).

In August 1987 corporal punishment was finally banned from schools.

7 Several pupils throughout the period of interviews, including as adults, recalled Mr David and spoke about him with affection and respect.

CHAPTER TWO *Classroom behaviour*

1 Clarricoates was concerned with the *effect* of stereotyping but not with the processes involved which she did not regard as problematic. In order to avoid falling into the trap of stereotypes about boys, the process of stereotyping needs full recognition.

2 This is an illustration of 'exampling' as defined by Glaser and Strauss in 1967 whereby a theory is supported by empirical data. I examine this and other questions relating to the role of 'experience' in the course of discussing experience in some detail (Wolpe, 1988).

CHAPTER THREE *Girls and boys at school*

1 This concept has appeared in a variety of disparate texts. Foucault (1982) asserted that resistance was a direct and inevitable consequence of any disciplined situation. Genovese (1972) in his mammoth study of slavery in America accounted for many of the actions of the slaves in terms of resistance and accommodation. Willis (1977) in analysing the apparent willingness and collusion with which working-class lads move into their restricted no-prospect occupations also employed a highly sophisticated version of resistance and accommodation.

2 Humphries (1983) differentiated between three types of truancy, recognizing that there could be a certain degree of overlap between them: opportunist, retreatist and subsistence. Opportunist truancy was not consistent and was occasional and spontaneous absenteeism. An example would be taking a day off from school on a bright summer's day and going to an outdoor swimming pool. Retreatist truancy was defined by Humphries as a deviant form, 'incessant and deeply ingrained, inspired by a profound aversion to various aspects of school'. He recognized the difficulty of being precise in his definition of this category. The third, subsistence, was 'provoked essentially by poverty and social deprivation'. While social conditions today have altered and school children need not go picking up waste bits of coal,

there are still numbers of pupils, mainly girls, who do not attend school because of domestic responsibilities.

Note to Introduction to Part II

1 There is a wide range of different theories on sex and sexuality from Freudianism to behaviourism. Within feminist literature there has been, as Segal (1987) points out, a preoccupation with the application of analytical theory which has been hotly debated (Wilson, 1981, Snitow *et. al.*, 1984).

CHAPTER FOUR *Sexuality and moral order*

1 An examination of the titles of articles published in the *Journal of Moral Education* since 1974 reveal that very few articles are devoted specifically to sex education.
2 The whole formulation is in the process of change as a direct consequence of the potential threat of AIDS to heterosexual relationships.
3 I have drawn extensively on my article 'Sex in Schools: Back to the Future' in *Feminist Review* No 27, 1987.
4 Following the media coverage on sex education in 1986, and in particular ILEA's book dealing with a homosexual couple bringing up a girl, there was a spate of letters and articles often opposing the teaching of sex education, including anything relating to homosexuality. For example S. Horsford in a short article in the *Guardian* (16 September 1986) strongly opposed any such teaching.
5 Farraday (1985) reviews Havelock Ellis who commented on 'crushes'. He regarded these as a form of 'arrested development' which could result in 'permanent artificial homosexuality'. She points out that following his work a succession of writers canvassed for co-education schools on the grounds that single sex schools could lead to homosexuality – amongst boys as well as girls. This view was held also by Marie Stopes, who Farraday describes as suffering from a 'lesbian angst' on 'the incipient threat of the spinster at school'.

CHAPTER FIVE *Sexuality in the school*

1 According to DES Statistics the following are the figures for male and female teachers in England:

	1985		
	Full Time	Part Time	Full Time Equivalent of Part Time
Male	18,803	2,432	894
Female	18,885	13,035	5,938

The difference in part time numbers is to be expected.

2 Miller and Fowlkes (1980) are critical of Simon and Gagnon in their lack of concern with marital sexuality because they say that these two men see marriage 'less as an entry into adult society and sexual roles than as the end product of childhood and adolescent social- ization' (p. 263).

CHAPTER SIX *Sex and everyday life*

1 Davies (1984) who was concerned with gender and deviance in school discussed teachers not only acting as role models for pupils, but also, in the case of young women teachers, as being potential rivals. To support this she gave a verbatim report by one girl on an older woman teacher, claiming that it was the 'teacher's age which precluded the girls seeing her as a rival; it was her lack of propriety in fact which infuriated them'. To substantiate this she quoted the following tran- scription of one girl's comments:

> Mrs S. was the one; her was about 82 years old . . . her was filthy, her used to sit with her legs open, didn't her? All the chaps would be sitting in front of her on the floor lying down like this. Vultures. Every time I looked at her, I could kill her (p. 29).

2 Informal discussions I have had with a psychoanalyst who has worked for many years with adolescents who experience a wide range of sexual disturbances suggest this is not the case. He asserts that it is not the norm for adolescents to fantasize about rape.

3 It should be noted, in passing, that homosexuality was only referred to in terms of boys. At no stage did the question of lesbianism arise and no one offered any comments on this except Shirley when inter- viewed as an adult. She spoke about the fact that girls are much more affectionate than boys and so cling to one another. 'You tend to love a girl' she said. But she did not equate this with lesbianism. She said she knew nothing about lesbianism until she was close to leav- ing school.

4 Adam was also racist in his views. He said:

> The black community in my mind isn't very good. They are people – there are one or two people – only about two, three, four black people who are in this school and are friendly people. The others are just thick, mindless people who – I blame their parents really because their parents didn't give them such a strong upbringing and if you notice in the papers these days you will find a lot of black youths going around the streets

mugging and they are not people who you can sort of have a fight with. They have instruments of torture, knives and they go around in gangs of forty which I think they are insecure. They don't really know what they want to do, they sort of funk their exams, they don't care less, they just sort of go around mugging people as they like. And there is a black community centre according to the grapevine that is going to open.

CHAPTER SEVEN *Knowledge and control*

1 Curriculum studies is relatively new sociologically speaking as Whitty (1985) has said. He delineates M. Young's book *Knowledge and Control* (1971) as the moment when the role of the curriculum was conceptualised as a form of transmission of knowledge related to aspects of social control: access to knowledge constituted a major element in attaining power and control. Arising out of this development in what became known as the New Sociology of Education was a spate of research in which, as Whitty points out, conclusions were reached which demonstrated how 'definitions of school knowledge could help to reproduce society'.

Whitty identifies two distinct approaches to this area of study, neither of which has appeared to have had an impact on the other, Marxist, neo/Marxist and Phenomenological. In the course of making this identification Whitty has ignored a third approach which reflects the work of feminist writers.

2 The development reflected in the work of Bowles and Gintis has been criticized over the years with a recent assessment (Cole, 1988). One of the major grounds for criticism has been the monolithic relationship established between the ideology relating to the work ethic as transmitted during the course of schooling and the labour process. Sharp and Green (1975), for example, emphasised the need to consider overall power relations in the broader social structure. As Whitty (1985) points out, the break from the notion of this monolithic relationship was none too successful and he points to the different theoretical thrusts derived from the work of Foucault and discourse theory which superseded this type of analysis.

CHAPTER EIGHT *The curriculum at Berkeley*

1 Given the complexity and range of activities covered by technology and technological skills, one could argue that the mere attendance of woodwork and metalwork classes would not necessarily lead girls into technological fields of work and, indeed, the same may be said to apply to boys. Furthermore, it simply is not known to what extent advanced technology will require more skilled man and woman power: the contrary seems to be the case.

2 Hargreaves (1977) produced a slender argument linking the provision of PE to capitalism. He suggests that PE is offered because it might well contribute an 'ideological means of helping to perpetuate the status quo and this demonstrates an interesting link between the subject (i.e. PE) and the capitalist mode of production' (p. 22).

EPILOGUE

1 In an earlier article (1978) I examined this relationship in great detail.

Bibliography

Aggleton, P.J. and Whitty, G. (1985), 'Rebels without a cause? Socialisation & subcultural style among the children of the new middle classes', *Sociology of Education*, Vol. 58, No.1, Jan., pp. 60-70.

Althusser, L. (1971), 'Ideology and ideological state apparatuses' in *Lenin and Philosophy and other Essays*, London, New Left Books.

Anyon, J. (1983), 'Gender, Resistance and Power', in S. Walker and L. Barton (eds), *Gender, Class and Education*, Lewes, Falmer Press.

Apple, M. (1981), 'Social structure, ideology and curriculum', in M. Lawn and L. Barton (eds), *Rethinking Curriculum Studies*, London, Croom Helm.

Apple, M. (1982), *Education and Power*, London, Routledge & Kegan Paul.

Aries, P. and Bejin, A. (eds) (1985), *Western Sexuality*, Oxford, Blackwell.

Arnot, M. (1984), 'How shall we educate our sons?' in R. Deem (ed.), *Co-Education Reconsidered*, Milton Keynes, Open University Press.

Arnot, M. (1986), 'State education policy and girls' educational experiences' in V. Beechey and E. Whitelegg (eds), *Women in Britain Today*, Milton Keynes, Open University Press.

Aronowitz, S. and Giroux, H.A. (1986), *Education under Siege: The Conservative, Liberal and Radical Debate Over Schooling*, London, Routledge & Kegan Paul.

Ball, S. (1981), *Beachside Comprehensive: A Case-Study of Secondary Schooling*, Cambridge, Cambridge University Press.

Baron, S., Finn, D., Grant, N., Green, M. and Johnson, R. (1981), *Unpopular Education*, London, Hutchinson.

Barrett, M., Corrigan, P., Kuhn, A. and Wolff, J. (eds) (1979), *Ideology and Cultural Production*, London, Croom Helm.

Barton, L. and Walker, S. (eds) (1983), *Education and Social Change*, London, Croom Helm.

Bates, I., Clarke, J., Cohen, P., Finn, D., Moore, R. and Willis, P. (1984), *Schooling for the Dole*, London, Macmillan.

Beechey, V. (1978), 'Women and production: A critical analysis of some sociological theories of women's work', in A. Kuhn and AM. Wolpe (eds), *Feminism and Materialism*, London, Routledge & Kegan Paul.

Beechey, V. (1982), in S. Wood (ed.), *Degradation of Work*, London, Hutchinson.

Bellaby, P. (1974), 'The distribution of deviance among 13–14 year old students' in J. Eggleston (ed.), *Contemporary Research in the Sociology of Education*, London, Methuen.

Bourdieu, P. (1971), 'Systems of education and systems of thought' in Young, M.E.D., (ed.), *Knowledge and Control*, London, Collier-Macmillan.

Bourdieu, P. and Passeron, J.C. (1977), *Reproduction in Education, Society and Culture*, London, Sage.

Bowles, S. and Gintis, H. (1976), *Schooling in Capitalist America*, London, Routledge & Kegan Paul.

Brake, M. (1980), *The Sociology of Youth Cultures and Youth Subcultures*, London, Routledge & Kegan Paul.

Brake, M. (ed.) (1982), *Human Sexual Relations*, Harmondsworth, Penguin Books.

Brown, R. (1984), 'Education for what work?', *British Journal of Sociology of Education*, Vol. 5, No. 1, pp. 97–101.

Browne, P., Matzen, L. and Whyld, J. (1983), 'Physical education' in J. Whyld (ed.), *Sexism in the Secondary Curriculum*, London, Harper & Row.

Bury, J. (1984), *Teenage Pregnancy in Britain*, London, Birth Control Trust.

Centre for Contemporary Cultural Studies, Education Group (1981), *Unpopular Education, Schooling and Social Democracy in England since 1944*, London, Hutchinson.

Chandler, E.M. (1980), *Educating Adolescent Girls*, London, Allen and Unwin.

Chetwynd, J. and Hartnett, O. (1974–5) 'A review of schooling & sex roles with particular reference to the experience of girls in secondary schools', *Educational Review* 27(3) pp. 165–78.

Chisholm, L.A. and Holland, J. (1986), 'Girls and occupational choice: anti-sexism in action in a curriculum development project', *British Journal of Sociology of Education*, Vol. 7, No. 4, pp. 353–66.

Church of England Board of Education (1962), *Sex Education in Schools*, London, Church Information Office.

Clarricoates, K. (1980), 'The Importance of Being Earnest . . . Emma . . . Tom . . . Jane. The Perception and Categorization of Gender Conformity and Gender Deviation in Primary Schools' in R. Deem (ed.), *Schooling for Women's Work*, London, Routledge & Kegan Paul.

Bibliography

Cohen, S. (1972), *Folk Devils and Moral Panics*, London, MacGibbon & Kee.

Cole, M. (1983), 'Contradictions in the educational theory of Gintis and Bowles', *The Sociological Review*, Vol. 31, No. 3, pp. 471–88.

Cole, M. (ed.) (1988), *Bowles and Gintis Revisited: Schooling and Capitalism Ten Years On*, Lewes, Falmer Press.

Cornbleet, A. and Libovitch, S. (1983), 'Anti-sexist initiatives in a mixed comprehensive school', in AM. Wolpe and J. Donald (eds), *Is There Anyone Here From Education? Education After Thatcher*, London, Pluto Press.

Corrigan, P. and Frith, S. (1976), 'The politics of youth culture', in S. Hall and T. Jefferson (eds), *Resistance through Rituals*, London, Hutchinson.

Crowther Report, See Report of the Central Advisory Council for Education.

DES (1977), *Health Education in Schools*, London, HMSO.

DES (1981), *The School Curriculum*, London, HMSO.

DES (1986), *Health Education from 5–16*, London, HMSO.

DES Welsh Office (1983), *Curriculum 11–16: Towards a Statement of entitlement*, London, HMSO.

DES Statistics 1984, *Statistics of Education School Leavers, CSE and GCE* 1984.

Dallas, D.M. (1972), *Sex Education in School and Society*, National Foundation for Education Research.

David, M. (1980), *The State, the Family and Education*, London, Routledge & Kegan Paul.

Davidoff, L. and Hall, C. (1987), *Family Fortunes: Men and Women of the English middle class, 1780–1850*, London, Hutchinson.

Davies, L. (1984), *Pupil Power, Deviance and Gender in School*, Lewes, Falmer Press.

Dawson, P. (1981), *Making a Comprehensive Work*, Oxford, Blackwell.

Deem, R. (1978), *Women and Schooling*, London, Routledge & Kegan Paul.

Deem, R. (ed.) (1980), *Schooling for Women's Work*, London, Routledge & Kegan Paul.

Deem, R. (ed.) (1984), *Co-education Reconsidered*, Milton Keynes, Open University.

Delamont, S. (1980), *Sex Roles and the School*, London, Methuen.

Denscombe, M. (1984), 'Control, Controversy and the Comprehensive School' in S.J. Ball (ed.), *Comprehensive Schooling: A Reader*, Lewes, Falmer Press.

Eaton, M. (1986), *Justice for Women, Family, Court and Social Order*, Milton Keynes, Open University Press.

Ehrenreich, B. (1983), *The Hearts of Men*, New York, Doubleday & Company.

Eppel, E.M. (1963), 'The Adolescent and Changing Moral Standards' in W.R. Niblett (ed.), *Moral Education in a Changing Society*, London, Faber & Faber.

Entwistle, H. (1970a), *Child-centred Education*, London, Methuen.

Entwistle, H. (1970b), *Education, Work and Leisure*, London, Routledge & Kegan Paul.

Farraday, A. (1985), *Social Definitions of Lesbians in Britain 1914-1939*, Ph.D. Dissertation University of Essex, March–April 1985, Sociology Department.

Farrell, C. (1978), *'My Mother Said', the way young people learned about sex and birth control*, London, Routledge & Kegan Paul.

Foucault, M. (1982), *Discipline and Punish*, London, Peregrine Books.

Foucault, M. (1985), 'The Battle for Chastity', in P. Aries and A. Bejin (eds), *Western Sexuality*, Oxford, Blackwell.

Fuller, M. (1980), 'Black Girls in a London Comprehensive School', in R. Deem (ed.), *Schooling for Women's Work*, London, Routledge & Kegan Paul.

Furlong, A. (1986), 'Schools and the structure of Female Occupational Aspirations', *British Journal of Sociology of Education*, Vol. 7, No. 4, pp. 367–78.

Genovese, E. (1972), *Roll Jordan Roll: The World the Slaves made*, New York, Vintage.

Glaser, B. and Strauss, A. (1967), *The Discovery of Grounded Theory*, Chicago, Aldine.

Gordon, L. (1984), 'Paul Willis – Education, Cultural Production and Social Reproduction', *British Journal of Sociology of Education*, Vol. 5, No. 2, pp. 105–16.

Grant, M. (1983), 'Craft, Design and Technology' in J. Whyld (ed.), *Sexism in the Secondary Curriculum*, London, Harper & Row.

Hall, S. and Jefferson, T. (eds) (1976), *Resistance Through Rituals*, London, Hutchinson.

Halsey, A.H. (1963), 'The Sociology of Moral Education' in W.R. Niblett (ed.), *Moral Education in a Changing Society*, London, Faber & Faber.

Halsey, A.H., Floud, J. and Henderson, C.A. (eds) (1961), *Education, Economy and Society*, London, Collier-Macmillan.

Harding, J. (1980), 'Sex differences in performance in Science examinations' in R. Deem (ed.), *Schooling for Women's Work*, London, Routledge & Kegan Paul.

Hargreaves, D.H. (1967), *Social Relations in a Secondary School*, London, Routledge & Kegan Paul.

Bibliography

Hargreaves, D.H. (1974), 'Deschoolers and New Romantics' in M. Flude and J. Ahier (eds), *Educability, Schools and Ideology*, London, Croom Helm.

Hargreaves, D.H. (1977), 'Sport and physical education: autonomy or domination', in *Bulletin of Physical Education*, 13.1.

Hargreaves, D.H., Hester, S.K. and Mella, F.J. (1975), *Deviance in Classrooms*, London, Routledge & Kegan Paul.

Hebdige, D. (1979), *Subcultures – The Meaning of Style*, London, Methuen.

Hindess, B. (1973), *The Uses of Official Statistics in Sociology: a critique of positivism and ethnomethodology*, London, Macmillan.

Holland, J. and Chisholm, L. (1985), *Girls and Occupational Choice: A brief description of the first eighteen months of the project*, Girls and Occupational Choice Project, Working Paper No. 6, 1985, Sociological Research Unit, Department of the Sociology of Education, Institute of Education, University of London.

Holly, L. (1985), 'Mary, Jane and Virginia Woolf: Ten year old girls talking', in G. Weiner (ed.), *Just a Bunch of Girls*, Milton Keynes, Open University Press.

Humphries, S. (1981), *Hooligans or Rebels? An Oral History of Working-Class Childhood and Youth 1889–1939*, Oxford, Basil Blackwell.

Jackson, M. (1984), 'Sociology and the universalisation of male sexuality' in L. Coveney, M. Jackson, S. Jeffreys, L. Kaye, M. Mahony (eds), *The Sexuality Papers*, London, Hutchinson in association with the Exploration in Feminism Collective.

Jackson, S. (1978), 'How to make Babies: Sexism in Sex Education', *Women's Studies International Quarterly*, Vol. 1, pp. 341–52.

Jones, C. (1985), 'Sexual Tyranny: Male violence in a mixed secondary school' in G. Weiner (ed.), *Just a Bunch of Girls*, Milton Keynes, Open University Press.

Kamm, J. (1965), *Hope Deferred*, London, Methuen.

Keddie, N. (1971), 'Classroom Knowledge' in M.T.D. Young (ed.), *Knowledge and Control: New Directions for the Sociology of Education*, London, Collier-Macmillan.

Kelly, A. (1981) (ed.), *The Missing Half: Girls and Science Education*, Manchester, Manchester University Press.

Kelly, A., Whyte, J. and Smart, B. (1984), *Girls into Science and Technology: Final Report*, GIST, Department of Sociology, University of Manchester.

Kohlberg, L. (1963), 'The development of children's orientations towards a moral order: 'sequence in the development of moral thought', in *Vita Humana*.

Kuhn, A. and Wolpe, AM. (eds) (1978), *Feminism and Materialism*, London, Routledge & Kegan Paul.

Lawton, D. (1975), *Class, Culture and the Curriculum*, London, Routledge & Kegan Paul.
Lees, S. (1986), *Losing Out Sexuality and Adolescent Girls*, London, Hutchinson.
Litewka, J. (1977), 'The socialised penis', in Snodgrass, *For Men Against Sexism*.
Lobban, G. (1978), 'The Influences of the School on Sex-Role Stereotyping', J. Chetwynd and O. Harnett (eds), *The Sex Role System, Psychological and Sociological Perspectives*, London, Routledge & Kegan Paul.
Longford Committee (1972), *Pornography: The Longford Report*, London, Coronet.

Maccoby, E.E. and Jacklin, C.N. (1974), *The Psychology of Sex Differences*, Stanford, Stanford University Press.
MacDonald, M. (1981), *Class, Gender and Education*, E353, Block 4, Milton Keynes, The Open University Press.
McLoughlin, A. (1984), 'The Golden pathway', in A. McRobbie, and T. McCabe, (eds), *Feminism for Girls, An Adventure Story*, London, Routledge & Kegan Paul.
McRobbie, A. (1978), 'Working Class Girls and the Culture of Femininity', in Women's Studies Group, Centre for Contemporary Cultural Studies, *Women Take Issue*, London, Hutchinson.
McRobbie, A. (1980), 'Settling Accounts with Subcultures: A Feminist Critique', *Screen Education*, Spring, No. 34.
McRobbie, A. and Garber, J. (1975), 'Girls and Subcultures: An exploration' in S. Hall and T. Jefferson (eds), *Resistance through Rituals*, London, Hutchinson.
McRobbie, A. and McCabe, T. (eds) (1981), *Feminism for Girls: An Adventure Story*, London, Routledge & Kegan Paul.
Mahony, P. (1985), *Schools for the Boys? Co-education reassessed*, London, Hutchinson in association with The Explorations in Feminism Collective.
Miliband, R., Panitch, L. and Saville, J. (eds), *Socialist Register*, London, The Merlin Press.
Miller, R.Y. and Fowlkes, M.R. (1980), 'Social and Behavioural Constructions of Female Sexuality', in C.R. Stimpson and E.S. Person (eds), *Women, Sex and Sexuality*, Chicago, University of Chicago Press.
Millman, V. (1985), 'Breadwinning and Babies: A redefinition of careers education' in G. Weiner (ed.), *Just A Bunch of Girls*, Milton Keynes, Open University Press.

Bibliography

National Child Development Study, *Growing up in Great Britain* (1983), K. Fogelman (ed.), London, Macmillan.

Niblett, W.R. (ed.) (1963), *Moral Education in a Changing Society*, London, Faber & Faber.

Pearson, G. (1975), *The Deviant Imagination: psychiatry, social work and social change*, London, Macmillan.

Pearson, G. (1983), *Hooligan: A History of Respectable Fears*, London, The Macmillan Press.

Perkins, T.E. (1979), 'Rethinking Stereotypes' in M. Barrett, P. Corrigan, A. Kuhn and J. Wolff (eds), *Ideology and Cultural Production*, London, Croom Helm.

Peters, R.S. (1963), 'Reason and Habit: The Paradox of Moral Education' in W.R. Niblett (ed.), *Moral Education in a Changing Society*, London, Faber & Faber.

Phillips, A. (1983), *Hidden Hands: Women and Economic Policies*, London, Pluto Press.

Platt, A. and Whyld, J. (1983), 'Introduction' in J. Whyld (ed.), *Sexism in the Secondary Curriculum*, London, Harper & Row.

Plummer, K. (1975), *Sexual Stigma, An Interactionist Account*, London, Routledge & Kegan Paul.

Plummer, K. (1982), 'Symbolic Interactionism and Sexual Conduct: an emergent perspective' in M. Brake (ed.), *Human Sexual Relations*, Harmondsworth, Penguin Books.

Poulantzas, N. (1975), *Classes in Contemporary Capitalism*, London, New Left Books.

Reid, D. (1982), 'School Sex Education and the causes of unintended teenage pregnancies – a review' in *Health Education Journal*, Vol. 41, pp. 4–11.

Report of the Central Advisory Council for Education, *15–18*, Ministry of Education, Vol. 1 (1959), London, HMSO (The Crowther Report).

Rich, B.R. (1986), 'Feminism and Sexuality in the 1980s, Review Essay', *Feminist Studies*, Vol. 12, No. 3, pp. 525–63.

Riley, D. (1983), *War in the Nursery, Theories of the Child and Mother*, London, Virago.

Samuel, J. (1983), 'Mathematics & Science – Introduction' in J. Whyld (ed.), *Sexism in the Secondary Curriculum*, London, Harper & Row.

Sarap, M. (1982), *Education, State and Crisis*, London, Routledge & Kegan Paul.

Segal, L. (1987), *Is the Future Female? Troubled thoughts on Contemporary Feminism*, London, Virago.

Schofield, M. (1963), *The Sexual Behaviour of Young People*, London, Longmans.

Schofield, M. (1973), *The Sexual Behaviour of Young Adults*, Harmondsworth, Allen Lane.

Shacklady Smith, L. (1978), 'Sexist assumptions and female delinquency', in C. Smart and B. Smart (eds), *Women, Sexuality and Social Control*, London, Routledge & Kegan Paul.

Sharp, R. and Green, A. (1975), *Education and Social Control*, London, Routledge & Kegan Paul.

Sharpe, S. (1976), *'Just like a Girl': How Girls Learn to be Women*, Harmondsworth, Penguin Books.

Shaw, J. (1984), 'The politics of single sex schools' in R. Deem (ed.), *Co-Education Reconsidered*, Milton Keynes, Open University Press.

Simon, W. and Gagnon, J. (1971), 'Psychosexual Development' in D.L. Grummon and A.M. Barclay (eds), *Sexuality: A Search for Perspectives*, New York, Van Nostrand Reinhold Co.

Smart, C. and Smart, B. (eds) (1978), *Women, Sexuality and Social Control*, London, Routledge & Kegan Paul.

Smith, M.J. (1975), 'Discipline in the Classroom', *Comprehensive Education*, No. 30, Summer 1975.

Smith, S. (1984), 'Single-sex setting' in R. Deem (ed.), *Co-Education Reconsidered*, Milton Keynes, Open University Press.

Snitow, A., Stansell, C. and Thompson, S. (eds) (1984), *Desire: The Politics of Sexuality*, London, Virago.

Spender, D. (1980), 'Disappearing Tricks' in D. Spender and E. Sarah (eds), *Learning to Lose, Sexism and Education*, London, The Women's Press.

Spender, D. (1982), *Invisible Women: the schooling scandal*, London, Writers and Readers Co-operative.

Stanley, L. and Wise, S. (1983), *Breaking out: Feminist Consciousness and Feminist Research*, London, Routledge & Kegan Paul.

Stantonbury Campus Sexism in Education Group, Bridgewater Hall School (1984), 'The realities of mixed schooling' in R. Deem (ed.), *Co-Education Reconsidered*, Milton Keynes, Open University Press.

Stanworth, M. (1983), *Gender and Schooling*, London, Hutchinson, in association with the Explorations in Feminism Collective.

Stebbins, A. (1987), 'Review Symposium', *British Journal of Sociology of Education*, Vol. 8, No. 1, pp. 83–6.

Stimpson, D.R. and Person, E.S. (eds) (1980), *Women, Sex and Sexuality*, Chicago, University of Chicago Press.

Urwin, C. (1985), 'Constructing motherhood: the persuasion of normal development' in C. Steedman, C. Urwin and V. Walkerdine (eds), *Language, Gender and Childhood*, London, Routledge & Kegan Paul.

Walden, R. and Walkerdine, V. (1982), *Girls and Mathematics: The Early Years*, Bedford Way Papers 8, London, University of London Institute of Education.

Bibliography

Walker, J.C. (1986), 'Romanticising Resistance, Romanticising Culture, Problems in Willis' theory of cultural production', *British Journal of Sociology of Education*, Vol. 7, No. 1, pp. 59–80.

Walkerdine, V. (1981), 'Sex power and pedagogy', *Screen Education*, No. 38, pp. 14–25.

Webster, P. (1981), 'Pornography and Pleasure' in *Heresies, Sex Issue*, No. 12, pp. 50–51.

Weeks, J. (1981), *Sex, Politics and Society*, London, Routledge & Kegan Paul.

Weeks, J. (1985), *Sex, Politics and Society: The Regulation of Sexuality since 1800*, Harlow, Longman Group Limited.

Weiner, G. (ed.) (1985), *Just a Bunch of Girls*, Milton Keynes, Open University Press.

Weitz, S. (1977), *Sex Roles, Biological, Psychological and Social Foundations*, Oxford, Oxford University Press.

Whitbread, A. (1980), 'Female Teachers Are Women First: Sexual Harassment at work' in D. Spender and E. Sara (eds), *Learning to lose*, The Women's Press, London.

Whitty, G. (1981), 'Ideology, politics and curriculum', Block 3, The Politics of Cultural Production, Educational Studies, E353, *Education and the State*, Milton Keynes, Open University Press.

Whitty, G. (1985), *Sociology and School Knowledge*, London, Methuen.

Whyld, J. (ed.) (1983), *Sexism in the Curriculum*, London, Harper & Row.

Whyte, J., Deem, R., Kant, L. and Cruickshank, (1985), *Girl Friendly Schooling*, London, Methuen.

Williams, R. (1961), *The Long Revolution*, Harmondsworth, Penguin.

Williamson, J. (1981–2) 'How does Girl Number Twenty Understand Ideology' in *Screen Education*, No. 40, Autumn, Winter, pp. 80–87.

Willis, P. (1977), *Learning to Labour*, Farnborough, Saxon House.

Willis, P. (1979), 'Shop floor culture, masculinity and the wage form' in J. Clarke, C. Critcher, and R. Johnson (eds), *Working Class Culture*, London, Hutchinson.

Wilson, D. (1978), 'Sexual Codes and Conduct' in C. Smart and B. Smart (eds), *Women, Sexuality and Social Control*, London, Routledge & Kegan Paul.

Wilson, E. (1981), 'Psychoanalysis, Psychic Law and Order', *Feminist Review*, 8.

Wilson, E. (1987), 'Thatcherism and Women: After Seven Years' in R. Miliband, L. Panitch and J. Saville, *Socialist Register*, London, The Merlin Press.

Wilson, J. (1975), 'Moral education: retrospect and prospect' in *Journal of Moral Education*, Vol. 9, No. 1, October 1979, pp. 3–9.

Wilson, J. (1979), *Moral Thinking*, London, Heinemann.

Wolpe, AM. (1977), *Some Processes in Sexist Education*, London,

Women's Research and Resources Centre Publications.
Wolpe, AM. (1978), 'Education and the Sexual division of Labour' in A. Kuhn, and AM. Wolpe (eds), *Feminism and Materialism*, London, Routledge & Kegan Paul.
Wolpe, AM. (1983), 'Moral Order and Discipline', in AM. Wolpe and J. Donald (eds.), *Is There Anyone Here from Education, Education After Thatcher*, London, Pluto Press.
Wolpe, AM. (1985), 'Schools, Discipline and Social Control' in L. Barton and S. Walker (eds), *Education and Social Change*, London, Croom Helm.
Wolpe, AM. (1987), 'Sex and Schools: Back to the Future', *Feminist Review*, No. 28, October.
Wolpe, AM. (1987), 'Experience as Analytical Framework: Does it account for Girls' Education?' in M. Cole (ed.), *Bowles and Gintis Revisited: Schooling and Capitalism Ten Years On*, Lewes, Falmer Press.
Wolpe, AM. (1988), ' 'Experience' as analytical framework: does it account for girls' education?' in M. Cole (ed.), *Bowles and Gintis Revisited*, Lewes, Falmer Press.
Wolpe, AM. and Donald, J. (1983), *Is there Anyone Here From Education? Education After Thatcher*, London, Pluto.
Wood, J. (1984), 'Groping Towards Sexism: boys' sex talk' in A. McRobbie and M. Nava (eds), *Gender and Generation*, London, Macmillan.
Wood, S. (ed.) (1982), *Degradation of Work*, London, Hutchinson.
Wright, D. (1976), Editorial: 'Some thought on moral education', *Journal of Moral Education*, Vol. 5, No. 2.

Yates, J. (1977), 'Ideology in Physical Education', *Bulletin of Physical Education*, Jan.
Young, M. (ed.) (1971), *Knowledge and Control*, London, Collier-MacMillan.

Index

academic curriculum: and gender differences, 248; and non-academic curriculum, 202; school's contribution to boys' rejection of, 237; women's disadvantages, 235
AIDS, 105, 113
Althusser, L., 7, 103, 181
Anyon, J., 9
Apple, M., 180, 181
apprenticeships, 223, 230
Arnot, M., 19, 43, 58, 212
Aronowitz, S. and Gioroux, H.A., 9, 59-61
attainment: perception by pupils, 66, 71, 75, 79; linked to behaviour, 75, 92

Ball, S., 7
Bates, I. *et al*, 228
Beechey, V., 229, 234
Bourdieu, P. and Passeron, J.C., 7, 180
Bowles, S. and Gintis, H., 7, 8, 9, 59, 181, 272n.
Bowlby, J., 39
boy friends: girls' views on, 145-8; outings with, 152-3
boys' behaviour: aggression, 79; afterschool activities, 253-4; characteristics of, 40, 41

passim; determined by patriarchy, 58; disruptive in classrooms, 58; girls' perceptions of, 71-2, 151-2; girls victims of, 99, 247; greatest threat to discipline, 124; perception of themselves, 78
Brake, M., 120
Brown, R., 228
Browne, P., *et al*, 208
Bury, J., 113

career guidance, 256, 269
Centre for Contemporary Cultural Studies (CCCS), 231
Chandler, E.M., 106
Chetwynd, J. and Hartnett, O., 38
Chisholm, L. and Holland, J. 249
Church of England Board of Education, 105
Clarricoates, K., 40, 44, 274n.
classroom control, 32-3, 34; gender of teachers important in, 87-8; and masculinity, 124; and sexuality, 123-7, women's ability in, 123; see also discipline
co-education, 84-6, 93, 98
Cole, M., 277n.
community school, 182
Cornbleet, A. and Liebovitch, S., 43

corporal punishment, 28ff., 35;
applicable only to boys, 30
correspondence principle, 8, 9, 181
Corrigan, P. and Frith, S., 272n.
craft courses, 206-7, 248;
contributing to breakdown of
gender barriers, 185-6, 191,
206-7; and girls, 185-6, 191,
206-7; as home oriented and
hobby activity, 207, 223;
parents' views on girls doing,
192-3; pupils' views on, 242-3
Crowther Report, 105, 106
'crushes' by pupils, 119-20
cultural capital, 7, 180
cultural reproduction, 8, 181; and
resistance, 9
cultural deprivation, 183
curriculum: discourses on, 180-82;
division between academic and
non-academic, 202; class
differentiation and, 202; 180-1,
248; and cultural capital, 180;
and cultural deprivation, 183,
184, 185, 197; ideology of, at
Berkeley, 182ff; integrated, 183-
4, 199, 221, 224-5; interventions
in, 249; and gender
differentiation, 181, 183, 248;
and link with employment, 227;
sub-division of, at Berkeley,
190-1; teachers' views on
integrated programme, 189, 191,
224, 225; as transmission of
cognitive and value systems, 2,
15; see also Craft, Design for
Living, Hidden Curriculum,
Home Economics, Humanities,
Mathematics, Physical
Education, Science

Dallas, D.M., 107, 110, 111
David, M., 103
Davidoff, L. and Hall, C., 13
Davies, L., 43, 82, 90, 276n.

Dawson, P., 22, 26
Deem, R., 12, 97
Delamont, S., 44
Denscombe, M., 20
Design for Living, 187, 188, 269
De Waal, 273n.
discipline: absence of in working
class homes, 28; boys as
greatest threat to, 124;
examinations as form of, 23, 34;
core of school organization, 15;
ignored by sociologists, 20;
liberal form of, 33-4;
marginalization as form of, 33;
'normalizing judgements'
effective tools of, 23; as
physical constraint of pupils,
14, 246; as regulatory restraint
on human behaviour, 23, 31;
self-discipline, 26ff, 188-9;
sexuality and, 124-8; simple
instruments of, 23; strategies
adopted at Berkeley, 25; success
of in Berkeley, 30ff; tone and,
26; traditionalist form of, 31ff
see also classroom control;
truancy

Eaton, M., 108
employment: assessment of
schemes for, 229; boys' views
on their future, 239; and City
and Guilds qualifications, 260;
of girls, 189; girls ignorance of
job opportunities, 256; initiative
by school for, 228; low level of
boys' aspirations for, 258; low
level of girls' aspirations for,
257-8; of parents, 251-2; pupils'
aspirations for, 251, 255-61;
relations between schooling
and, 228, 248-9, 269; women's,
250; see also LAP; TVEI; MSC
Entwistle, H., 23, 31
Eppel, E.M., 104

experiential accounts by girls on education, 12

family life: boys' views on marriage, 75–6; children's domestic duties, 252; determines girls' occupational aspirations, 250; gender differences and expectations of, 270; having children as proof of women's capabilities, 263; ideology of, 108; as main goal for girls, 121; male responsibilities in, 268; pupils' views on, 121, 262–8; women's duties in, 2
Farraday, A. 120, 275n.
femininity and teachers' control, 123, 125–8, 141
football: boys' domination of playground through, 51; as part of male culture, 52; girl's attempt to play football, 53
Foucault, M., 21, 22, 25, 105
Fuller, M., 58
Furlong, A., 249–51, 269

GCSE (General Certificate of Secondary Education), 24
gender stereotyping: see stereotyping
Genovese, E., 274n.
girl friends, 160–4
girls' behaviour; aggressive, 35, 90–1; assumed passivity of, 36, 41; characteristics of, 40ff, 64, 67; counter school, 36, 37ff; and deviance, 43; dominated by boys, 36, 45–6, 98; fighting, 64–7; in playground, 50–1; non-stereotypical, 52–3, 55, 56, 70; as oppositional, 61ff, 238
girls' occupational aspirations, 249
GIST (Girls into Science and Technology), 213
Glaser, B. and Strauss, A., 274n.

Gordon, L., 9
Grant, M., 206

Haigh, G., 273n.
Halsey, C., 103
Harding, J., 212
Hargreaves, D.H., 7, 20, 208, 277n.
hidden curriculum: 2, 8, 13, 201–2, 219, 225, 248; in craft classes, 221–2; in Humanities, 220; scripted forms of, 220–3; tension with policy of integration, 221
Hebdige, D., 272n.
Hindess, B., 5
Holly, L., 51
Home Economics: 185, 199, 203–6, 224, 248; and boys, 186, 190, 204, 205, 248; and deviant boys, 127, 206; ideology of, 204, 205; parents' views on boys doing, 192; pupils' views on, 243–4; as useful knowledge, 202; see also Needlework
homosexuality, 169–73; equating with pro-school culture, 173
Humanities: 217–19; content of, 218; failure of interdisciplinary approach, 196; headteacher's tactics to demoralise group, 196; hidden curriculum in, 219; historical 'facts' in, 218; as interdisciplinary programme, 193–4, 198; teachers of, constituted unified group, 195
Humphries, S., 82, 83, 272n., 273n., 274n.

illegitimacy, 106, 107
independent behaviour: of boys, 71; of girls, 67
interaction process, 7

Jackson, S., 114
Jones, C., 128, 145

Kamm, J., 203, 208
Keddie, N., 181
Kelly, A., 212, 213
knowledge: as control mechanism, 8; and gender differentiation, 15; male forms of, 12
Kohlberg, L., 103

LAP (Lower Attainers Project), 228
Lawton, D., 191
Lees, S., 99, 100, 105, 132, 145, 156
link scheme, 183
Litewka, J., 98
Lobban, G., 201
Longford report on pornography, 108

Maccoby, E.E. and Jacklin, C.N., 38
MacDonald, M., 10, 12, 44, 59
Mahony, P., 10, 19, 43, 45, 50, 98, 99, 100
male youth culture and drinking, 81–2
manual labour: equated with masculinity, 237–8; reasons for boys' acceptance of, 237–8; and shop floor culture, 238
marriage: see family life
Marxist analyses: feminist criticism of, 10, 59
masculinity: and boys' sporting ability, 72; and classroom control, 124; and control over girls, 124–5; equated with successful discipline, 123, 141; exaggerated form amongst teenagers, 98; and manual labour, 237; see also Home Economics; Needlework; homosexuality
maternal deprivation, 39
mathematics, 212–14; accounts of

girls' low attainment in, 213–15; at Berkeley, 213–14; comparison between boys and girls pursuance of, 236; pupils' views on, 241ff; single-sex teaching of, 212
McRobbie, A., 60, 145
McRobbie, A. and Garber, J., 9
Miller, R.Y. and Fowlkes, M.R., 131
Millman, V., 229
mixed ability teaching, 183, 187
Mode III examinations, 187–8, 198
moral actions and rationality, 103
moral codes: acquisition by children, 103–4; create consensus, 103; delineation of, by schools, 120; education to teach, 103; teaching of, 14
moral education: 104; equating with marital life, 113; and sex education, 113
moral order, 15, 102ff; philosophers' concept of, 103; relation to sexuality, 100
motherhood: girls' perception of, 67–8

Needlework: boys doing, 184, 185, 190, 205; as creative subject, 185, 205; parents' views on boys doing, 192; pupils' views on boys doing, 244–5 see also Home Economics
new vocationalism, 228
Niblett, W.R., 103
normalizing judgements, 23, 187, 198
Nuttall, D., 24

observation techniques, 5
oppositional behaviour: to academic subjects by pupils, 237–9; forms of, 69, 90; to

Index

school uniform, 62-3; *see also* resistance

pastoral system: 23; augmenting discipline, 23

patriarchy: 58, 59, 98, 99; as applied to girls' education, 12; as main account of women's subordination, 10; as universal phenomenon, 11; and women's sexuality, 10

Pearson, G., 22, 272n.

Perkins, T.E., 38

Peters, R.S., 103

Phillips, A., 235

Physical Education (PE) and games: gender specific aspects of, 211; failure of integrated programme in, 209-10; and integrated programme, 186, 208, 224; and football, 210; ideology of, 208, 210-11; sexuality in, 210, 211; unpopularity of games with girls, 210

playground activities, 50ff; and cultural factors, 52

Platt, A., and Whyld, J., 229, 230, 231, 234

Plummer, K., 120, 130

Poulantzas, N., 7

progressive education at Berkeley, 26

qualifications: City and Guilds, 260, 261, 269; definition of at O and CSE level, 231; in examinations, 233-4; and gender differences, 234; improvement amongst girls, 234; levels of, 233, 248; relation between and labour market, 234, 249

research method, 5ff.

reproduction of capitalist relations of production, 7

resistance and accommodation: 59-61, 246; confusion of, with oppositional behaviour, 60; and cultural formations, 60; by girls, 246; to schooling, 9

Rich, B.R., 121

Riley, D., 39

Sarah, E., 97

Sarap, M., 23

Schofield, M., 107, 111

school organization structure, 2

Science: 196; comparison between boys and girls in, 235-6; gender differentiation of, at Berkeley, 215-17; ideology of at Berkeley, 214-15; single sex teaching of, 212; teaching of, 214-17

Segal, L., 10, 275n.

sex: girls' views on, 154-8; boys' views on, 165-8

sex education: 102, 247; at Berkeley, 108-12; and birth control, 108; differentiated on basis of class, 107; effectiveness of, 114; girls' views on, 153-4; and health, 104, 114, 115; identification with marriage, 108, 110, 111; as form of moral education, 104; official statements on, 105, 111, 112; and physical reproduction, 104, 109, 110, 120-1

sexual oppression of girls, 12; harassment of girls by boys, 19, 59, 93; of women teachers, 128-9

sexuality: acceptable forms of sexual behaviour, 14, 101; between male teachers and senior girls, 129-30; as breach of discipline, 135-7, 142; conceptualization of, by teachers, 116-18, 134-41;

sexuality (*cont.*)
    control of girls' and boys', 14,
    99, 102, 124–8; essentialism of,
    132; and gender identity, 15;
    and gender differences, 104,
    120; and girls' reputations, 99,
    105, 121, 156; heritage of
    Victorian values, 106;
    heterosexuality as norm, 121;
    and male teachers, 73, 157–8;
    manifest in schools, 97, 247; as
    moral and political battlefield,
    104; as normal development,
    137, 138, 141, 142, 247; and
    power relations, 97, 100; and
    schoolwork, 68, 158–9;
    sexualisation of deviancy, 107–
    8; social construction of, 99,
    131; and teenage sex, 113
Shacklady Smith, D., 107
Sharp, R. and Green, A., 277n.
Sharpe, S., 250
Shaw, J., 212
Simon, W. and Gagnon, J., 130–1,
    132, 142, 276n.
single-sex schooling: advantages
    for girls of, 41
skill: concept of, 229–30, 231;
    vocational skills for girls, 230
Smith, S., 212
Snitow, A. *et al*, 275n.
social scripting: 122, 130–1, 132;
    in Berkeley, 132–4, 142
Spender, D., 19, 43, 44, 97, 145
sporting ability, 81; and
    masculinity, 72
Stanley, L. and Wise, S., 13
Stantonbury Campus Sexism in
    Education Group, 213
Stanworth, M., 43, 44
Stebbins, A., 7, 20
stereotyping: boys' acceptance of
    female stereotypes, 76, 93; of
    boys' behaviour, 12, 35, 37, 40,
    92, 219, 247–8; definition of, 38;

factors contributing to gender,
    2; of girls' behaviour, 35, 37, 40,
    51, 53–5, 90, 91, 219;
    popularization of, 39; of
    teachers' behaviour, 88, 89, 93
style: 62, 63, 74, 78, 148–51, 164–5

teachers' behaviour: determined
    by boys' behaviour, 46;
    favouring boys, 44;
    generalizations on, 43–5;
    interrelated with pupils'
    responses, 58; perceptions of
    pupils, 86–9, 91, 250; variability
    of, 45, 55
TVEI (Technological and
    Vocational Education Initiative),
    227, 228, 269
tomboy behaviour, 69–70
truancy: 28, 82; at Berkeley, 83ff;
    boys and home economics, 127,
    206; means of combatting, 28;
    opportunistic, 83–4; rates of, 28;
    see also discipline

underachievement of girls, 19
Urwin, C., 115

vocational/technical subjects, 237;
    pupils views on, 242–5;
    relevance of, for pupils, 245

Walden, R. and Walkerdine, V.,
    181
Walkerdine, V., 58
Weeks, J., 104, 108
Weiner, G., 19
Weitz, S., 38
Whitbread, A., 123
Whitty, G., 181, 277n.
Whyld, J., 181
Williams, R., 185
Willis, P., 5, 8, 11, 105, 120, 121,
    173, 181, 197, 237, 251, 274n.
Wilson, E., 275n.

Index

Wilson, J., 122
Wolpe, A.M., 20, 97, 103, 234, 250, 272n., 274n., 275n.
women's employment: and labour market, 234–5
Wood, J., 97, 160
Wright, D., 104

Yates, J., 208
Young, M., 7
youth culture: 8; absence of girls from studies of, 9; spectacular male, 9